A Favored Man

A Favored Man

AN AUTOBIOGRAPHICAL JOURNEY
OF AFFLICTIONS, BETRAYAL, HOPE,
SURVIVAL, AND CHRISTIAN FAITH.

COUNTED WORTHY BY GOD,
TO SUFFER FOR HIS PURPOSE.
THE JAMES LANDON STORY.

James Landon

A Favored Man
Copyright 2014 by James Landon

ISBN: 0991664175
ISBN 13: 9780991664177
Library of Congress Control Number: 2015953045
Plant Publications LLC , Empire, CO

The word "cestus" is Latin and means, "to strike."

Ancient Greek and Roman gladiators wore cestus gloves. Metal studs and spikes on their gloves increased the brutality of their hand-to-hand competitions.

During times of personal injustice, or when the storms of life buffet me, I metaphorically use cestus gloves in battle with my inner man, because within, insidious deceit often weakens my faith, hope and integrity. With Cestus gloves, and the Word of God, I fight, preserving faith, hope, and the fidelity of my walk before man and God.

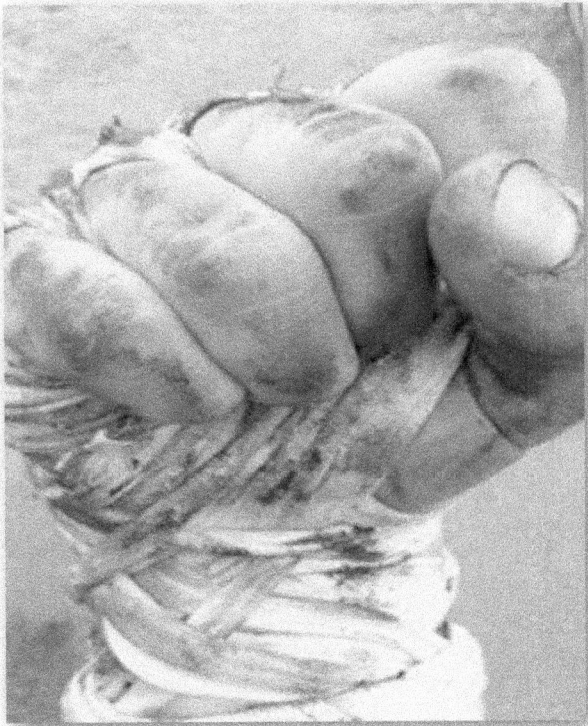

This is a rendition of a "poor man's" cestus glove

To my dear daughters:

*Nicknamed Sprinkle, Pretty Meadow, and Kitty
You are my lifelong dreams and the desires of my heart.
I love you so very much!*

To my dear friends Richard, Pete and Sophia:

*I am grateful for your heart-felt sacrificial improvements to my life,
and to this book.*

To those locked in sorrows, sufferings, and losses:

*This time will pass. The Father is hope and comfort.
He is able to open doors for you that no one can close.
Ignore logic and psychology. Wait for Him.*

Table of Contents

If you wish to schedule us for a speaking engagement or a book tour, you may contact us at our Call of Faith Ministries website: COFMinistries.com

Author's Notes

⁓

Regarding the injustice committed against me in this story, I am allowed under Fair Use Doctrine to state the true names of the people and business's I have a quarrel with, as long as my purpose is for personal defense. In addition, Fair Use Doctrine also permits me to quote from their documents if my intent is for the purpose of analysis, or criticism that leads to the establishment of truth. However, in that my story is volatile, stating true names, and quoting documents might cause unjustified court actions against me, and our publisher. Therefore we will not mention true names, or quote directly from the 240 documents that I possess. Prudence inclines us to give everyone in this story a symbolic name, and to assign our story to a factious place. We earnestly request that if you know the true names of business's, places or people referred to in this story; please do not reveal those names, because we do not wish to harm anyone's business, name or reputation.

NOTE: The views and opinions expressed in this book are not those of the publisher.

Unless otherwise indicated, all scripture quotations are from the Holy Bible: The 1599 Geneva Bible (Copyright © 2006-2010 by Tolle Lege Press, permission granted), KJ Thompson-Chain Reference Bible (Copyright © 1988 by B. B. Kirkbride Bible Co, Inc.), and The MacArthur Study Bible NKJV (Copyright © 1977 by Word Publishing, a division of Thomas Nelson, Inc). Other quotations are from The Wycliffe Bible Encyclopedia (Copyright

The KJ Thompson Chain-Reference Bible states in the "Origin and Growth of the English Bible" section that the Geneva Bible is a "very scholarly version." After my five year critical word study in the Geneva Bible I am able to confirm that the Geneva Bible is a "very scholarly version."

Matthew Henry (1662–1714) was an expert in critical analysis of biblical interpretation, and served as a pastor. His commentaries, and other devotional works, describe with great depth of insight, the rich meaning and abundant beauty of God's word.

When I read Isaiah 6, and by faith see the brilliant seraphim angels above God's throne, and then behold our great and glorious Creator upon His throne, this great sight inspires within my heart the greatest awe and reverence for God, enlarging my heart with an immeasurable desire to understand more about our Creator. My desire is well satisfied when I read Matthew Henry's Commentary. His profound thoughts about God, fills my heart and mind with deep, reverent wonders about our great God.

As grateful children of God, we believe this book is an excellent means whereby we may introduce many to Matthew Henry's Commentary, and begin the careful process of understanding great awe and reverence for our glorious God.

Why You Should Read my Book

IN THIS LIFE, THE SOFT PART OF THE OYSTER is wounded during the slow process of making the highly prized pearl. So from within, the hidden work of affliction will, at the proper time, adorn many with transient beauty.

When I step from this life into heaven; finally into life with no sorrows, sufferings, or losses, the Gates of Pearl will always remind me that during my travel toward this city, trials often wounded my heart, revealing weaknesses in strength, patience, and faith, influencing my will in the slow process of making a godly character. So from within, the hidden work of affliction, and the transforming influence of God's word, increasingly adorned me with only a hint of my Father's transcendent beauty, until finally, when my Father called me into heaven and renewed me with His divine beauty.

Oh, come with me and walk worthy of the gates of pearl

And I saw a new heaven,...
REVELATION 21:1

And God shall wipe away all tears...
REVELATION 21:4

And the twelve gates *were* twelve pearls, and every gate is of one pearl,...

REVELATION 21:21

The following true story explains why God designs for us and allows us to have sorrows, sufferings, and losses before we pass through His Gates of Pearl. I have no doubt that my Father allowed me to suffer cruel injustice so that according to His word, my long term sorrows, sufferings, and losses may become a great warning to offenders, and a strong inspiration for the offended.

Jonah and the Apostles might say that in God's word, we learn why God designs the storms of life for the disobedient and the obedient.

James was the first born of four children, and though his father provided very well for the family, his father did not give himself to his family, because his addictions to alcohol and Vicodin kept him occupied, distant, and sometimes abusive.

When James was in the early prime of his life, before he became a Christian, God spoke to his heart, saving him from a potentially fatal motorcycle accident. Then after six years of riding his Harley like a dirt bike, parties, and street fights, God again showed kindness to James.

In February of 1979, when James was twenty three years of age, God began the adoption process with James, enabling him to repent and become a born again Christian, taming his heart with an earnest desire for God. James' spiritual birth was immediately evident to many because of his insatiable hunger for the Word of God, his new nature, his obedience to God, his righteous principles, and his holy affections for Godliness.

Through the first seven transforming months, the effect of God's presence, and the influence of His Word, inspired James to hand the reins of his heart to God. He then abandoned his job and the woman he hoped to marry and traveled 1,200 miles away to a Bible College. However, within the first few minutes of his first class James knew that he must return home, because the teaching pace of the professor was much too fast, as if a miner, in haste, strikes the ore, passing over rare treasure.

Back at home, James read and studied his Bible as the Bible teaches us to do; slowly, and circumspectly, as one digs in the earth for silver and gold. Though family, and some at church, disapproved of James' return from Bible College, James continued to learn about providential guidance and the approval of Almighty God.

James' affectionate communion with God, and remarkable answers to his prayers, increasingly inclined him to mature in the wisdom, knowledge, and understanding of God. However, one year after God had warned James that the godly woman he again planned to marry would someday turn from him and from God, James followed Eve's logic, and became one with her in marriage.

A year later, James and his new wife traveled across four states so that both of them could attend a Bible College. After completing a one year course, his wife achieved a 97.5 grade point average, and James almost failed. James' low scholastic score was because he often chose to neglect his college work assignments so that he could open the Word of God to classmates, edifying and warning them about their walk before God.

A few weeks before graduation, the College Dean asked James if he would give the commencement speech. As the Dean began to mention restrictions upon James' message, James realized that he did not have the freedom to say what God might have him say, so James declined the offer. The graduation ceremony was performed before an audience of 2,500 and four TV cameras. And James was very proud of his wife when she was honored with Valedictorian, Presidents List, and special achievements.

After graduation James accepted an offer from that College President to serve as his right-hand man. However, about a month later when James learned that the College President was not honest about money received during a telethon, James resigned. As a result, James and his wife returned to their home state.

After about a year they went back to the state where they had attended collage so that James could serve as a right-hand man to a famous National Evangelist. However, after a few months when it became clear to James that the Evangelist was consistently a great hypocrite, James resigned. This endeavor with the Evangelist put James into a debt of about $15,000.

Shortly before James and his wife returned to their home state, they learned that James' beloved wife was pregnant. Family and friends were also happy about the pregnancy, but very concerned about James because of his numerous failures; his first return from Bible College; his very low academic score at his second Bible College; and his inability to work with a college president, and a famous evangelist. Though family concerns troubled James, he was at peace with God, because he confidently understood that his apparent failures were very important aspects of God's training of him, equipping him for future service.

In 1986, James and his wife were blessed by the birth of their second daughter. And James was very fortunate to work as a carpenter for his dad, who was a very successful contractor-engineer. Through the previous fifteen years, James received special training from his dad, preparing him to someday work in his office. All was well, until his dad offered him that position in the office, guaranteeing James of up to $300,000 a year. James did not accept his dad's gracious offer, because responsibilities of that magnitude would require the neglect of his family, his Bible studies, meditation, and prayer.

When family and relatives learned that James declined his dad's offer, their gossip was confirmed; that James fails every time an excellent opportunity is offered to him. However, James was assured that God had the reins of his heart, and was leading him according to His purpose.

After James' dad almost died because of an overdose of Vicodin, James learned that a local refinery was hiring carpenters, so he applied and was hired. Generous paychecks subdued struggles and worries, issuing thankfulness to God. The questions to God began when one day at work James climbed a four story ladder, stepped onto a platform, and into a toxic gas. Though authorities understood that James needed medical attention, they told James to go to the carpenter shack and rest until his shift ended at midnight. Through the following three years, continuous denial of medical help allowed the onset of a diagnosed severe terminal nerve disease. The slow death of his nerves, threatened a rapid cascading death of life-long dreams of family and marriage. And then, happiness entered the hearts and arms of James and his family when their third daughter was born.

About three years later when James was completely disabled, and in great need of his wife, she divorced him. James immediately gave ninety eight percent of their possessions to his wife and family, and made his home in his truck, often bathing in a river.

Just as God had warned James, after his wife turned from him, she also turned from God. She stopped her church attendance, and the reading of her Bible, so that she could pursue the true desires of her heart; western bars and self-indulgence. The true character of her heart became evident when she and James' mother began to manipulate James' life so that they could legally establish that James was mentally unstable. However, God warned James about their manipulations, and protected him. Thirteen years before James' former spouse brought the first of many great delights to James' heart, and after the divorce she filled his heart with the greatest sorrows, sufferings, and losses.

As James' health deteriorated, his Workers' Compensation claim was denied because of documented physician fraud. While James waited for

Disability benefits, he moved into a garage, and then lived in a back yard, and when he moved into a shed, he replaced his truck for a wheel chair. A neurologist then informed James that his disease was incurable, and that he should prepare to die in a nursing home. James' anguish increased when medical fraud turned judges, lawyers, doctors, and even some of his family against him.

Three years after James filed for Social Security Benefits, monthly disability payments were issued to him because Social Security doctors determined that he was one hundred percent disabled. James' nerve disease was strongly developing in the back of his brain, dulling his discernment, and discipline. And throughout his nervous system he was losing control of his motor-sensory functions. His spirit began to weaken when he also developed a sleep disorder, and severe unrelenting pain in the back of his head, legs and feet.

Through eleven years of Workers' Compensation Court battles, numerous medical reports, and various medical tests clearly established that James' nerve disease was work related. However, the documented physician fraud prevented justice for James. And when James learned that his attorney was involved in the fraud, he fired him, and sat in his seat at the next hearing. All present at that hearing will never forget James' words and performance.

James' declining health forced him to often lie down; and his spirit was further weakened when his tongue began to jerk, and his eyes became very painful and red, preventing him from looking into the eyes of another during conversation. The absence of his beloved daughters caused him to have a fast sad beating heart, and an unrelenting lump in his throat.

The following paragraph is from his book: "How many blows or insults can a man take before he throws in the towel, especially when he is suffering from enormous mental and physical difficulties? As a constant flowing river erodes a strong rock, so do my unrelenting trials wear me down. I can feel it every day as my heart cries; my situation is hopeless. I feel so heavy because the many cruel Workers' Compensation puppets, and my many afflictions, have clothed me with exhaustion. I know it, because I wear it every day. No doubt, this is an opportune time for Satan to take advantage of my weak, hopeless state, and easily convince me that there is no hope because of the logic and psychology of my trials. This is truly a convenient, logical time for Satan to shake me until I fall into a state of hopeless despair. However, God's presence indwelling me, and His Word open to me, inspires me, sustaining me with uncommon heavenly might, and God honoring faith, and hope against all hope. This is a great opportune time for me, because trials open my ears, and incline my heart to the mind and will of God. And no doubt, God uses trials to shake me from this world, which means that I must let my trials humble me…"

Note: I will now switch from speaking to you in third person, and speak to you from my heart.

Why did God allow my chemical exposure? Why! I was intimate with Him, and He graciously loved me. He saw me when I stood at the bottom of the ladder. He knew about the toxic gas up on the platform and He knew that I had a wife and two daughters at home. So why did He allow me to climb up into a gas that made me cry for many years? Why!

Through many years I enjoyed health, prosperity and happiness until God closed the door on all of it. I wept as I tried to push that door back open. The harder I pushed the more stressed and distraught I became, until through God's Word, I understood His mind and will for me. And with God's help I stopped pushing on that door, submitted to His purpose, and became truly spiritually healthy, prosperous and happy.

After twenty two years of great physical and emotional sorrows, sufferings, and losses, God enabled me to completely recover my health, and my life, by a proper diet, and earnest prayer.

My book is an inspiration from me and God because we see that many are not able to obtain true comfort, purpose, or peace with Him, even though after Jesus returned to Heaven God sent the Comforter, the Holy Spirit, to the earth. As He graciously cared for me He may also care for you.

Through my book you will better understand Gods mind and will, His providential influence, and why He allows sorrows, sufferings, and losses; His purpose in trials, and how to benefit from them.

From God's Word, this book clearly declares a strong warning to the offender, and a great inspiration for the offended. My many offenders have not repented to me; therefore, I have not forgiven them, because God does not forgive unless one first repents. I am however, happy and content, because I am harmonious with God, His purpose, and His Word.

The Well Wisher of Your Soul,

James Landon

CHAPTER 1

My First Protection from God

⁓

A DISASTROUS FLIGHT ON A HARLEY

DECEMBER 1974: I AM SEVENTEEN YEARS OLD

OH...IT'S ONLY THREE MINUTES LATER than it was the last time I looked at the clock! And another glance out the window. *Good deal!*

My increasing pulse makes me draw deeper breaths because all day I have watched our chilly December change to better weather for riding my motorcycle.

Another peek at the slow clock, *Good deal. Almost there! Three...two...one!* When the last school bell finally sounds, my flame is lit.

Ignition! On the way up from the desk, my hand feels my pocket. *Yep, my key!*

A lively good-bye to my classmates carries the hint that I am late to ride my motorcycle. With a spirited turn to my left, and a swift bolt to my locker, I put tonight's homework on the shelf, and consider my jacket. But the sounds of an awakening parking lot enlarge my heart with a desire to join them and play, so there is no time to put on my jacket.

After I slam the locker door and hear the crisp click of the lock, I finally step through the school door. At the sight of my bike, I develop unusually long steps. However, halfway there I clearly hear within my heart, "Go back and get your jacket."

But my Lewis-and-Clark westward stride will not turn back to the east, so I respond, *No way. Today is a good day for riding without my jacket!*

My advance continues, more determined than Apollo 8's reach for the moon. However, this being the third time for me to hear, "Go back and get your jacket," I finally obey and head for my locker. Anxious to resume my good advance toward my bike, yet slightly distracted by the odd detour, and curious as to why I should get my jacket. I finally arrive at my locker and feel as if now I am the only one in school. So I open the locker door with record speed and quickly slip into my leather jacket. Then from the parking lot, I hear sounds like a departing happy parade, and say to myself, *I'm outta here!*

After the click of my lock, my return is almost at a gallop, and finally as my leg swings over my bike a thought fills my heart. *Fighter pilots must experience this same thrill as they climb into the cockpit.*

I feel so fortunate to finally sit on this seat. As both hands reach for the handle-grips, my heart lowers my head and I look deep into the paint of the fuel tank, still not believing that I own a new 1973 Harley Sportster. Some people think that when I am seated on this machine, I glow brighter than its new chrome. I feel like I do! I worked hard and long to pay $2,310 in cash for this beauty.

My elevated heart rate commands my thumb to push the starter button!

As I make contact with the button, my mind and heart unite, so thrilled to ignite 1000 cc's of famous Harley power. My thumb then presses the button, and my ears are so pleased with the favored Harley sound. No doubt, the sound of this engine is worth every penny I spent. Now my bike and I are ready to play. So, with an authoritative roll of the throttle, we join the parade and make a right turn onto the main road. As usual, traffic moves slowly at about fourteen miles per hour for a little more than a quarter mile.

My heart rate increases as I consider, *The ramp! Should I? Yes, today I will do it!*

My excitement rises higher than when I talk to a cute girl, because toward the end of this long line of cars there is a drainage ditch parallel to the road with a double-wide driveway crossing the ditch. On each side of the driveway, dirt is sloped from the bottom of the ditch to the top of the driveway, creating the ramp.

As I finally approach the area of the ramp, my heart questions my attempt to fly a Harley. However, my grip tightens as I veer to my right, down into the ditch, and with a roll of the throttle, traffic next to me is blurred, raising my heart rate as high as my Harley's RPM. With a cautious but rapid glance at the speedometer and a slight touch to the brake, we are at the perfect speed of sixty miles per hour. The sound of the engine is in no way timid in this endeavor, and we are number one on the runway.

The jump is good and the flight is long. However, when my 450-pound Harley lands hard at sixty miles per hour, the left handle grip comes off and the bike and I hit the dirt hard — the kind of hard that makes me think that I should not have done this. The bike then falls on top of me and we begin a violent tumble. During our brawl, I hear a loud bang as we slam into the side of a passing car, which deflects us back to the dirt and 110 feet later our tumbling stops.

I briefly lie unconscious while my nervous system struggles to keep me alive. My frantic nerves yank me out of unconsciousness and my eyes snap open in alarm. Still stunned, I instantly realize that my nervous system is screaming for attention, and I am horrified as I cannot breathe because my Harley is on top of me. I am face down, pressed hard to the ground with the engine on my upper back. Fortunately, the engine stops. And because the engine is only about an inch above my right ear I can easily hear the "tink, tink, tink" of cooling metal.

Within my heart are strong cries from sudden threats of death. The weight of my Harley and the stirred-up dust make it almost impossible to draw even a small sip of air. And the little air that I do draw in is instantly consumed due to my exceedingly high heart rate. *I'm losing! I'm in trouble! If my bike is not pulled off me in a few seconds, I will die!*

Each second my increasing nerve activity rises to higher critical levels. And because my pulse rate exceeds safe limits, my blood pressure may now break my heart. And even worse, my nervous system is losing control.

The traffic stops, and with a limited range of vision, I'm only able to see the feet of gathering classmates. *They are just staring at me. No one is picking the bike up off me!*

I understand that I possess only seconds to live and that I might have only one chance to cry out for help. So with an earnest effort I cry, "Get the bike off of me!"

However, because my voice is weak they do not hear me.

My heart begins to lose hope. However, my mind refuses to give up. My eyes desperately roll to my right searching for some hope. I then see my right foot pinned tightly behind my right ear. I become more desperate because it seems that my leg must have been pulled from my hip. But my resilient, determined mind ignores my strong desperate emotions, and I again look for hope. Through the spokes of the slow-turning back wheel, I see four or five classmates jump from the back of a truck and run toward me. A few heartbeats later, they lift the rude elephant off my back and I hear my right leg flip over to the ground.

Good! It's still attached!

As I roll over, my starved lungs suck all the air from this city. All of my senses are so relieved, and I am thankful that I'm face up. As extremes abate, frightened and stressed nerves moderate as triumphant jubilation fills my heart with deep gratitude. I am so very thankful that I am still alive because at the tender age of seventeen I am not ready to die.

As I peer into the deep blue sky, the sounds of my classmates fade as I ponder, *I'm alive! I am alive and my leg is still attached!*

When I taste blood, I put my hand to my mouth, *Oh great! My lip and my chin are bleeding!*

I am hurt and bleeding from a number of places, and yes, my leg hurts. Some areas of my leather jacket have been shredded all the way through.

I am so thankful that I put on my jacket!

And, I am also thankful that yesterday when I rode my Harley during a sleet storm, and walked into a Harley Davidson store with black-and-blue marks across my face and forehead caused by the sleet, my good friend and coworker handed a face shield to me and said, "Put this on your helmet!"

"Thanks buddy!" I told him.

Still lying in the dirt, I check myself for damage and roll my head to the left for a look at my bike, also wounded and lying not far from me. It is so odd to see my bike on its side.

Then my heart sobers when I hear the approaching ambulance.

Oh great! How am I going to hide all of this from Mom and Dad?

When the ambulance medic finally stands next to me, I ask him, "How much does it cost for a ride to the hospital?"

He says, "Thirty-five dollars."

I respond, "Thirty-five dollars! No thank you! My friend Jeff will take me."

They leave, probably thinking that I am very weird.

As I stand, the extension of my young life evaporates the anxious apprehension of my peers. Now all their expressions are exuberant, as if I were Evel Knievel at Caesar's Palace. Pride again lifts my heart, not for my Sportster, but for me. I begin to speak about my courageous (stupid) jump as if I were indeed Knievel.

However, during my boast I clearly hear within my proud heart, "You are alive because I allowed it."

I am astonished, but all my senses understand that the statement is from God.

God! The same voice that told me to get my jacket!

I am so amazed that I say to my classmates, "I'm only alive because God above allowed it."

I am as surprised as they are at this statement. This is truly amazing because I am not a Christian and I do not attend church.

I think empty impressions from the TV and movies inspire my foolish vanity.

Jeff takes me to the hospital, and then home.

[Gold Statement #1: In 1956 the average price of gold was $34.99 per ounce. And now in 1973, the average price is $97.39 per ounce.]

Entering the second week of December, Christmas happiness in all the people begins to gallop toward a brief suspension of wasteful, foolish living; giving rise and room for expressions of love and the offers of simple fun and laughter.

Well, I am for sure not at a gallop. Because of my recent stupid stunt, it seems as if I am to be forever here in this bed. My young body does not like to be stuck in bed, and it seems as if I might have an escape when I hear my family preparing to go cut firewood. Nevertheless, Dad will not let me go.

"No James, the doctor says that you're supposed to stay in bed."

"But Dad, the accident didn't kill me, but if I stay in bed another minute, I feel like I will die."

I ask Dad a few more times if I may go, and he finally says yes, as long as I stay on the tailgate of the truck.

Finally, out in the field, the December chill feels so good, and the chainsaw smell reminds me of autumn. However, it is not good that I sit on this tailgate while Mom, Dad, two younger sisters and my younger brother work. So eventually, I help load the truck as much as I am able.

On the way home, Mom reminds us about her homemade chili in the refrigerator, and I say, "Yum!"

This will be a great evening, with promises of a nice warm fire, endless cornbread and bowls of hot chili. As we drive home, we are aglow with simple December happiness.

We pull into our driveway and there we sit in stunned silence. In our absence, fire has completely destroyed our home. It is almost two weeks before Christmas, and all is gone. Mom and Dad have only enough insurance to cover Mom's piano and organ. We have suffered a great loss. If I had remained at home, sedated and in bed, I likely would have died because the kitchen fire started right under my bedroom.

After Christmas, we rebuild our home, sell it, and move to the east coast of America where Mom's family lives.

This unexpected change in the course of our lives makes our eyes drop, because our dreams have turned to ashes like our beloved home. However, in this new journey, with our heads up, through squinted eyes, we see new good things.

CHAPTER 2

The Power of Visual Examples

⟶

TRAINING FROM A CHAMPION BOXER

Thou therefore suffer affliction as a good soldier of Jesus Christ. No man that warreth, entangleth himself with the affairs of *this* life, because he would please him that hath chosen him to be a soldier. And if any man also strive for a mastery, he is not crowned, except he strive as he ought to do.

2 TIMOTHY 2:3–5

The great care of a soldier should be to please his general; so the great care of a Christian should be to please Christ, to approve ourselves to him. The way to please him who hath chosen us to be soldiers is not to entangle ourselves with the affairs of this life, but to be free from such entanglements as would hinder us in our holy warfare....We are striving for mastery, to get the mastery of our lust and corruptions, to excel in that which is good, but we cannot expect the prize unless we observe the laws. In doing that which is good we must take care that we do it in a right manner, that our good may not be evil spoken of.

MATTHEW HENRY

AUTUMN 1974: I AM EIGHTEEN YEARS OLD

JOHN ALACRITY IS AN UNCOMMON man. He shows me, a common dreamer, his champion spirit. His accomplishments strongly define his unique personality. He is a former state boxing champion who, as a professional boxer had fought a title fight in New York at Madison Square Gardens. [A partial definition of John's last name alacrity, is the cheerful willingness of a warrior as he advances toward his enemy.]

His spirit excites my heart with champion dreams, inspiring my pursuit of his powerful skills. Before John begins the process of honing my aim to fight as skillfully as he fights, he mentions a long list of things that I must not do, such as drink alcohol, date, eat junk food, take long hot showers, or stay up past ten-o'clock. After I quickly say, "Okay, anything else?" John says that he now owns me; and that these activities drain my energy. When I train with him I will need a lot of energy. Each evening I train three to four hours at John's house, with four other men who also seek for the advance of their champion dreams. We all consider the abuse of John's training a privilege. I feel like a young buck with new short antlers, learning to spar with tree branches. It was my first handshake with John Alacrity that ignited my dreams to become a boxer. Every morning, and through each day, I am also inspired with dreams about George Forman, Joe Frazier, and Mohammad Ali.

In the gym I begin my first four-minute round on what I think is the most inspiring piece of equipment in the boxer's gym; the speed bag. In motion or at a standstill this small item communicates the great pride and soul of boxing. However, today my boxing pride is not so great because during my third round I am slightly frustrated because I cannot deliver the bag to the envied rhythm at hyper-speed. However, very determined, I continue like a logger hard at work with a dull axe. That is until what seems like a northbound Santa Fe train strikes my right side, knocking me out from under the speed bag.

It's John!

He strikes me so hard with his elbow that I go flying. And before I can recover myself, all my nerve endings interpret the abrupt blow as good communication that now brings me to vital instruction. My piqued anticipation readies all my senses, and as I spin back around and fix my eyes upon him, he places his hands in front of the idle speed bag and within a second, the bag easily skips at an excellent rhythm, and with impressive velocity. As my eyes focus, and my nerve endings intensify, my heart is inspired with his champion spirit. So after about sixteen seconds, I strike John with my elbow, knocking him out from under the bag. As he falls out from under the bag, I step in, and with authority, I raise my enlightened hands to the bag. Within a second, the bag easily skips with an excellent rhythm and impressive John Alacrity speed. Tremendous energy flashes through my nervous system with an outburst of triumph, enabling me to keep the bag at an enjoyable high RPM, feeling as if I could push it to warp speed. But wisely I don't because the link that connects the bag to the platform would melt.

After four and a half years of training, John schedules me for a main event fight in a large city one hour away. The morning of the event, before breakfast, a struggle has already begun within my heart; a battle between my self-confidence, and the unknown skills of my opponent. However, my confidence gains the victory because of the 1,642 days of training from John, and numerous skilled sparing partners and opponents.

I am ready!

Later in the afternoon, the unknown warrior and I arrive for our great contest. And when we slip through the ropes, the auditorium noise fades when our sober dark eyes lock on each other. Our nervous stares at this moment are like that of a fighter pilot on his first approach to a pitching aircraft carrier.

However, noise from the arena's large audience draws my attention, so I turn to my right and squint through bright lights. And like the unfortunate sailor who beholds the approach of a large wave, I see the large crowd and begin to feel numb. *There are so many people here!*

I make a nervous glace to my left, and what seems like a moment later a loud crash slowly awakens me. *Someone is yelling at me. It's John and he is very mad at me!*

My open eyes finally begin to see that I am standing in the locker room. I then understand that the loud crash was from a chair that John threw against the wall. I slowly begin to realize that I had blacked out due to stage fright while in my corner, and now somehow I stand here before John. To say that my humiliation is severe is an understatement, and I feel like my only solution is to live the remainder of my life in a monastery with a bag over my head. My exaggerated strength of heart and mind has proved false.

[Note: Visual examples touch the senses, yielding change, enabling ambitions with abilities beyond common limits. So dear reader, I pray that as your eyes fix upon this story of my life that your heart will be inspired with hope and ability; enabling your good dreams to reach beyond the difficult, the adverse, and what seems to be impossible. You will see the hand of God in my life, and hopefully examine your own, and identify God's providence. So stay with me through these pages and I will tell you more good stories. As you read my words, it is my hope that your thoughts will connect like the links of a chain eventually forming a good understanding and a strong hope for you.]

CHAPTER 3

The First of Many Calls from God

_6

CALLED OUT OF A PARTY

The preparations of the heart _are_ in man: but the answer of the tongue is of the Lord.
                    PROVERBS 16:1

God easily can, and often does, cross men's purposes, and break their measures.
                    MATTHEW HENRY

The heart of man purposeth his way: but the Lord doth direct his steps.
                    PROVERBS 16:9

But let men devise their worldly affairs ever so politely, and with ever so great a probability of success, yet God has the ordering of the event, and sometimes directs their steps to that which they least intended.
                    MATTHEW HENRY

To all things _there_ is an appointed time, and a time to every purpose under the heaven.
                    ECCLESIASTES 3:1

That every change concerning us, with the time and season of it, is unalterably fixed and determined by a supreme power; and we must take things as they come, for it is not in our power to change what is appointed for us.

MATTHEW HENRY

AUTUMN 1978: I AM TWENTY-TWO YEARS OLD

TWO WEEKS AGO, I SAW a pretty girl who adhered to my heart, and now I always think about her. Oh how she makes my adrenalin flow.

A moment ago, I meet that pretty girl, and learned that her name is Mara. After a few weeks of dating, she surprises me when she says, "The Gideon's came to my school and gave this Bible to me. I don't want it. Do you want it?" Feeling as if no one should deny a Bible, I gladly accept the little red Bible.

Four months later:

For a brief moment, my senses are relieved as I throttle around the last corner and finish my turn. The January 1:30am cold burns. But a look down the street warms my heart. *Good deal! I can't believe how many cars are here!*

I ride my Harley right up to the front porch and turn the engine off. The window next to me is vibrating because inside "Steve Miller" is at full volume.

Oh, my hands are so cold. I don't think that I can hold a beer!

I pull my gloves off and place them on the fuel tank. I then extend both hands low, and lightly touch the warm engine, as if in front of a nice hot wood stove. While my hands thaw and my ears fill with excitement from the party inside, my heart is like a spirited racehorse bumping its chest on the gate. *Open so that I may run!*

Powerful sounds from inside the house draw and arouse me, enticing my heart with irresistible desires to party with my friends. With little effort the bellow inside raises my aspirations to a full mighty blaze, causing me to stand and place my gloves under my left arm, and as I pull my jacket zipper down, I am now fully prepared to step into this party.

The music and party are so amped up I can barely hear myself think. No doubt, this is worth the freezing cold ride. During a drop in the level of music, someone from the back porch near the keg of beer says, "Harley's here!"

Two other friends from different parts of the house further lift my pride when they say, "Harley Dude is here!"

Here at this party I am as grand as John Wayne, because everyone knows that I ride my Harley like Evel Knievel and train with a top-ranked contender. As I press through the crowd toward the keg, the reception I receive is very good, especially from the girls because they do love my southern accent. As shy as I am, I need all the help I can get.

Then I hear so clearly within my heart, "Go home and read your little red Bible."

I am so amazed, and my heart responds, *God! I heard this same voice at my accident five years ago. My Gideon Bible?*

For a few seconds all my senses turn from the party and focus on my amazed, curious heart. Feeling a sense of uncommon reverence, my nerve endings cannot fully measure this second visit from God. I clearly understand that I have now had another rare encounter with God. However, the imma-ture inclinations of my heart insist that I continue my advance toward the keg. Slightly distracted as I go toward the keg, I clearly hear again, "Go home and read your little red Bible."

I am astonished to hear God again. My body feels the heavy pulse of loud music, yet I hear God very clearly within my heart as if all were silent. This highly unusual moment is beginning to change the disposition of my heart with feelings of submissiveness. However, the power of the party commands my steps, and when I am about halfway to the keg I hear again, "Go home and read your little red Bible."

I am now as single-minded as when one is chosen for a special rare mis-sion. As powerful mixed messages flood my being, the lust of my eyes and the pride of my ears push my advance two or three more steps toward the keg. I then hear again, "Go home and read your little red Bible."

A strong sense of divine purpose instantly stops my motion and my desires for this party. Now that I have stopped my advance toward the keg, submis-siveness fills my heart as thoughts of obedience enter my mind. This powerful transformation is so amazing and odd. I feel as if this party and these friends are meaningless, and now it is time to go. As I quickly turn away from the keg, slightly to my right is one of my friends. His stare questions the amazing change in me. So I step close to him, and when the music drops I say to my friend, "You're not going to believe this, but I have to go home and read my little red Bible."

Confusion widens his eyes, and yet with military style I break from him and march to my cold bike.

All the way home, I think about the amazing odd experience. I ride my Harley right up to the patio door and turn off the engine. The little red Bible is just inside my room. My puppy, HD (short for Harley Davidson) is asleep. Hoping not to wake him, I slowly slide the door open and quietly push my Harley into my bedroom. HD lifts his sleepy little head, and with his tail wagging, he trots over to greet me. After putting down the kickstand, I reach down and playfully pick him up, drawing him in for a late-night hug.

"Hey little buddy. Sorry to wake you."

The lively licking of his little tongue and his very happy wagging tail affirms that it is okay.

I put HD into his warm bed, and then with crude reverence, pick up the little red Bible and say, "Thanks Mara."

So, very thankful to have this Bible in my hand, I place my thumb on the edge and open to Genesis 1, and my curious eyes slowly scan the page. Though I am very tired, I feel a little revived because this Bible inspires me with reverence. Through the past two weeks, I have looked through this Bible a few times. However, this time is very different because this Bible now feels like it is alive and actually communicating with me. *Amazing!*

With the curiosity of a treasure hunter, my thumb reaches again and this time opens to Matthew. For a brief moment, my very tired brain is puzzled as I read the long genealogy. *Oh, I'll try one more time.*

My thumb reaches deeper, all the way to Colossians, and I then read:

For though I be absent in the flesh, yet am I with you in the spirit,...
Colossians 2:5

I say, "Absent… yet am I with you in the spirit,…this is Jesus talking, so these words are supposed to be in red." [Later, upon becoming better acquainted with the scriptures, I learn that this is Paul speaking, not Jesus.]

Confused, and by now very, very tired, I put my little red Bible on the table and melt into my bed, unaware of the adoption process in progress. The reason God drew me out of the party and to His Word, is clearly stated in the following verse:

No man can come to me, except the Father, which hath sent me, draw him: and I will raise him up at the last day.
JOHN 6:44

CHAPTER 4

Heaven's Adoption Process in Progress

_⟶⟶_

Enter in at the strait gate: for it is the wide gate, and broad way that leadeth to destruction: and many there be which go in thereat. Because the gate is strait, and the way narrow that leadeth unto life, and few there be that find it.
MATTHEW 7:13–14

The account that is given of the bad way of sin, and the good way of holiness. There are but two ways, right and wrong, good and evil; the way to heaven, and the way to hell; in the one of which we are all of us walking: no middle place hereafter, no middle way now: the distinction of the children of men into saints and sinners, godly and ungodly, will swallow up all to eternity...if many perish, we should be the more cautious.
MATTHEW HENRY

Strive to enter in at the strait gate: for many, I say unto you, will seek to enter in, and shall not be able...There shall be weeping and gnashing of teeth, when ye shall see Abraham, and Isaac, and

Jacob, and all the Prophets in the kingdom of God, and your-selves thrust out at doors.
LUKE 13:24–28

We have reason to wonder that of the many to whom the word of salvation is sent there are so few to whom the word of salvation is a saving word…It concerns us all seriously to improve the great truth of the fewness of those that are saved.
MATTHEW HENRY

And if the righteous scarcely be saved, where shall the ungodly and the sinner appear.
1 PETER 4:18

The gate is so strait and the way so narrow.
MATTHEW HENRY

LATE WINTER 1979: I AM TWENTY-THREE YEARS OLD
ONE WEEK LATER ON FRIDAY, a Baptist preacher speaks with Mom and Dad about heaven and hell. Neither Mom nor Dad is Christian, so talking about hell frightens both of them. Mom tells me about their talk with the preacher and says, "Your Dad and I are going to church in the morning. Your brother and sister are going with us. Would you like to go with us?"

I'm sure that Mom can see that she is causing a riot in my mind. *Church! I'm going out with Mara this evening. If I go to church, I'll have to go to bed early tonight!*

Mom then says, "James, ask Mara if she would like to go to church with us."

Mom knows just what I am thinking. I'm a little embarrassed to ask Mara to go to church, and it would be odd to go to bed early on a Saturday night. I would like to say no. But Mom is standing there so serious. So I say, "Yes, I'll go. I'm going to Mara's house at noon, so I'll ask her if she'll go to church with us."

No doubt, Mara will go with me because since our first date almost six months ago we have spent almost every evening together. However, I cannot believe Mara when she says no.

I can't believe she said no! Great! I've already told Mom that I would go!

Through the day and into the evening, I feel a deep, growing regret as the close of our day draws near. Finally, I am pained when on my watch I read 9:31. We begin to say good night, and then at 10:16, our strong emotions of parting from each other give in, and we say good-bye. I am going to church tomorrow, and Mara is going to a party tonight. I turn toward the light of church, and Mara goes out to the darkness of a party.

All the way home my heart echoes; *I can't believe I've left Mara early on a Saturday night!*

A disturbance then enters my mind. *She's going to a party! As cute as she is, someone will flirt with her!*

My heart almost turns me around until I think of Mom, and the possibility of falling asleep in church because I stayed out late the night before. When I finally park in our driveway, my heart is so worked up that I almost go back to Mara, until I notice that all the house windows are dark.

Everyone is already in bed. Well, I might as well just climb into bed.

When I step inside, I'm still thinking about leaving Mara early and her at a party. I think for sure that my pounding heart will wake everyone, except for my brother. So I move through the house in slow motion. Finally, in the room I now share with my brother, I quietly undress as my heart races with thoughts about so many men flirting with Mara.

Great! I'll probably lie awake all night thinking about Mara!

As I climb into bed, I feel like I should go to the party. However, my head upon the pillow sets in motion man's ordained pause, and when I pull the covers up to my chin, my day closes.

The clock's hour hand circles almost eight times, and as a new day begins, my eyes open.

Early sounds of Mom and Dad in the kitchen put a hint of excitement in getting dressed.

This morning there is a better feeling in our house, and I feel good because I feel like I'm about to do something that's right.

The two-day rain finally stops during sunrise. After breakfast, HD and I go out to the front porch. And as I stand enjoying the clean, fresh morning air, my little brother comes out and says, "James, we're going to church now."

He is like a big neon sign that says, *"Look at me!"*

Because of his extra clean appearance, his walk is a little different. So I must say, "My my, look at you. I don't think I've ever seen your hair combed so neatly."

His face turns a little red. "Very funny! Come on. Mom and Dad are on their way out."

I turn to HD, and as he feels my affectionate touch upon his young head, I say, "See ya later buddy."

Before my second step I think, *I'd better make sure that I don't walk like my brother!*

Dad's starting of the car brings my sister out of the house, and as all of us climb into the car, I feel we must look a little like a Norman Rockwell Sunday morning family picture.

All the way to church, my curious thoughts make me unusually quiet, and as my heart and mind share sentiments, Mom says, "We're almost there."

With an eager shift to the left, I can see around Mom's puffy hair. Then, a few heartbeats later, Dad turns into the church parking lot. As a sailor studies each wave, I look at each person across the parking lot and realize that these people are different, and seem to be simple and happy. *This is good.*

We finally park, and as we walk toward the church, embarrassment builds within my heart because of my long hair and secular appearance. But the lure of this old-fashioned Baptist church kindly invites me to step inside. As we draw closer, my embarrassment fades when friendly, happy sounds reach through the door and touch my heart. The appeal of new beautiful sounds draws me in with desires for all that is inside.

After a few steps through the door, I clearly understand that I am in a different culture. As I realize these great differences, all my nerve endings fire new, different messages to my very active brain.

The abundant grace of these people compels my earnest survey of them. As I behold these amazing people, I am so impressed because they seem simple and so very happy.

Then I notice the door to the sanctuary. As I slightly lean left, my eyes are able to reach in, and my heart follows, moving my steps toward the door. To my surprise, after a few more steps, Mom and Dad slip around me and venture inside, and us kids follow close behind like timid little chicks.

The charm and reverence in this old sanctuary are very pleasing, and after we sit down, I curiously look around and am filled with so many rich impressions. Moments later, the pastor steps up to the pulpit and into my heart. *He seems like a grandpa whom everyone would love. He seems like a good, simple, tender man—a true godly man.*

After his excellent message, the pastor steps from behind the pulpit down to the floor and says, "Please stand, and as we sing our hymn, if there is anyone who would like to pray and become a Christian, please step forward, and one of our members will be happy to pray with you."

During the pastor's sermon, I decide that I would like to become a Christian. *Yes! I should run down the aisle!*

It must be a devil that says to my heart, *What will Mara think?*

As embarrassment and concern about Mara increases the rate of my pulse, everything within me still says, *Go!*

Everyone seems so happy, but within my young heart, a great war begins when Heaven above draws, and earth below pulls. I have not experienced this great conflict before. I should just run down the aisle, but my natural inclinations will not bow to heaven's invitation. As the hymn draws near its end, I feel my chance slip away. A great remorse grips my heart as if I had just heard, "Sorry sir, only women and children are allowed in the lifeboat."

As all leave, my wavering heart cries, *Just talk with the pastor!*

I do not know why I begin to follow everyone out away from the pastor. As I step through the front door, my fear of hell intensifies. Halfway out to our car, I feel like a desperate man out in the cold ocean, so very far from land, struggling against violent, heavy seas, and for some insane reason I have just refused the offer of a life preserver.

Later in the day I hear so clearly within my heart, "You're not special; if you die without Jesus, you will go to hell."

Held in a state of fright, heaven's warning weakens as concern about Mara strengthens.

Monday morning I awake very much afraid of hell. As I prepare to go to work, my mind considers the day, and the many ways that I could easily die and go to hell. *I think it's better for me to stay here in my room. Yeah right! Next Sunday I'm going to church, and when the pastor invites people to pray, I'll go forward. No doubt, I will go forward!*

During that next day at work and each following day, I am very much afraid of hell. So I mention to Mara that I am afraid to die and go to hell, because I think for sure that my fear will encourage her to go to church. But again she says no.

My passage through the week seems so slow, because my approach to next Sunday is only minute-by-minute. But now that I have finally arrived at Saturday evening, I'm so happy because I feel as if I am finally almost there. I am happy to go to bed early on a Saturday night. I know it is odd for me to go to bed early on a party night, but it seems as right as when I was a boy and jumped into bed early on Christmas Eve.

Early Sunday morning as my eyes open, my heart is already considering the day and the many good impressions I received at church last week. The fast pace of my getting dressed, a short breakfast, and an early good-bye as I drive my own truck to church, reveal the true desire of my heart, which is to learn more about God.

As I finally walk across the church parking lot, I realize, *This just seems right, and it's so good to see these people again.*

After a few steps through the church door, a kind, elderly man warmly greets me. "Well hi there. I remember you. You were here last week." As I place my hand in his, he smiles and says, "I'm Ed Thomson."

His simple affection kindles a new flame within my heart, one that I so wish would burn bright in my life.

As I turn toward the sanctuary, others kindly greet me and make me feel much greater than John Wayne, because these Christians must know that I am a sinner responding to heaven's invitation. As I press through the crowd toward the sanctuary, these redeemed sinners warmly greet me, because they are rich with God's love. I am happier when I see my family step through the church door, and after we sit down together, we eagerly wait for another excellent message.

During the first hymn, I think again, *I am ready to go forward when the last hymn is sung. No doubt, I will bolt like a deer!*

So why during the last hymn do I freeze and not go forward? Is it because I am so much like our first parents Adam and Eve that I too run and hide (Genesis 3:7–13).

A few times through the next week, I hear within my frightened heart, "You're not special; if you die without Jesus, you'll go to hell."

The following Sunday I go to church again without Mara, because she thinks it is best for her to stay at home.

Through the past two weeks, my hell-frightened heart has stared into eternity, sowing into my young, fertile mind warnings about worldly, temporal values in contrast to the inspirations of eternal godly values. I understand the rewards of both invitations, and I know that the scale is not balanced. I think, *I'm going to pray and become a Christian. I am going to do it!*

But after the pastor's message when all stand to sing a heartfelt hymn, my heart rate rises. And as I am about to freeze again, my desperate pounding heart cries, *No! Just go!*

As the old hymn fills the sanctuary, the weight of judgment and hell is very heavy upon my heart. My heart and mind that are so desperate to live in heaven someday, begins a survey of eternity. And from heaven, divine love takes pity upon me in my poor helpless state. Mercy and grace then enable me to close the hymnbook and slip it back into its slot. When my eyes come back up and look forward, I feel enabled to go. Oh, but the battle is not over! My little brother to my right, and the man to my left must surely hear my heartbeat, and I am sure that those behind me can see the beating pulse in my neck.

As everything within me says, *Go!* I take my first step toward Heaven. And now with everyone behind me, the pastor is straight ahead. His kind expression draws me to his extended hand, and a few heaven-bound steps later, our hands unite. Just as I thought, his big hand feels as gracious as his warm smile.

Then the pastor hands me to a member of the church staff, Jim, who kindly greets me and leads me to a Sunday school room. I am impressed with Jim's pleasant nature and strength of good character.

After we sit down, we introduce ourselves and briefly speak about our families. I then mention that I am afraid to die and go to hell.

[Note to you, dear reader: The following conversation with Jim is my way of explaining to you my understanding of what might have occurred in the Garden of Eden.]

Jim opens his Bible so that I can read verses about why I deserve to be thrown into hell. Then he asks, "Do you understand why God will not allow you to enter heaven? Do you understand why God will not allow you to enter into his city?"

I answer with a hint of soberness, "Is it because I'm a sinner?"

He answers, as one offering a remedy, "Yes, but that's only part of the reason."

By lifting my eyes to him, I signal a question. So Jim says, "Okay James. Let's go back to the beginning of man's problem. On the sixth day, the Creator made the animals, and then the man called Adam. Adam was a most amazing man, because he was made with similar qualities like those of our Creator. That means that Adam's essential nature was like God's nature. So Adam was sinless and pure. I think because Adam was made in God's likeness that he was also clothed with God's glory. Therefore, his body likely glistened with brilliant white light, just like God. It must have been so amazing!

The Creator then planted a garden called the Garden of Eden and then God must have said to Adam that this garden is your home. How amazing. The garden must have looked like a beautiful park, decorated with so many pretty colors. Their first walk into the park must have been so very amazing, the Supreme Being and Adam, both glistening among so many pretty colors. Amazing! There in the garden the Supreme Being communed with Adam. I am sure that animals and angels must have watched with amazement.

And I think…well, it's just my personal belief, but I think very early the next morning as dawn evolves from night, God walked into His slumbering park and found Adam sound asleep in his favored place, and said to him,

Good morning my son. Let's go for a walk and watch the sunrise. The slow progression of the early morning must have set the pace of their slow walk. And when the new sun was finally brightly shining, the great Creator said to His darling son, My love for you is brighter than the sun. And for the first time, man pulled God into his arms, close to his heart, and said, Ohhh God, as your early morning flowers open for you, so has my heart opened for you. And with eternity before them, they continue their short walk through the pretty park.

And maybe later when Adam was alone caring for the garden, his thoughts were much about two horses standing together, not far away in a meadow."

Jim then asks, "Have you even seen two horses stand close together?"

I answer with a strong hint of country pride, "Oh, yes. We owned three horses when we lived out in farm country."

Jim's smile carries his words so well. "Good for you. So you've probably seen two horses stand facing each other, with each horses head next to the others' shoulder?"

I answer, "Yes, that's funny when they do that."

Jim slides to the edge of his chair, and his hands are now much involved in his talk. "Have you seen them when they stand like that and nip back and forth at each other's shoulders?"

Jim's animation draws me to the edge of my seat. "I have, but I don't know why they do that!"

Jim then mellows and slides back into his chair. "I don't either, but my point is there must have been a day when Adam was alone, busy caring for the garden, and his thoughts were much about two horses standing close together out in a meadow. And maybe when they started nipping back and forth at each other's shoulders, Adam stood straight and tall and fixed his eyes on them. Their playfulness must have caused him to stare curiously. In that moment, the amazing blessed man must have realized his need when he thought, *Where is someone for me?* Maybe through the day as Adam cared for the garden he also realized his need for help. Well, the Creator heard the thoughts in Adam's heart. I think later when God and Adam walked in the garden in the cool of the day (Genesis 3:8); the Creator said to Adam, It's not good that you are alone. So I will make a help meet for you (Genesis 2:18). That same day, the Creator fashioned a woman for His man. Amazing!

Adam and his woman finally stood before each other; glistening with divine excellence, and by increasing degrees admired each other because of their holy innocence. Their perfect agreement of masculinity and femininity must have harmonized, as notes vary in song. And though they were encompassed by so many delights and comforts, they beheld the best delight and comfort in each other.

So with great affection they reach out for each other, uniting their hearts with deep lifelong love. They then must have turned to our kind Creator and expressed their deep, heartfelt gratitude for each other. Amazing!

And maybe a few moments later Adam said to the woman, who he named Eve, see the two horses in the meadow? He must have then explained how their playfulness enlarged his heart with great need for her. No doubt when the three of them began their first walk, Satan continued his vigilant watch. You can read about this here, in Genesis 2:8 to the end of chapter three."

I glance at his open Bible and thank him. Then Jim continues, "I'm sure that Satan's powerful intellect easily devised a simple plan, as he continued his careful watch. During their walk through different parts of the garden, the rich beauty must have revealed the Creator's great strength, love, and provision for them. There must also have been an abundance of good food and sweet fellowship."

Then the different animation of Jim's face and the hint of his playful smile prepare me for a new thought. "I know that I say 'amazing' a lot, but that's because everything about the garden story is so amazing!"

I smile and say, "I agree. It is amazing!"

Jim then brings us back to the most important part of our talk. "One of the most amazing things about the garden was a certain tree in the middle of the garden. That tree represented a test, a serious test."

I say, "A test?"

As Jim answers, I move closer to the edge of my chair.

"Yes, in the middle of the garden there was a tree representing the test of obedience. First, I should mention that Adam and Eve understood that they could eat from every tree in the garden, except from that one tree in the middle of the garden. Right there in the middle of the garden, right where they could see it every day. Adam and Eve knew that if they obeyed God's command- ment and did not eat from that one tree, they would enjoy the Creator's favor. They understood that their happiness would continue only if they continued in obedience. They also understood the threat of severe punishment, and the consequence of disobedience (Genesis 2:16–17; 3:2–3). So they avoided the tree by staying in a safe current, but they were unaware of a developing riptide.

Satan's superior mind understood the chain of their thoughts. So with angelic speed of thought he devised a simple, logical plan. Now with his scheme readied, he waited until the opportune time. It was only a short time until he saw Eve alone near the forbidden tree. He then emerged from his concealed place of observation, and approached his victim. He is a seductive artificer, so the dethroned liar greeted Eve with an attitude of innocence. As he had thought, his contrived concern for her drew her into his dangerous conversation. Satan believes that when he purposely misquotes God, Eve's heart and mind will acquiesce to his subtle influence. So he said,

…Yea, hath God indeed said, ye shall not eat of every tree of the garden?
GENESIS 3:1

And as he also perceived, she was quick to engage in the conversation and correctly quote God:

…We eat of the fruit of the trees of the garden. But of the fruit of the tree which is in the midst of the garden, God hath said, Ye shall not eat of it, neither shall ye touch it, lest ye die.
GENESIS 3:2–3

Eve's developing consent encouraged the devil. So as she weakened, he strengthened his ploy by asking if it is a sin or not if you eat this fruit?

And as he planned, questioning the absolute further weakened her will. So Satan then fixed more of his influence upon her heart and mind when he said,

…Ye shall not die at all,… and ye shall be as gods, knowing good and evil.
GENESIS 3:4–5

With the assurance of no danger, and the promise of being as a god, she finally surrendered her heart and mind. And because of Satan's artful process of persuasion, she no longer feared the threat from God.

As the devil had planned, he easily lured Eve into temptation. His entice-ments now easily drew her into shameless defiance of divine law. Because seditious seduction summons vulnerable desires, she now considered the forbidden fruit as 'good' and 'pleasant.' And as she extended her hand, divine favor ebbed from her.

James, I think that when the fruit was in her hand, she must have thought, he's right. There's no harm! So she lifted the fruit to her mouth and for a moment pressed it against her lips. As a flood of adrenalin raced into her heart, she opened her mouth for the fruit. I think when her tooth broke the skin of the fruit, her glistening then vanished. And as she bit, perpetual happiness dissolved, as spiritual death evolved.

The onset of mortality must have stunned her senses, filling her heart with terror. As her first tears left her eyes, she then must have understood that her advisor was an agent of spiritual death. And I am sure that she then spit his instrument of death to the earth and ran.

Now, as before, when Satan hid, she now hid, filling the garden with strong deep cries.

For the first time Adam heard her cry, touching his senses with alarm, causing him to stand, as he also looked with a questioning stare. The strange sound from 'his delight' caused him to walk rapidly and then run toward his wife. Before he arrived his eyes reached out, and embraced her, throwing his heart and mind into greater commotion, because for the first time she was sobbing and without her glow. This strange sight slowed his run so that his true manliness might tame his heart and mind for her. Adam then finally stood next to his wife, but she did not rise or lift her face from her hands until his hand touched her shoulder. She then must have sprung up into his arms, expressing a most sad cry. And for the first time, man pulled a broken woman into his arms, close to his heart.

Eve's now carnal nature easily began to weaken Adam's godly sense, facilitating his defiance of God's law, initiating harmony with his wife.

Adam must have been curious about the different nature of his wife, which slowly made him susceptible to Eve's wrong suggestion. After Eve told Adam that she did eat of the forbidden fruit, she handed the fruit to Adam (Genesis 3:6). And after he ate the fruit, impending doom alarmed his heart, as spiritual death alienated him from God. He must have then spit the poison out. James, their consequence was:

...in the day that thou eatest thereof, thou shalt die the death.
GENESIS 2:17

It is very sad. The very moment that Adam and Eve sinned, divine purity faded from them as corruption filled them. At that moment their pious nature died. That was their consequence. But our consequence is...well, I'll turn to the verse and let you read it. Here it is."

As Jim pulls his finger down the page, he says, "Right there. Verse twelve."

...by one man sin entered into the world, and death by sin, and so death went over all men: in whom all men have sinned.
ROMANS 5:12

Jim then says, "Before we talk about this verse, read verse eighteen."

So I say, "Okay."

...by the offense of one, *the fault* came on all men to condemnation,...
ROMANS 5:18

Jim then says, "Now we're beginning to see man's problem. Do you see it?"

My mind searches for a good answer, and I then wisely say, "Uh."

Jim knows that I do not know the answer, so he kindly says, "Adam and Eve's defiled nature infected their children through conception (Job 14:4, 15:14–16, 25:4; Psalm 51:5). In the same way, their children passed corruption to all generations. That means that at the moment of conception, all babies inherit uncleanness from Adam and Eve. And that is man's problem."

[Note to Reader: Pastor and teacher John MacArthur has written an excellent book titled *Age of Accountability*. In addition, sermons from Pastor MacArthur's ministry and other information are found at Grace to You, www.gty.org or by calling 1-800-55-GRACE]

As Jim turns a few Bible pages, he says, "James, that means that you and I inherited uncleanness from our parents. Here it is. Read this verse, and you will understand why uncleanness is a serious problem. Just read the first sentence."

And there shall enter into it [heaven] **none unclean thing,...**
REVELATION 21:27

When my eyes meet with Jim's, I am sure that he can see my hell-frightened heart.

Jim then sobers and says, "James, now do you see man's problem?"

From my heart I respond, "I do, I do. All people are born unclean, and God will not allow any unclean person to enter heaven. I know that there are people in heaven. So my question is how did they become clean so that they could enter heaven?"

"James, first my question is do you really believe that everyone is born as an unclean thing?"

Before I answer, Jim says, "Just consider man's nature. Because of our defiled nature, our understanding is darkened (Ephesians 4:17–19). That is why we are often wrong. It is because our senses are corrupted. And because our senses are corrupted, we naturally give ourselves to vanity and not godliness. The reason that we give ourselves to vanity is because our capacity to love God is ruined. That's why we increasingly love perversion and not God. So because of our corrupt nature, this world is burdened with sorrows, sufferings, and losses (James 4:1–2).

We are completely ruined. We are born as unclean things and love it (John 3:19). Because we are born unclean, and naturally love ungodliness, all people are condemned. However, because God intensely loves us, He offers a way that man may become clean and enter His city.

God looks on us with empathy because He does love the world (John 3:16). He has abounding sympathy for us, and because of His tender compassion to us, He offers a remedy for us. Our remedy comes to us through Jesus (John 14:6; 1 Timothy 2:5–6). God sent Jesus, His own son, to pay the penalty for our uncleanness (Romans 5:10; 2 Corinthians 5:18), but not with money (1 Peter 1:18–19). Jesus offered His own life as payment (Matthew 20:28). The reason His payment was acceptable to God, is because when Jesus was born, He was born clean, and He then lived a clean, sinless life (Hebrews 4:15; 1 Peter 2:22). His birth and life was a pure devotion to God. That is why God accepted His death as payment for our penalty.

Jesus offered His clean righteous life as payment. So now God offers the clean righteous life of Jesus to us as a pardon for our sins (Romans 5:18–19). So all of your uncleanness, all of your sins, can be placed on Jesus (Colossians 2:14; 1 Peter 2:24), and His righteousness can be placed on you (2 Corinthians 5:21). And that is how God makes a person clean.

But you must be very careful and accept God's offer according to His terms, or He will not make you clean (Romans 2:16; Galatians 1:8–9).

There are many who truly believe that God has cleansed them, but after they die, they will learn that they are not clean (Matthew 7:21–23; Luke 13:23–28; Acts 18:24–26; 1 Peter 4:18). James, think about how easily we are deceived. How many times have you thought that you were truly right and later learn that you were truly wrong? Well, here is a frightening thought about deception. Lucifer, also known as Satan, did not discern his own self-deceit. A third of the angels did not discern Satan's deceit that ruined them (Revelation 12:9). And when Eve's nature was like God's nature, she did not discern the devil's deceit that ruined her (1 Timothy 2:13-14). Their superior minds did not discern deceit. And so, because of our corrupt minds, it is so much easier for us to be deceived (Jeremiah 17:9). You must make sure that you understand God's offer and what God requires of you to enter heaven."

Jim explains that I cannot earn my entry into heaven just by doing a religious deed or by living a good life (Romans 3:20, 9:11, 16, 18, 11:6; Galatians 2:16), and reads the following verses to me:

…not of yourselves: it is the gift of God, Not of works,…
EPHESIANS 2:8–9

Not by the works of righteousness, which we had done, but according to his mercy he saved us,…
TITUS 3:5

But we have all been as an unclean thing, and all our righteousness *is* as filthy cloths,…
ISAIAH 64:6

Jim further explains that the Hebrew word "filthy" means a woman's menstrual flux. The word is symbolic of the menstrual cloths used during a woman's menstrual cycle to picture uncleanness.

Jim then shocks me when he says, "James, would you pick up a soiled menstrual cloth and then say to God, 'I'll give this to you if you will make me clean'?"

Now I am just silent, so Jim further explains, "The point is that our best devotions to God are soiled by our uncleanness. A defiled, unclean sinner cannot say to the Holy Supreme Being, 'I will give my filthy righteousness to you if you will make me clean.' That is not an acceptable exchange with God, not for salvation. God knows that we are ruined, completely destitute of the ability to make ourselves clean or even earn cleanness.

If you wish to make sure that you will live in heaven and not perish in hell, then you must understand 'amend' or 'repent.' Because these two words are part of what is required of you to enter heaven."

Jim then found the place in the Bible so that he could tell me the requirements to enter heaven.

...but except ye amend your lives, ye shall all likewise perish.
LUKE 13:3

The King James Bible states:

...But, except ye repent, ye shall all likewise perish.
LUKE 13: 3

In *The New Strong's Concordance of the Bible*, which includes Hebrew and Greek dictionaries, "repent" is defined in the following way:

to think differently ...(1) "to change one's mind or purpose." (1a) always, in the NT involving a change for the better, an amendment, ... (4) The three steps found in [the Greek word for repent] *[are] (4a) new knowledge (4b) regret for the previous course, displeasure with self, and (4c) a change of action.*

"Amend" is described in the *American Dictionary of the English Language*, Noah Webster 1828 as to correct, or to rectify by correcting a mistake, to reform by stopping a bad habit, or to make a moral situation better.

"Repentance" is so well defined by Carl G. Kromminga in the *Wycliffe Bible Encyclopedia:*

> *...that inward change of mind, affections, convictions, and commitment, rooted in the fear [Luke 12:5], of God and sorrow for offenses committed against Him, which when accompanied by faith in Jesus Christ, results in an outward turning from sin to God and His service in all of life.*

Then Jim says, "James, God knows that you are not able to truly amend your life or repent because you are so depraved. So if you are able to truly amend your life or repent it is because God draws souls by giving them grace and strength and a heart to come to Him (John 6:44, 65; Ephesians 2:1–3; 2 Corinthians 4:4; 2 Timothy 1:9).

And the other requirement is:

For if thou shalt confess with thy mouth the Lord Jesus, and shalt believe in thine heart, that God raised him up from the dead, thou shalt be saved:
ROMANS 10:9

James no one can truly amend his life or repent unless God 'draw him' or 'except it be given to him' (John 6:44, 65). So my question to you is do you have an earnest, true desire to repent or amend your life?"

I say, "I do."

Jim says, "Very good. And do you also truly believe that Jesus is the Supreme Authority, like a king, and that if He accepts your prayer, then you must die to self and live for Him" (Luke 14:26–27; Romans 6:2)?

I nod my head with a heartfelt yes.

Jim says, "Very good. Do you also believe that God raised Jesus up from the dead?"

My heart now beats a little faster because I feel as if I am about to be adopted by God (Ephesians 1:5). So from an earnest heart I say, "Yes, I do."

We bow our heads for prayer so that I may confess to God my repentance and belief regarding Romans 10:9. After asking God to forgive my sins, Jim says, "Well, if God accepted your prayer, then you are now His child. You are a Christian! [Many are not accepted, and these verses describe this: Luke 13:23–28; Matthew 7:13-14, 21–23; 1 Peter 4:18.]

If you are accepted, then God has put His spirit within you (Romans 8:9; 1 Corinthians 3:16, 6:19–20). If God's spirit is within you, His presence will change every part of your life (2 Corinthians 5:17). The presence of God's spirit will change you. The change will be so obvious that your family and friends will think that you are a different, new man (Ephesians 2:1–5). This change will be so great that it will be as if you are 'born again' (John 3:3) with a new life. If God's spirit is within you, your ungodly character will weaken, and God's 'divine nature' will become more evident in your life (2 Peter 1:2–4)."

We then notice how quiet the church is so Jim says, "Sure is quiet out there. We might be the only ones here."

As we say good-bye to each other, Jim invites me to come back to church Wednesday evening or Sunday morning. As we shake hands, I say, "I don't know about Wednesday, but I will for sure come back on Sunday. Well, bye-bye. I'm going to go tell my girlfriend that I am a Christian."

I then hurry out.

As I begin my walk through the church, my pace picks up because I am in a hurry to tell Mara that I'm a Christian. However, my pace slows just a little when I begin to realize that I do not feel any different.

When I finally start my truck, I remain in the parking space for a moment, and ponder why I still feel like I did before my repentance.

It is new for me to sit and ponder the thoughts of my heart. As my thoughts ebb and flow, the increased level of my happiness causes me to push the clutch in, release the brake, and head for Mara's house.

I am surprised to find that she is still in bed. After she comes out to the dining room, I speak as if God had just adopted me.

"I don't know what you're going to do, but I'm on my way to heaven. I prayed, and now I'm a Christian."

She does not seem interested in hearing about my new steps toward heaven, so after a few minutes, I say good-bye and head for my house. During my drive, I think a lot about Jim and my prayer, and wonder why I feel the same as before.

When I finally pull into our driveway, I turn the engine off and hurry to my bathroom. As I stand at the toilet, I am surprised to hear so clearly in my heart, "Look at your bathroom. It is filthy."

I immediately recognize the voice and say to myself, *God! This is the same voice that I heard at the party and through the past three weeks!* I feel so embarrassed because it seems as if someone is standing at my bathroom door looking at my filthy bathroom. As I slowly look around, I feel humbled as I say to myself, *It is filthy.*

I feel so embarrassed, but for the first time, I am happy to clean my bathroom and make it look better than new. I think, *Let's see. I'll need a bucket, Pine Sol, and a brush. I think they are in the kitchen—no, the utility room.*

I hurry to the utility room and quickly return with the cleaning items. As I begin to clean, I feel a strong new desire to read the Bible. After about a minute or two, I stop cleaning and go look for Mom's Bible. *Just where I thought it would be.*

I find it in the dining room on the shelf. After I blow the dust off of it I open Mom's Bible, and I feel a happy harmony with God, and realize that I can know Him through the Bible.

My desire to read is amazing because during my thirteen years in school (third grade twice—Mom held me back), I had only read two books—one in third grade, and the other in sixth grade.

A few minutes later, the aroma of Pine Sol draws me back to the bathroom. During my hour of cleaning, I can feel the influence of the Bible in the other room, just as in December when the influence of the Christmas tree is felt throughout the house.

After the bathroom is clean, I stand in the doorway and stare, so very happy with my bright, clean bathroom. I feel proud of myself. I then quickly put the cleaning supplies away and return to Mom's Bible. I pull a chair from the kitchen table, and then sit and open the amazing King James Bible. I do not even know where to start reading. As I glance at the index, I think, *Revelation! Oh, that will be good to read!*

I turn to the book of Revelation and begin to read, and soon discover a new difficult word, well at least for me. And for the first time in my twenty-three years, I have an interest in the dictionary. So I grab Mom's dictionary and then go back to the table and begin to look for the difficult word.

Mom steps from the hallway into the kitchen and says to me, "What are you doing?"

Just as a theologian might say, I reply, "Studying the Bible."

Mom is as amazed as I am because she has never seen me sit with two open books, so willing to study.

I am happy to realize that I am forming new desires and new habits, because God changed me almost three hours ago. My new insatiable hunger for spiritual nourishment is like that of a newborn baby's hunger for its mother's milk.

As newborn babes desire that sincere milk of the word, that ye may grow thereby,
1 PETER 2:2

My amazing change is, being newly born, a new spiritual babe, I instinctively crave spiritual milk.

Through the following week, each day my heart and mind are occupied with the Bible stories that I read the evening before, inspiring new godly thoughts and honorable habits. I am so pleased to learn that my daily reading of the Bible is developing a genuine happiness within me.

However, I am not happy about the pastor's recent comment about Mara. Saturday morning Mom mentions to me that the pastor said I should stop dating Mara. I now have a problem with this pastor. In defense of Mara, I quickly say, "What? Stop dating?"

After six months of dating Mara, I am in love with her. I am sure that Mom can hear a hint of irritation in my voice when I ask, "Why does the pastor think that I should not date Mara?"

Mom says, "The pastor says that Christians are not supposed to date or marry someone who is not a Christian, and that Mara is not a Christian." (2 Corinthians 6:14–18; 1 Corinthians 7:1–40, especially verse 39).

I am so happy to answer the pastor's troubling comment with a good response. With confidence I say, "Well, Mara said that she will go to church with me in the morning."

The next morning at church, during the last hymn, Mara whispers to me, "I'm going to go talk to someone about how to become a Christian."

Amazing! I am very thankful and so amazed to see her step forward. Jim's wife greets Mara and takes her to a Sunday school room. Their long visit greatly encourages me, and gives me some time to dream about a long, good life with my future Christian wife. Finally, when the door opens, my dreams are felt, as Mara says, "James, I prayed, and now I'm a Christian!"

We greet each other as happy citizens of heaven. Then I notice that we are about the only ones still in the church. So I say to Mara, "Are you hungry? C'mon, let's go get something to eat!"

After our meal we begin our journey toward heaven by reading the Bible together, which thereafter becomes a daily habit (2 Timothy 2:15).

We now attend church Sunday morning and in the evening, and again on Wednesday evening, because:

Not forsaking the fellowship that we have among ourselves, as the manner of some *is*: but let us exhort *one another*, and that so much the more, because ye see that the day draweth near.
HEBREWS 10:25

For where your treasure is, there will your heart be also.
MATTHEW 6:21

Because God is the treasure of our hearts, the character of our lives is changing every day. We are now always aware of God, and sensitive to anything that would offend Him. Our daily desire is to please God and avoid sin (Philippians 2:12; Ephesians 5:3–6; Romans 12:1–2).

My favorite music was Lynyrd Skynyrd, Creedence Clearwater Revival, and Steppenwolf; and Mara's favorite music was soft rock. Now we love the old hymns. Since my Harley has been like a god to me, it is now up for sale. And boxing...well, I've turned from it because I am now a man of peace. Our change of heart and mind are so great that we are beginning to appear as if we are pilgrims from another country (1 Peter 2:11).

Now that my citizenship is in heaven, my affections are also there (Philippians 3:20; Colossians 3:2). My daily correspondence with heaven weakens my affections for the things of this life on earth. I often consider that it would be very sad if my devotion to Jesus were less than my previous total commitment to John Alacrity.

CHAPTER 5

Learning to Follow God's Overruling Providence

A SERIOUS FISTFIGHT IS STOPPED

For the ways of man *are* before the eyes of the Lord, and he pondereth all his paths.

PROVERBS 5:21

The ways of man, all his motions, all his actions, are before the eyes of the Lord, all the workings of the heart and all the out goings of the life,...

MATTHEW HENRY

For the eyes of the Lord behold all the earth, to show himself strong with them that are of perfect heart toward him:...

2 CHRONICLES 16:9

[God's] eye directs his hand, and the arm of his power; for he shows himself strong...that those whose hearts are upright with him may be sure of his protection and have all the reason in the world to depend upon it.

MATTHEW HENRY

Thou hast enlarged my steps under me, and mine heels have not slid.

2 Samuel 22:37

August 1979: Six months after my conversion

This weekend, the main park in our city is full of booths and hundreds of curious people. So, late Saturday morning Mara and I melt into the crowd, and as we walk up to an interesting booth we hear, "Mara! Mara!"

The fast approach of happy giggles turns both of us around. Mara and her dear friend greet each other with a great big hug. As they begin to calm down, I stare at five or six men across the park that look like Hell's Angels. They hold my attention because they act as though they might possibly cause trouble. While my stare is fixed on them, I remember Ephesians 4:17–19 and consider, *They are in darkness; they do not know what they're doing.*

I think to myself, *There was a time when I acted as stupid as they are acting.*

Well, that for sure softens my heart, which makes me feel sorry for them. The girls' giddiness draws my attention back to them. However, a moment later the tallest of the unruly men purposely bumps into Mara's friend, and as he tries to collide with me, he misses because I roll my left shoulder out of the way. Before the next beat of my heart, I interpret the language of his intended strike as a threat to me. And before I turn back around, out of the corner of my left eye, I see him turn to face me. I am certain that it is not so he can share a doughnut with me. As I turn toward him, I already know my strategic approach, and within my heart, I laugh as I think, *This poor Philistine has no idea about my four and a half years of training as a boxer with John Alacrity.*

My soft appearance has deceived him. I look like harmless, easy prey because of my church-boy haircut, soft face, and nice clothes. He cannot see the highly skilled boxer now standing before him. If he had watched my last street fight almost a year ago, I am sure that he would apologize, and wisely walk away.

This street fight a year ago was with a famous black belt whom I challenged because he had hit a friend of mine; and who also thought that I was an easy challenge. We met in his territory behind a store at the appointed time of 1:30 a.m. And with about forty men circled around us, we displayed our skills. After my victory, while he was still horizontal, many of his friends rallied around me, asking, "Where did you learn to fight like that?"

If this unruly man had watched my command of that fight, I am sure that he would now shake my hand, turn, and leave.

By now, many people have gathered around us. I am for sure not going to take a nap in front of them, and especially not with Mara watching. My thought is, *I'm ready!*

All present are charged with anticipation. I can feel it because both of us have crossed a line and are about to inflict bodily harm on each other. His friends, also wearing black leather jackets, are gathered behind him, anxious for my demise. My Father, who is also watching, says so clearly to my heart, "I want you to learn to trust me."

Within my heart I say, *God!*

I understand that there is a purpose and a lesson that I must learn. So, I pray from my heart, *I won't touch him, if you will.*

The rude man must have noticed in my eyes that I was distracted, which encouraged him to draw both fists up tight and sway his upper body from side to side, indicating to me a surge of adrenalin. I realize, *He's going to hit me! I am not taking a nap in this park, not in front of Mara!*

I decided when it was time to end that fight with the black belt, and now it is time for me to stop this man now!

I then hear so clearly within my heart a verse that I had read a few times:

The King's heart is in the hand of the Lord, *as* the rivers of waters: he turneth it whithersoever it pleaseth him.
PROVERBS 21:1

The effect of God's presence and the influence of His Word produce an amazing change in my mind, enabling me to hand the reins of my heart to my Father. I say again to myself, *I know that there is a lesson here that I must not miss. I trust you. I will not touch him, if you will.*

In that moment, my opponent's hands fall open, and his swaying stops. His countenance also completely changes, as if God has seized control of him.

His sudden, amazing transformation convinces my brain that what I am seeing is true. Nevertheless, my cautious heart is not convinced. Then God confirms in my heart that it is actually true. I am so amazed at his change that I now feel as if we are alone in this park, and while his blank stare is fixed on me, I step up to him and say, "You wouldn't believe me if I told you. Have a nice day."

I turn and meet Mara, and as we walk away, I tell her how God interceded.

Last year, before Mara became a Christian, her high school scholastic achievements were very low. However, this year, after she became a Christian, she started her senior year at a Christian High School, and graduated as valedictorian. Her spiritual and academic growth in one year amazed everyone. That gives me great confidence that she will be a great wife, and mother.

[Gold Statement #2: On January 14, 1980, gold is valued at $660 per ounce. Six days later, on January 21, it is over $850 per ounce.]

1980: I AM TWENTY-FOUR YEARS OLD

SUMMER IS ALMOST HERE, and I'm finally parked in front of a small convenience store, hungry for another bag of Peanut M&Ms. But for a moment I remain in my truck, pondering the many summer evenings long ago when my friends and I stood in front of this little store, acting like young bucks at the edge of a mountain meadow. I then consider a more important thought, *Well, I should go in and get a bag of M&M's, no, two bags!*

As I get out of the truck, I am surprised when God says to my heart, "Look at all of the people."

Amazed, I think, *God!*

I realize that there must be a lesson for me to learn. While standing in this parking lot, and with great curiosity, I lay my right arm on top of the open truck door, and look across the parking lot towards a restaurant. I carefully look at the people over there, and continue to scan to the right at the supermarket parking lot. It is there, when I lay my eyes upon the last two people, a mother and her young daughter that God says to my heart, "Someday you are going to speak to many people."

My mind and heart respond as if struck hard with spurs, *I can't do that!*

As I begin to feel numb, my gaze into the parking lot intensifies, as a surge of adrenalin sweeps through my body.

I am afflicted again by the embarrassing moment of my boxing match when I blacked out in front of many people. Though I am sixty miles from the location of that boxing match, and eighteen months beyond that embarrassing moment, that humiliation is always painfully close within my heart and mind. I now look forward and consider another embarrassing moment before many people and wonder, *How am I going to speak to many people? I cannot do it! There is no way!*

A deep breath slightly slows my rapid heartbeat and stops my intense stare.

I can't do it! Well, I might as well go in. I probably look weird standing here.

Out of habit, I step right to the Peanut M&Ms and consider, *How am I going to speak to many people?*

Week after week, the thought of speaking to many people afflicts my heart like a splinter in my finger. And week after week, Mara and I fan the flames of our lifelong dreams together.

AUTUMN 1980: I AM TWENTY-FOUR YEARS OLD
I LOOK TO THE LEFT and then to the right. I then look straight ahead and say, "I'll never get across!"

Again, I am after a large bag of Peanut M&Ms in a store on the other side of a busy street.

Look to the left.

A gap!

A space in the traffic, and suddenly I am as bold as a rodeo clown. Running through this traffic will be so worth a mouth full of chocolate. So as the gap draws near, I slightly bend my knees and make myself ready to bolt. I am now like a .45 Long Colt revolver that is cocked and ready, and as I wait for the gap, I say, "Two bags!"

I leave the curb like a hot desert wind. It feels good to run again, yet after a short burst, I reduce my run at the other side. Now at a comfortable walk, I am on my final approach to the M&Ms. Then I notice a man to my left as he steps out through the door of another store. When my eyes first fix on him, I am surprised to hear God say to my heart, "Talk to him about the gospel."

I look with heavenly interest, as young Christian enthusiasm now enlarges my heart. *I will talk with him. He must be ready to repent.*

After a year and a half of bible study, I think I know what I should say, and I see that our direction of walk will cause us to meet in the middle of the parking lot.

Amazing! I'm ready.

My heart is aglow with heavenly duty, and I am thankful for this opportunity. As we draw near to each other, I keep my eyes fixed on him and think, *He must be ready to accept Jesus.*

When we are twenty feet apart, my heart begins to lose courage. Five feet from my noble duty, my eyes, full of failure, meet his. And as we pass by each other, I can only muster a few words. "Hi there."

Heavy disappointment floods my heart, and I say to myself, *I am so stupid! What is wrong with me? I should go after him! He must be headed for hell. That is why God told me to talk with him.*

However, in this moment I am just a coward. So I avoid my duty to urge him to eternal bliss, and surrender myself to my desire for chocolate.

Finally, the bags of candy are in my hand. However, I am not happy because I am so ashamed of myself. So here in the store, feeling as if I am truly before the Father, I bow my head, confess my sin, and ask, "Please Father, give me another opportunity with that man."

I pay for the candy, and as I step through the front door on my way out, a man to my right captures my attention as he steps out through the door of the store next-door. I realize that it is the same man, leaving the same store that he had stepped out of before. As I stare at him, I say, "No way! Amazing!"

Feeling like a navy pilot who must not miss his carrier landing, I know what to do. I know what I *must* do. I am so very happy to hand the reins of my heart to my Father. This time I will obey.

As before, the direction of our walk will cause us to meet again in the middle of the parking lot.

"Amazing! Father watch, this time I will not fail."

My heart is aglow with renewed heavenly duty, and I am thankful for another opportunity. As the Father and I draw near, I fix my eyes on the man, and settle the matter.

No doubt, I will talk to him about Jesus.

When we are twenty feet apart, my heart begins to gallop, not as a stallion, but as an obedient Christian. At ten feet, my heart is very determined with heavenly courage. Then, five feet from my noble duty the man must have understood the language of my heart through my eyes, because as I slow and extend my hand, so does he. My lively handshake shows him that I am happy to finally meet him. I am like the farmer who is happy about the arrival of spring, because like the farmer, I finally stand at the edge of my field with seed in my hand (John 4:35–38). I then sow the Word of God into his heart, telling him about heaven and hell, and God's offer of salvation. Moments later, as I walk away, I pray for him, and celebrate the occasion with two yummy bags of Peanut M&Ms.

CHAPTER 6

Trust in Eve's Logic

⤙∽

MY REACH FOR MARRIAGE AND CHILDREN

Therefore shall man leave his father and mother, and shall cleave to his wife, and they shall be one flesh.
GENESIS 2:24

Set me as a seal on thine heart, *and* as a signet upon thine arm: for love *is* strong as death:...
SOLOMON'S SONG 8:6

Let me never lose the room I have in thy heart; let thy love to me be ensured, as that deed which is sealed up not to be robbed...Let me be always near and dear to thee, as the *signet on thy right hand*, not to be parted with...Let thy power be engaged for me, as an evidence of thy love to me; let me be not only a *seal upon thy heart*, but a *seal upon thy arm*; let me be ever borne up in thy arms, and know it to my comfort....

MATTHEW HENRY

Love is a violent vigorous passion. It is strong as death. The pains of a disappointed love are like the pains of death;

MATTHEW HENRY

EARLY SPRING 1981: I AM TWENTY-FIVE YEARS OLD

THE SETTING SUN HAS MEASURED another day, and as the movement of night begins, Mara and I stay in the truck until the old hymn on the radio ends. After the hymn, I turn the radio off, and for a moment, we quietly sit and listen to the sound of the soft rain falling on the top of the truck. My heart then extends my hand to hers, and I say, "C'mon. I'll walk you to your door."

For thirty-one blessed months, I have walked her to her front door. Each time, I dream about the day when we may walk to "our" door. But for now I must leave her at her house. As we slowly head for the door, I am surprised to hear God say to my heart, "Years ahead she's going to turn from you and me."

Emotional strain instantly sobers my mind, extending my arm far enough in front of her to slow our pace, which stops us twelve feet from her door. Now, face to face, I say, "You're not going to believe what God just said to me. He said that years ahead you're going to turn from me and Him."

Her eyes express deep love for me, and as she takes careful aim at my heart, she says, "James, I love you. I wouldn't leave you, and I especially wouldn't leave God."

The language of her eyes and the charm of her pretty face weaken the warning (Proverbs 6:24–26), and her tender words easily turn my heart from simple truth, to deceitful logic. And so, the process of logic begins within me, as it did with Eve in Genesis 3:1–6.

Had God indeed said, "Years ahead she's going to turn from you and me"? She shall surely not turn from me. I clearly see that her love is good, and that our dreams are "pleasant to the eyes" both desired. With the logic of Eve, I ignore God's warning and plan for our marriage. Moreover, because I am so assured by this logic I say to Mara, "Don't worry. When you turn away, I'll do my best to bring you back."

The affectionate bond between us is like the inseparable union of a husband and wife. My proper care and nourishment of her prove my sacrificial and permanent love for her.

As Mara's Mother only provides minimal food and clothing for her. Therefore, I provide almost all of her unmet needs. That's okay, because of our spiritual growth and complete agreement about Bible doctrine, someday we will become "one" blessing each other as husband and wife.

When I was very, very young, before I learned to measure a year, continuous happy expressions entered my heart, setting a course for my life. As the years passed, wonderful dreams conceived, eventually giving birth to a very satisfying long view of my life. When I met Mara, she easily harmonized with my happy expressions and wonderful dreams, truly satisfying my long view of life. Together, we now reach for lifelong dreams.

EARLY SUMMER 1981
EARLIER TODAY, I ASKED Mara to be my wife for life. Her happy "yes" will deliver us to our bond of marriage next year.

A year later, the expressions of our love, and delights of our hearts, have become one in marriage.

[Gold Statement #3: In 1982, the low for gold is $296 per ounce, and the high is $488 per ounce.]

APRIL 23, 1982: I AM TWENTY-SIX YEARS OLD, AND MARA IS TWENTY-ONE
THE LAST BOX IS CLOSED, taped, and carried out to the truck. Now all of our possessions are in the back of our little Toyota pickup. We finally cast the

lines, and sail from our harbor. The treasure we seek is Bible knowledge. Our destination is a Bible college in mid-America.

Each morning, farmers in that state awake before first light, and almost two hours earlier the sun began to warm the east coast. However, we depart from the east coast and arrive in mid-America three days later. But our three day drive does not dull Mara's happy glow, and within a short time, she is a favorite of both faculty and classmates at the Bible College. I am not surprised!

Future Bible scholars arrive from all parts of the United States, each enthusiastic to make a little home in the dorm. Everyone's senses are heightened and eager for friendship because they are so far from home.

As Mara and I acquire Bible knowledge, we also gain an excellent friendship with classmates Jonathan and Sarah.

One day, while in our dorm room, I feel compelled to go across the hallway to Jonathan and Sarah's room. I knock on the door and Sarah opens the door. When I look into the room, I see Jonathan sitting in a chair in the middle of the room with his open Bible in his lap. He says, "James, come here and let me show you something." I step close to him and look over his shoulder as he begins to read from Act 3: 1-4, about when Peter and John walked up to the temple to pray, and there at the gate saw a palsied man asking for money. And when Jonathan read, "And Peter earnestly beholding him with John, said, Look on us." I instantly knew that God had cured me from my fear of talking to many people. So I begin to laugh, which causes Jonathan to stop his reading and turn around to look at me. I explain to him that God just cured me from my fears of speaking before many people, because some day He is going to give many people a reason to look to me as I preach His word. About a month later, I stand on stage before five television cameras and twenty-five hundred people as I speak about my Christian testimony.

One day, as the four of us begin our climb up the stairs to our college classroom, we see five or six classmates coming down the stairs. Compelled by maritime law, we sail to starboard and give the right of way to the larger vessel of our friends. However, their expressions suggest that they have something to say. So there in the middle of the channel, all of us stop, and one of them says, "James, you remind us of Hosea." [The Old Testament Prophet]

All of us laugh as concern enters my heart, I think, *Hosea's wife ran away from him. This is another warning from God regarding Mara.*

Still laughing, each of us says, "See ya' later!"

During our climb, I feel as if my doctor had said, "James, I'm sorry to tell you that you have terminal cancer. And if you tell anyone, even your wife, they won't understand, or believe you."

I do not share this private thought with anyone except God. Mara's Christian character and the strength of our affectionate harmony assure me that we will survive all agonies, and prevail as one.

The expiration of days delivers us to the end of our academic course. Our graduation is in three days, on December 22. Mara's great scholastic reach rewards her with a 97.5 grade point average, and her superior mental gymnastics lead her to the honor of valedictorian, the President's List, and to be cited as one with special achievements. I am very proud of her, but I am not surprised by her accomplishments.

The day after graduation, we board a plane pointed toward the east coast, and then enjoy Christmas with family.

After Christmas, we return to our Bible College because I had accepted the offer of the college president to serve as his "right-hand man." I fill the position for about a month and then quit because of my disapproval of what he had said to the public on television. During a telethon, he had told the public that we had not yet reached the ministry's financial goal for that hour. Mara was keeping an account of money received, and told him that we had already reached his goal, yet he continued to tell the public that the goal had not been achieved.

FEBRUARY 1984

THE CHILLY, STILL MORNING feels like the far northern Yukon, and within our little country home, we are warm and blessed by the good company of Jonathan and Sarah. The Saturday morning sun is barely up, and the kitchen already smells like a good farm breakfast. Mara and Sarah are busy in the kitchen while Jonathan and I sit in the family room, enjoying our talk and hot coffee. Finally, Mara carries in hot food, and when she walks by me, I mention the insight given to me from God in that moment, and say, "Mara, you're pregnant."

All three of them laugh at me. Mara turns as red as can be and says, "No I'm not!"

The next morning, we scurry into the bathroom and hold our breath as the pregnancy test affirms yes.

We soon pack, and drive all the way to the east Coast, because I think it best that Mara be near our families during her pregnancy and the birth of our first baby. We settle into a comfortable home not far away from our families.

NOVEMBER 10, 1984

FOR THE PAST NINE MONTHS, my dear wife has nurtured one of our dreams, and early this morning our daughter Lauren is born.

We are happy with our new life in this large old city, and we enjoy the small Baptist church we now attend with a congregation of about fifty people. Friendships in this little church forms easily and quickly, and all of us are happy at how fast church membership is now growing.

Mara joins the church softball team, and I often teach the children's and the adult's Sunday school classes. I am so proud of Mara because I have heard that some of the women in church have said, "If you want to know how to be a good mother, watch Mara."

Mara is certainly worthy of this gracious compliment. Because her thoughtful approach, and tender progression of motherhood, our home is blessed with sweet beauty. We have now reached the top and full measure of simple pleasure, so our fond desire is for more children.

July 2, 1986

Today, the east coast suffers a very hot day. Because of this heat, I pause at the foot of this ladder, which leans against a customer's house that Dad and I are remodeling. I absolutely do not want to work up in the hot oven that many call "the attic." I wish that I could just stand down here all day. But before my ascent up this dreaded ladder, I am called to the phone to hear my very pregnant wife say, "Honey meet me at the hospital!"

After a few hours Maribelle is born. She is another great blessing for us.

CHAPTER 7

Heaven is Silent

⎯⎯᮫⎯⎯

THE CHEMICAL EXPOSURE: A THREAT TO LIFELONG DREAMS

...in the world ye shall have affliction,...
JOHN 16:33

Examples from Bible references in which various afflictions occur:

1. Accidental death by another: Deuteronomy 19:4–5
2. Eighteen men die when a tower falls on them: Luke 13:4
3. David's adultery with Bathsheba, and the murder of her husband: 2 Samuel 11:1–27
4. Unrighteous Cain murders righteous Able: Genesis 4:1–8
5. David's military leader Joab deceives Amasa, and then murders him: 2 Samuel 20:8–10
6. Judas betrays Jesus: Luke 22:3–6
7. Lies about righteous Stephen, result in his death: Acts 6:11
8. Amnon deceives Tamar, and then rapes her: 2 Samuel 13:1–19
9. Thirteen encouragements regarding obedience to God; and thirty-two warnings about disobedience: Leviticus 26
10. Fifteen encouragements regarding obedience to God; and fifty-three warnings about disobedience: Deuteronomy 28

11. God punishes the Hebrew's because of their sins: Numbers 14:26–38
12. The Hebrew's sins, and punishments have become a warning to us: 1 Corinthians 10:6–12
13. God ends Moses's life early (in Deuteronomy 32:4–51) because he sinned: Numbers 20:1–13
14. Warnings that many are sick or have died early because of their sins: 1 Corinthians 11:30
15. God gives King Asa a disease in his feet because of his sins: 2 Chronicles 16:12
16. God gives King Jehoram a disease in his intestines because of his sins: 2 Chronicles 21:15
17. Satan afflicts Job and his family: Job 1:6–22, 2:1–13
18. Satan afflicts a woman's health: Luke 13:10–17
19. Long-term afflictions for Gods glory: John 9:1–3
20. Short-term afflictions for Gods glory: John 11:1–48

LATE AUTUMN 1987

NOW THAT WE HAVE TWO daughters, we wish more earnestly for economic stability. Because of the weak economy, many carpenters like me are not working. So I step into the Union Hall and sign page twelve of the very long out-of-work list. I am very surprised to see the hall stuffed full of idle men, yet busy entertaining each other with cards, and many exaggerated stories. These men sit here week after week waiting to be called for work assignments. Though I am harmonious with their plights, I am opposed to this mode of idleness, because I am responsible for the health and well-being of my family. Although the Union forbids us to look for work after signing the out-of-work list, I walk out in search for work.

Later in the day, I stand at the Bashan Oil Refinery thinking that I need to display my best confidence because I have never worked in an oil refinery before. Thankfully, Og Construction, the contracted company working within Bashan Oil Refinery, hires me as a carpenter. I start work Monday morning. The Father is so good to us.

[Note to the reader: The meaning of the word "Bashan" comes from Deuteronomy 3:13, which states that the area of Bashan was "the land of giants." Skeletal remains reveal that the Old Testament giants were eight to thirty-two feet tall. In addition, even more amazing is that my Father enabled common people to defeat many of them. The king of Bashan was a giant named Og (Deuteronomy 3:11). A most excellent book about Genesis 6 giants can be purchased at Steve Quayle.com.]

Mara truly believes that I will faithfully provide for the needs and dreams of our family. I fully trust that my wife will spend every penny for our good. Neither one of us has a reason to question the other because we are under the marriage yoke, pulling together.

On Monday morning, I think the sun rises a few minutes early and shines a little brighter on the first day of my new job, and I am very anxious to go to the Bashan Oil Refinery. I arrive at the refinery gate a little early and enjoy my wait as other men arrive. And right on time, the gates are opened, and all of us walk in.

After the mandatory safety meeting, I am surprised to see my good friend Gary. He was one of my groomsmen at our wedding, and on one occasion when Mara was out of town for the weekend, Gary and his wife kindly invited me to their home for dinner, and to sleep in a nice warm bed.

Gary is not a typical carpenter because of his superior intellect, persuasive leadership abilities, and command of carpentry. About three years ago, Og Construction made a wise decision when they provided Gary with additional education and training. Now my good friend is a senior foreman for Og Construction. No doubt, he is *my* favorite senior foreman.

Friday, May 6, 1988

I have worked with Gary for several months. Today, my two partners and I are building a scaffold for another crew on top of a large heater that is four stories tall.

Though my two partners are already on top of the heater, I am still on the ground considering all the equipment that we might need for our project. I think to myself, *I should take extra clamps.*

Because of this delay, I shout to one of my partners up on top of the heater, "Hey Jack, I'll be up there in just a minute. I'm going to grab extra clamps!"

Jack shouts back, "Okay, good idea!"

The clamps lock tube scaffolding together, each one weighing about four pounds. My tool bags are able to carry the weight because they are attached to leather suspenders. In addition, I am able to carry the weight because of the good meals that Mara packs into my large lunch box, keeping me very healthy and strong.

After a few steps toward the ladder, the heavy clamps and tools in my nail bags, which weigh about thirty-five pounds, convince me to pause at the foot of the ladder. As my hands reach out to hold the four-story tall ladder, I look straight up and pause; not to question my ability to climb, but to prepare for the climb, because I feel like a little tugboat, now ready to bear down and pull a big ship through a narrow shipping channel. Almost all of my 195 pounds is solid muscle on my five foot eleven frame, so this climb is not a problem for me. After a big deep breath, my climb is quick and easy; however, up on the platform I pause again, waiting for my breath to catch up with me. While I am breathing very deeply, the lead carpenter, Jack, says to me in a raised voice from the other side of the platform, "Hey James, do you smell that odor?"

Petroleum refineries are full of various odors; however, this odor is very distinct, and different.

So in a loud voice I say, "Yes I do! What is it?"

Jack does not answer me as he turns to the other carpenter standing near him, and from what I can see their talk is serious. My curious gaze quickly becomes a concerned stare. I wish that I could step over to them, but I cannot, because the platform is stacked with scaffold material. Though the distance between us is only about eight feet, I cannot hear their words because of refinery noise.

Concerned, I yell, "Jack, what is it?"

Neither of them will look at me, and their disregard of me makes me think that they know that we are in some type of danger. I understand why they do not include me in their talk. It is because I am only a novice in this type of work. Both of them have a lot of experience in refinery work. When they look down, so do I. I now understand that they hesitate to go down to the ground because another crew from a different trade is waiting down below for us to finish the scaffold, and also because our foreman told us to never leave our work site unless we know there is a threat to our safety.

After about five minutes both men conclude that there is a threat to our safety, and as they step over scaffold material, Jack says, "James, this is not a good gas. Let's get out of here!"

As the three of us now gather at the ladder, I say, "You men board the ladder first."

A strict refinery rule allows only one person at a time on the ladder. However, we are desperate to leave this area, so all three of us scramble down the ladder at the same time.

On the way down, my entire body begins to feel numb, and I feel dizzy. So I glance down to see how far I am from the ground.

Oh, I'm only halfway down!

Concerned that I might pass out and fall on my coworkers, I carefully place my hands and feet on each rung as I descend the ladder until my boots finally touch the ground.

However, at the bottom when my hands finally slip from the ladder, I discover how much more unsteady and dizzy I actually am feeling it's like I'm on drugs. I turn to the lead carpenter and say, "Jack, something is wrong with me. I feel drugged."

Jack looks directly into my eyes, and I say to him, "And I feel nauseous."

I am surprised at how fast twelve to fifteen Og Construction and Bashan Oil authorities arrive, most of them wearing white shirts and carrying radios. Fire and safety personnel, Gary, and Og Construction's other foreman also quickly arrive, and yet all remain at a safe distance from the exposure site. Gary and the other foreman meet with Jack and me and ask, "What happened?"

Jack explains that we were up on the platform when a bad smelling gas engulfed our work area. Gary turns to me and asks, "How do you feel?"

I am hesitant to mention my symptoms because the other foreman always loudly mocks me. To Gary I say, "I have a headache with strong tingling in the back of my head, and I'm nauseous. I also have pain and tingling in both arms and both legs, and I am not stable. I feel drugged."

Both foremen now change their attitude toward me. They are not as friendly, and speak with as few words as possible. After a short conversation with each other, they return to the authorities, and a moment later, they come back to us. Gary tells us to sit on the ground about thirty yards away, and they then return to the Bashan Oil and Og Construction personnel.

After we sit on the ground, we fix our gaze upon Gary because we believe that he is gathering important information for us. We are also expecting the "Sniffer" to arrive. After a gas release, the protocol is for a Bashan Oil operator to come to the exposure site, and with his handheld computer identify the odor. We have witnessed the Sniffer procedure many times, and before Gary's return, the Sniffer steps into the exposure site. And with a lowered voice, I say to Jack, "The Sniffer."

Jack responds, "Yep."

We remain silent, and with a high degree of interest, we watch the Sniffer.

This time, however, the Bashan Oil Sniffer turns off his computer and quickly runs from the exposure site back to the authorities. I ask Jack, "Have you ever seen a Sniffer run like that from an exposure site before?"

Jack says, "No!"

During my many months of working in this Bashan Oil Refinery, I have observed the Sniffer at least ten times when he has tested an exposure site. They have never hurried like this from an exposure site before.

I ask, "What does that tell you about what we were exposed to?"

Jack responds, "It's not good."

Then Gary and the foreman step toward us from the large group of Og Construction and Bashan Oil authorities. So I say to Jack, "Good deal. Gary must know what we were exposed to."

However, when they arrive, Gary does not mention what the Sniffer discovered. So, I ask him, "What were we exposed to?"

Gary does not answer my question, and within about a minute, both men return to the group of authorities, which gives me the impression that Gary is inquiring about the odor. A moment later, they step from the authorities, back to us. I ask again, "What were we exposed to?"

Gary says, "Your symptoms will pass. Don't worry about it."

I do not understand, but I do trust my old friend Gary. And I know that Bashan Oil and Og Construction are controlled by strict safety regulations, so I must trust them. I think to myself, *If they say that my symptoms will pass, then they will pass.*

Gary and the other foreman return to the group of authorities, and a moment later when they return to us, I again ask Gary, "What were we exposed to?"

Gary again avoids my question. Both men then return to the group, and a moment later, they return and say to us, "Get into a truck and hide until your shift is over."

Hiding employees after they are injured is common practice at Bashan Oil Refinery, so it is not unusual for us to be told to hide.

When I stand up, I am surprised at how unstable I am. So I say, "Jack, I'm not able to drive."

Jack says, "Okay, I'll drive."

Jack then drives us to a secluded area of the refinery where there are no other workers.

After Jack turns off the engine he says, "This is not the first time this has happened to me. I'm going to quit refinery work."

I have learned that many people in this refinery believe that Jack is a lifetime refinery man. "Jack, I'm surprised to hear you say that."

I ask Jack about my symptoms.

Jack responds, "Gary said we will be all right, so don't worry about it."

After almost an hour, Gary and the other foreman arrive and park their truck next to us. Gary asks, "How do you feel?"

Jack quickly says, "I feel nauseous."

I say, "I feel the same as I did at the exposure site."

For the first time since I started working for Og Construction, the loud mouth foreman keeps his mouth shut.

Gary says to us, "Go down to the carpenter shack for the remainder of your shift. We will go with you. Follow us."

When the four of us enter the carpenter shack, Gary says, "If you need to lie down, lie there on that table."

I feel a little embarrassed to lie on our dinner table, especially in the presence of that other foreman, because he always makes rude, crude remarks to me, and teases me every day. I just hope that when I lie on the table, he doesn't tease me. I don't think that he means any harm when he teases me. In fact, I know that he likes me, and I believe that he respects my carpenter skills. However, I think that if I changed and acted like him, he would fire me! So as usual, I must do what I must do and risk his rude remarks. I move a few lunchboxes and a jacket off the table, and I am so very thankful to finally lie down.

However, after only a moment I realize that there is no escape from what is tormenting me, *Great!*

I seem to feel more irritated when I lie down. The pain and tingling sensations in the back of my head and in both of my arms and legs are very strong. And besides, this plywood table is very hard. I roll off the table and step across the room for a drink of water.

Another problem in this room is the carpenter's pride that I am expected to express. Winter cold, summer heat, splinters, and cuts from nails temper long-term carpenters. Through the seasons, the elements and daily afflictions shape and fortify the carpenter. In the presence of these carpenters, my thought is to act tough and not show any concern. Especially after about an hour ago when Gary did tell us, "Your symptoms will pass. Don't worry about it."

After three hours in the carpenter's shack, I feel about the same as before. Thankfully, our shift is almost over, and I can finally go home. At 12:29 a.m., I say good-bye to all three men and walk out of the carpenter's shack to my truck.

It is so good to finally sit in my truck. While the engine warms up, I notice again that since my exposure, my heart rate has accelerated, and the pain throughout my body is still very strong. The thought again enters my mind, *How long will these irritations last?*

Gary's words: "Don't worry. Your symptoms will pass" encourage me to be patient.

However, I consider, *Don't worry?* I wonder how long I am supposed to not worry. My pain and dizziness are not going away.

The engine is now warmed up, so I say aloud, "Break release, throttle up." This is an expression from an SR-71 pilot to the reconnaissance man behind him as they begin their roll down the long air force runway.

As I begin to roll, I think, *Good deal, I will be home in twenty-three minutes.*

I hope that I will be feeling better tomorrow because that foreman's constant teasing has conditioned me to consider what might happen if tomorrow night I tell Gary that something is still wrong with me. *He will tease me and make me feel stupid in front of the other men. I should be grateful that Bashan Oil and Og Construction do not have a rude character like that other foreman.*

I decide that I am not going to worry about my exposure symptoms because I trust Bashan Oil and Og Construction. They *did* tell me that I would be all right.

SATURDAY, MAY 7, 1988 I AM THIRTY-TWO YEARS OLD, MARA IS TWENTY-SIX, LAUREN IS THREE, AND MARIBELLE IS TWENTY-ONE MONTHS OLD

THE NEXT MORNING AS MY EYES begin to open, I am alarmed at how fast and hard my heart is beating and how fatigued and terrible I feel. As I consider the exposure, and how I now feel, my concerns about the exposure increase my heart rate even more, causing me to take a deep breath. As my mind races with troubling thoughts, I then again remember Gary's encouraging words, "Your symptoms will pass. Don't worry about it."

Then from the family room and kitchen, I hear the happy Saturday morning sounds of my wife and two giddy little girls. I then consider, *I should tell Mara about my exposure.*

I am always very happy to hear my family, and am always drawn to them because they are my lifelong dreams. Though I feel as if I have a terrible hangover, I cannot help but roll out of bed and go to them.

A moment later, when I turn the bedroom doorknob, both of our girls scream, "Daddy Daddy!" as they run to me. And then, bump, bump, and each of them hug my legs. I go to my knees and give them a big Saturday morning hug.

Then from the kitchen, I hear Mara say to me, "Good morning!"

I head for the kitchen so that I can tell Mara about my exposure. As I give Mara a big good-morning hug, I also say, "The kitchen sure smells good!"

As she smiles at me, she can see that something is wrong with me. I begin to tell her about the exposure and my symptoms. Her smile fades, and after I mention part of my story she says, "James, it sounds like you should go to the doctor!"

I say, "I don't think that I should."

She turns from the stove to look at me and says, "It sounds like you should go today!"

I say, "Oh, I agree. But in our safety meetings we are told that if we are injured at work and go to an outside doctor, we'll be fired."

Her face and body stiffen as she says, "What?"

With my body language, I try to calm her as I say, "Gary said that I would be okay. He said that my symptoms will pass and that I shouldn't worry about it."

The look on Mara's face is as if she just saw someone purposely trip me. So I say, "If I'm going to be okay, it's not worth the risk of losing my job. I will be okay. I will just rest all day."

To ease her concern I smile and add, "Maybe a good breakfast will make me feel better!"

After we enjoy a delicious breakfast, the girls are eager to play, so they scurry back into our family room. While Mara and I clean up our messy kitchen, I cannot help but follow my heart into our family room, because my life-long dreams are playing in there. Before we finish cleaning, I say to Mara, "I'm going to go play with the girls."

Her smile encourages me to go. So, as I toss my rag, I turn and head toward the room that sounds as happy as Disneyland. However, as I step from the kitchen, new thoughts about my exposure stop me. For a moment, I listen to my heart, and then decide, *I should ask the Father for wisdom, knowledge, and understanding about my exposure* (James 1:5-6).

I am then surprised to find myself thinking, *Why did my Father allow me to be exposed?*

As this thought takes hold of my heart, I further ponder, *The Father has protected me before. When I stood at the bottom of the ladder and looked up, the gas was already there up on the platform. Why did my Father allow me to climb the ladder? He could have told me not to go up there. Why didn't He warn me? The absence of any warning must mean that there is a purpose and a lesson here for me to learn from this exposure.*

As my mind searches again for a reason, my heart decides, *I should go to our bedroom and ask the Father about this exposure and what lessons I must learn from it.* With eager anticipation I head for the bedroom, and as I step in and close the door, I feel as if my Father will now listen to only me. I step to the middle of the room where I may kneel and pray. However, as I stand for a moment searching my heart before prayer, I hear so clearly, within my heart, "I allowed it."

I am astonished when I realize that my Father *is* listening to my thoughts!

I am immediately embarrassed and humbled, as when someone discovers that someone else is looking at him. As I consider the intimacy between us, my will becomes agreeable with my Father's will for my life; like the accord of light and shade, one is not without the other. And with an attitude of consent I ponder, *The Father saw me at the foot of the ladder, and He knew about the gas up on the platform, so He allowed me to be exposed because...*

I begin to search for a reason, and am reminded that, *The Apostles sailed into a storm! It was God's will that they sail into a storm so that they could learn an important lesson. That's in... Matthew 14.*

I begin to understand why my exposure was allowed, and quickly grab my Bible and turn to Matthew 14. I see that the story begins at verse twenty-two and ends at verse thirty-three.

As I begin to read, I remember, *The other storm occurred first, so I should read about that one first.*

I then turn to Luke 8 and see that the story of the first storm begins at verse twenty-two and ends at verse twenty-six. As I stare at the verses, I begin to feel as if I am favored by my Father to learn special lessons. I then consider, *Special storms teach special lessons. Okay, then what are the lessons that I must learn?*

So, with great reverence, I bow my head and ask my Father for wisdom, knowledge, and understanding about the chemical storm I climbed up into. I then begin to read that Jesus and His disciples board a boat so that they may cross over to the other side of the Sea of Galilee. As they sail, Jesus falls into a deep sleep. During His sleep, the wind and waves develop into a violent storm filling their boat with water, and filling them with great fear.

Then they went to him, and awoke him, saying, Master, Master, we perish. And he arose, and rebuked the wind, and the waves of water: and they ceased, and it was calm. Then he said unto them, Where is your faith? and they feared, and wondered among

**themselves, saying, Who is this that commandeth both the winds
and the water, and they obey him!**

I stare at the page and ponder; *Some of these men were experienced mariners.
If they thought that they were going to die, then the storm must have been very
bad. Since the storm was so severe, it would have been logical for them to believe that they were going to die. So I don't get it. Why did Jesus ask, 'Where
is your faith?' I don't get it. That storm was severe; there was no hope. That's
it! That's it! When there is logically no hope, when the heart and everything
within you tells you that there is no hope, like when the apostles were out in
their storm, there is hope in Jesus. So when Jesus asked, 'Where is your faith?'
He was asking, Where is your trust in me? Amazing! Jesus put the Apostles
into an extreme trial so they would learn to trust in Him, and not trust just
in themselves.*

I then ponder again, *Special storms teach special lessons, leading to special
service for God. Amazing! The apostles had no idea about the special service that
would be required of them after Jesus returned to heaven. My special storm is
preparing me. But for what?*

As I stare at the page, I see the words of Jesus: "Where is your faith?"

I then say with a soft voice, "Wow."

I look up to heaven and say aloud, "Father, I trust you."

I look down at my Bible to check my thought and see that Jesus fell asleep
before the storm developed. I then look back to heaven and say, "I know that
you did not fall asleep before I climbed up into my storm. You allowed me to
be exposed, but why did you allow me to be exposed, and what lessons do you
want me to learn? Some of the lessons must be about faith."

With eagerness, I turn to Matthew 14:22–33 and read about the second storm. In the second storm, Jesus told the apostles to get into a boat and cross over to the other side of the Sea of Galilee. He then went up on a mountain to pray. During the night, as Jesus prayed, a violent storm developed, and again the apostles thought that they were going to perish. However, at about three in the morning, Jesus walked on the water out to the frightened Apostles, and calmed both them and the storm.

I then consider, *When Jonah was out to sea, a storm developed because of his disobedience; and when the obedient apostles were out to sea, a storm developed to teach them lessons about faith. Therefore, the storms of life are designed for both the disobedient and the obedient. During the first storm, Jesus was in the boat with the apostles. However, during the second storm, Jesus was not in the boat; the apostles were alone. It seems to me that Jesus teaches us by degrees of increasing difficulty. During the second storm, Jesus came to the apostles at about three in the morning. That means that the apostles struggled against the storm through much of the night. So I understand that I must not give up during my storm, even though it continues long through the night, or will continue for a long time.*

I then realize that at the proper time, and only at the proper time, Jesus will come to me when I am in a storm of life.

I hear my girls at the bedroom door calling for me, so I close my Bible and go to them.

After another night of suffering a lot of painful pressure throughout my body, I arise Sunday morning to take my family to church, because I am setting a good example for our young daughters.

SUNDAY, MAY 8, 1988

AT CHURCH A FRIEND ASKS, "James, do you feel okay? You look as if something has happened to you."

I must look as bad as I feel, so I say, "Yes, Friday night I was exposed to chemicals at work. I don't feel good."

My friend asks, "What kind of chemicals?"

I say, "I don't know. They wouldn't tell me."

We then break from each other as our Sunday school begins. I am usually very involved in Sunday school discussions. I am famous for the large amount of Bible knowledge stored within my heart and my many memorized Bible verses. However, this morning I am quiet because my exposure symptoms are so severe that I am not able to pay attention to the Sunday school lesson. This situation is frustrating, and I ask myself, *Why did I leave the house?*

Through the years I have learned to endure pain because of two motorcycle accidents at sixty miles per hour, twelve other motorcycle accidents at between thirty and forty miles per hour, a bad accident in Dad's truck, and four and a half years of boxing. However, my pain from this exposure is different. It is very difficult to endure.

Early Sunday evening Mara suggests that I call my dad and tell him about my exposure and the symptoms I am experiencing. Moments later, I call him, and after I tell him my story, he suggests that I go to the hospital, even if the visit to an outside doctor will put my job at risk. So, I heed his advice and go to the hospital emergency room.

After the ER doctors' examination, he prescribes Vicodin and rest.

The documented record of his examination, dated Sunday, May 8, 1988, states that I have been exposed to "gas leaks," which was the cause of my head and abdominal pain, and aches and numbness to both of my legs.

Thankfully, the Vicodin relieves enough pain so that I am able to go to work the next day. I am confident that because of my exposure symptoms, I will likely work slower than usual, but my coworkers will understand and compensate for me.

During my shift the following day, a laborer accidently drops a heavy six foot long piece of wood from about fifteen feet above me, which strikes my left elbow. The injury almost brings me to tears. A few minutes later, Gary and the other foreman arrive, and after examining my arm, they suggest that I go to the hospital.

Because of the pain in my arm, I am not able to unbuckle my tool belt. So as I look at Gary, I smile because I know that my request will embarrass him, especially in front of the other foreman. A questionable smile develops on his face when he says to me, "What?"

I cannot help but laugh as I say, "I can't unbuckle my belt! Will you do it for me?"

As Gary turns red from embarrassment, the other foreman and I laugh. Gary steps over to me, and with a glowing red face unbuckles my belt.

A few moments later, as an Og Construction man drives me to the hospital, I ask him, "What hospital are we going to?"

When he mentions the same hospital that I went to last night, I say to myself, *Oh great! The nurse that cared for me last night! If she is there, she will say something about my visit last night! She will mention my exposure, and ask how I feel. Then this Og Construction man will tell someone in the office that I went to an outside doctor because of my exposure, and I will be fired!*

So, I pray an earnest prayer from my heart. *Father, if the nurse is there, please tell her to not say anything about my visit last night.*

When we finally walk into the ER, I am a little nervous as I look around for that nurse. After a brief wait, my name is called. The Og Construction man and I follow this nurse to a little room, and that nurse then says, "Wait here, and in a few minutes a nurse will take a look at your arm."

I think, *Oh no! A nurse! I hope it's not my nurse from last night!*

When I say, "Thank you." with a hint of nervousness in my voice, my concern is that the nurse and the Og Construction man might begin to question why I am nervous.

Minutes later, my nurse from last night steps into the room! My adrenalin begins to flow as if I were in the dentist chair!

When the Og Construction man introduces himself, I seize the moment, and as I begin to offer another prayer, God reminds me about Peter. His faith enabled him to walk on water until he saw the mighty wind, which weakened his faith of logic, causing him to begin to sink (Matthew 14:22–32). I then consider how strong my faith was when I prayed in the truck as we drove to the hospital. But now, before this woman, I begin to sink. In this moment, my faith is tested, and I realize my weak trust in God. I lower my head because I feel so embarrassed before God. I know that "without faith, it is impossible to please God" (Hebrews 11:6). In this moment, I know that God hears the thoughts of my heart, and I am thankful that He will hear my now renewed confidence in Him. So I pray from my heart, *Father, I know that you heard my prayer in the truck.*

In this moment, my trust in God strengthens. I now know that my Father will direct the heart of this nurse so that she will not mention my visit last night. Thankfully, the ER nurse did not say a word about my visit the night before. Thank you Father.

My elbow injury is just what I need, because I now have another prescription for Vicodin. It will help me for both my elbow pain, and for my exposure pain. And because of this injury, Og Construction will place me on light duty for a few days.

Through the next few weeks, I again tell Gary about my continual symptoms related to the exposure. On a Friday after the safety meeting, Gary raises his voice and asks me, in front of the men, "How do you feel?" His question pleases me because I think that he is finally sincere about my exposure symptoms. So I say, "I'm not feeling well. I need to see a doctor."

Gary and the other foreman laugh at me, as if I am a whiny kid. Gary then says, "The flu is going around. You probably just have the flu."

Almost two weeks later, I tell Gary that I am still struggling with symptoms from the exposure, and the next day Gary tells me that I can visit a Bashan Oil doctor. However, I answer, "I would rather visit a doctor who is not on Bashan Oil's payroll."

Gary's comment surprises me as he says, "Don't rock the boat, or you'll lose your job."

I start thinking that if my symptoms are going to pass, that maybe I should not worry about how I feel. I will just quietly suffer through the process of recovery and not risk my job, because during the winter Bashan Oil refinery employs many out-of-work carpenters.

The exposure occurred about twenty-one days ago, so for over five hundred long hours, I have suffered from exposure symptoms. My complaints embarrass me, and confuse my family because my symptoms change from day to day. Life is now even more difficult because I develop a sleep disorder. Now I am always physically, mentally, and emotionally exhausted, which harms our home life. Because I am always so stressed, our home does not feel as secure, or as blessed, as it once was.

At this point, I have no choice but to trust Bashan Oil and Og Construction. However, I am beginning to question their integrity because of the reactions of the foreman and the white shirted authorities at the time of my exposure. Shall I trust that they will do the right thing?

CHAPTER 8

Employee Trust and Employer Betrayal

⤖

SPECIAL STORMS OF LIFE TEACH SPECIAL LESSONS

And straightway Jesus compelled his disciples to enter into a ship, and to go over before him, while he sent the multitude away. And as soon as he had sent the multitude away, he went up into a mountain alone to pray: and when the evening was come, he was there alone. And the ship was now in the midst of the sea, and was tossed with waves: for it was a contrary wind. And in the fourth watch of the night, Jesus went unto them, walking on the sea. And when his disciples saw him walking on the sea, they were troubled, saying, It is a spirit, and cried out for fear. But straightway Jesus spake unto them, saying, Be of good comfort, It is I: be not afraid. Then Peter answered him, and said, Master, if it be thou, bid me come unto thee on the water. And he said, Come. And when Peter was come down out of the ship, he walked on the water to go to Jesus. But when he saw a mighty wind, he was afraid: and as he began to sink, he cried, saying, Master, save me. So immediately Jesus stretched forth his hand, and caught him, and said to him, O thou of little faith, wherefore didst thou doubt. And as soon as they were come into the ship, the wind ceased.

MATTHEW 14:22–32

Peter was very stout at first, but afterward his heart failed him. The lengthening out of a trial discovers the weakness of faith.

MATTHEW HENRY

Faith grows when it is exercised.

MATTHEW HENRY

I have seen the travail that God hath given to the sons of men, to humble them thereby.

ECCLESIASTES 3:10

There is indeed no profit *in that wherein we labour;* the thing itself, when we have it, will do us little good; but, if we make a right use of the disposals of Providence about it, there will be profit in that…not to make up a happiness by it, but *to be exercised in it,* to have various graces exercised by the variety of events, to have their dependence upon God tried by every change, and to be trained up to it, and taught both *how to want and how to abound,* Phil 4:12. Note, (1) There is a great deal of toil and trouble to be seen among the children of men. Labour and sorrow fill the world. (2) This toil and this trouble are what God has allotted us. He never intended this world for our rest, and therefore never appointed us to take our ease in it. (3) To many it proves a gift. God gives it to men, as the physician gives a medicine to his patient, to do him good. This travail is given to us to make us weary of the world and desirous of the remaining rest. It is given to us that we may be kept in action, and may always have something to do; for we were none of us sent into the world to be idle. Every change cuts us out some new work, which we should be more solicitous about, than about the event.

MATTHEW HENRY

LET US NOW CONSIDER THE following information about "good" and "evil" people. We must learn to properly judge because by their skill, and will, we may know their heart and character, as either "good" or "evil." [2 Corinthians 2:15; John 7:24; Matthew 7:5, 15–20; Proverbs 20:11, 27:19]

In the following comment, Jesus defines "good" and "evil" people:

Either make the tree good, and his fruit good: or else make the tree evil, and his fruit evil: for the tree is known by the fruit...For of the abundance of the heart the mouth speaketh. A good man out of the good treasure of his heart bringeth forth good things: and an evil man out of an evil treasure, bringeth forth evil things. But I say unto you, that of every idle word that men shall speak, they shall give account thereof at the day of judgment. For by thy words thou shalt be justified, and by thy words thou shalt be condemned.

Matthew 12:33–37

From The MacArthur Study Bible we gain a better understanding about Verse 36:

The most seemingly insignificant sin, even a slip of the tongue, carries the full potential of all hell's evil (cf. James 3:6). No infraction against God's holiness is therefore a trifling thing, and each person will ultimately give account of every such indiscretion. There is no truer indication of a bad tree than the bad fruit of speech (vv. 33, 35). The poisonous snakes were known by their poisonous mouths revealing evil hearts (v.34; cf. Luke 6:45). Every person is judged by his words, because they reveal the state of his heart.

Matthew Henry has this comment about Matthew 12:33–37:

The heart is the root, the language is the fruit (v.33); if the nature of the tree be good, it will bring forth fruit accordingly. Where grace is the reigning principle in the heart, the language will be the language of Canaan, and, on the contrary, whatever lust reigns in the heart it will break out; diseased lungs make an offensive breath: men's language discovers what country they are of, *so likewise what manner of spirit they are of: Either make the tree good, and then the fruit will be good;* get pure hearts and then you will have pure lips and pure lives: or else the tree will be corrupt, and the fruit accordingly. You may make a crab-stock to become a good tree, by grafting into it a shoot from a good tree, and then the fruit will be good, but if the tree be still the same, plant it where you will, and water it how you will, the fruit will be still corrupt. Note. Unless the heart be transformed, the life will never be thoroughly reformed.

The heart is the *fountain,* the words are the streams...as the streams are the overflowing of the spring. A wicked heart is said *to send forth wickedness, as a fountain casts forth her waters,* Jer 6:7... evil words are the natural, genuine product of an evil heart...The people looked upon the Pharisees as a generation of saints, but Christ calls them a *generation of vipers, the seed of the serpent,* that had an enmity to Christ and his gospel. Now what could be expected from *a generation of vipers,* but that which is poisonous and malignant? Can the viper be otherwise than venomous? Note. Bad things may be expected from bad people.,.

The heart is the *treasury,* the words are the things brought out of that treasury (v.35); and from hence men's characters may be drawn, and may be judged of.

It concerns us to think much of the day of judgment, that *that* may be a check upon our tongues; and let us consider, How particular the account will be of tongue-sins in that day: even *for every idle words,* or discourse, *that men speak, they shall give account.* This intimates (1.) That God takes notice of every word we say, even that which we ourselves do not notice....

We must not pardon evil or disapprove of that which is good because:

He that justifieth the wicked, and he that condemneth the just, even they both are abomination to the Lord.

PROVERBS 17:15

Matthew Henry's excellent comment about Proverbs 17:15 says:

This shows what an offence it is to God, 1. When those that are entrusted with the administration of public justice, judges, juries, witnesses, prosecutors, counsel, do either acquit the guilty or condemn those that are not guilty, or in the least contribute to either; this defeats the end of government, which is to protect the good and punish the bad, Rom. 13:3, 4. It is equally provoking to God to *justify the wicked*, though it be in pity and in *favorem vitae- to safe life*, as *to condemn the just*. 2. When any private persons plead for sin and sinners, palliate and excuse wickedness, or argue against virtue and piety, and so *pervert the right ways of the Lord* and confound the eternal distinctions between good and evil.

In 2 Corinthians 5:10–11, God says through the Apostle Paul that every Christian will appear before the judgment seat of Christ and give account for the good and the bad that he or she did on earth. This Christian judgment is going to be frightful!

Revelation 20:11–15 says that every non-Christian will stand before the judgment seat and give account for every word, and every action. This judgment will be overwhelmingly horrifying.

One single word may cause love or hate; edify or destroy. So, if a single word is stated for the purpose of offense or damage, the offended should take comfort because God has also heard that word. If that word makes the offended heart cry, the offended heart should take comfort because God hears that cry. If that word is not called to account in this life, the offended should take comfort, because God will demand an account of that word on the judgment day.

The documents cited in the following chapters were filed in Workers' Compensation Court as part of my appeal to the law for justice. Each referenced document speaks for itself and will reveal the skill and will of its author, as either good or evil. In addition, these will also reveal willful collaborators as either good or evil.

After my exposure, there was an incident report written on May 6, 1988, by a Bashan Oil Refinery operator who is called the Sniffer, (Document #7), that was written without my knowledge.

In his report he states that at about 9:55 p.m. a crew operator called stating that Og Construction people who were working on top of a heater reported an odor that was giving them upset stomachs.

The operator investigated the matter and found the source to be an overhead cooler of which all of the cooler plugs were pulled in preparation for water blasting. It was reported to the operator that the cooler has steamed all day, and that the direction of the wind was carrying the steam odor to the heater. The operator suggested that the people on the heater should wear yellow cartridge respirators because what they breathed was only a nuisance odor.

Now consider the impressive chain of evidence from my own observations, which will show that the named odor was far more dangerous than just a "nuisance odor" that was reported by the Sniffer. In my opinion, the following account is *more likely than not*:

1. Before the Sniffer arrived, he had been informed that an unidentified odor had caused two men to have upset stomachs.

2. When the Sniffer arrived, he clearly saw the two unstable men sitting on the ground.
3. The Sniffer stood with the investigators and both foremen. Therefore, he heard about our exposure symptoms.
   And most importantly,
4. The Sniffer entered the exposure site, tested the air, and quickly ran from the area.

Something relatively serious occurred, and this Bashan Oil refinery operator chose to omit vital facts in his report. His false description now provides protection for future defendants, such as Bashan Oil, and creates injustice for my family and me.

CHAPTER 9

My Lawsuit Brings Hope and a Threat From Big Oil

⎯⎰⎯

THERE ARE DECEITFUL ARTIFICERS WHO CONTRIVE SHAMEFUL SKILLS AGAINST THOSE WHO ARE IN FAVOR WITH MAN AND GOD.

When they were at the great stone, which is in Gibeon, Amasa went before them, and Joab's garment, that he had put on, was girded unto him, and upon it was a sword girded, which hanged on his loins in the sheath, and as he went, it used to fall out. And Joab said to Amasa, Art thou in health, my brother? and Joab took Amasa by the beard with his right hand to kiss him. But Amasa took no heed to the sword that was in Joab's hand: for therewith he smote him in the fifth *rib*, and shed out his bowels to the ground, and he smote him not the second time: so he died:...

2 SAMUEL 20:8–10

...but Joab there took an opportunity to kill him with his own hand; and he did it subtilely, and with contrivance, and not upon a sudden provocation. He girded his coat about him, that it might not hang in his way, and girded his belt upon his coat, that his sword might be the readier to his hand; he also put his sword in a sheath too big for it, that, whenever he pleased, it might, upon a little shake, fall out, as if it fell by accident, and so he might take it into his hand, unsuspected, as if he were going to return it into the scabbard, when he designed to sheath it in the bowels of Amasa. The more there is of plot in a sin the worse it is. He did it treacherously, and under pretence of friendship, that Amasa might not be upon his guard. He called him *brother*, for they were own cousins, enquired of his welfare *(Art thou in health)* and *took him by the beard,* as one he was free with, to kiss him, while with the drawn sword in his other hand he was aiming at his heart....

MATTHEW HENRY

The lying lips are an abomination to the Lord: but they that deal truly *are* his delight.

PROVERBS 12:22

JANUARY 1989: LAUREN IS FOUR YEARS OLD, AND MARIBELLE IS TWO YEARS OLD

THROUGH THE PAST FOUR MONTHS, my exposure symptoms have become so much worse. I visit another outside doctor, and with his electromyography, he confirms a developing nerve disease. He also documents my complaints of exposure symptoms in my arms and legs.

I experience sharp pains, numbness, and tingling in my feet, legs, hands, arms, and head. I also have a strong "electrical" feeling in all of my extremities. I often feel as if I have the flu, and sometimes my extremities feel painfully cold. There is no reason or pattern with my symptoms, and therefore my family is very confused about my exposure complaints. I understand their confusion about me; it is probably because of my healthy, strong appearance, which was noted by the emergency room doctors' report (noted previously as Document #10) regarding my examination, which refers to me as "a well-nourished, well-developed male."

FEBRUARY 16, 1989

TODAY AT NOON Mara called me, asking me to meet her at the hospital because she is about to deliver our third baby. Today Madeline is born, another tender blessing.

APRIL 1989

AS MY SYMPTOMS GROW WORSE, I speak to as many people as possible about how I am suffering. On a visit to my chiropractor, I mention how much I am suffering from the ill effects from a chemical exposure. I am so thankful, because she listens to me as if I were her own son. My frustration becomes her frustration. She strongly suggests that I contact an attorney, and she cautions me that I only have twelve months after the exposure to file a lawsuit. That means that I only have one more month until the statute of limitations runs out. I cannot believe that no one else has told me about a time limit to file a lawsuit. Therefore, I call an attorney, and he agrees to meet with me.

Eleven months after my exposure, Bashan Oil and Og Construction know that my symptoms are growing worse, but offer no help.

On April 18, 1989 Og Construction's Safety and Loss Control Administrator, Mr. Breach, wrote a letter to Bashan Oils' insurance company, (Document #15).

In the letter Mr. Breach states that about one month ago Gary Betray, Og Construction's carpenter foreman informed Mr. Breach that I had been evaluated by a doctor regarding the incident that occurred on May 6, 1988, and as a result I have several doctor bills.

This letter also states that I am concerned about my headaches that have persisted ever since the incident. And after my doctor preformed several tests, my doctor told me that I was losing power in my legs.

The letter also mentions that my doctor believes that my chemical exposure at work is the cause of my problems.

Mr. Breach states that he went to Mrs. Taint, Bashan Oil's Senior Industrial Hygienist and was informed that the material I inhaled would not have any long-term effects from a one-time exposure.

After I read this letter I was amazed that the Bashan Oil hygienist does not actually name the "*material*" that I was exposed to that fateful day.

On April 19, 1989, a handwritten note (by a possible Og Construction authority) regarding a telephone conversation between him and Mr. Breach was written (Document #16).

The note states that Mr. Breach called regarding my exposure and that they had talked in March about me and decided that they will not do anything, and that I am now claiming that I have a loss of power in my legs.

Because Bashan Oil Refinery and Og Construction will not offer proper medical help, my symptoms and frustrations grow worse.

Late April 1989

I meet with Mr. Gap, an attorney, whose office is in a large prominent city. After I tell him about my exposure, he laughs and says, "If what you're telling me is true, your pockets are full."

He quickly files a lawsuit with full assurance of winning my case. He also makes an appointment for me to see a new doctor named Dr. Bismarck. I am so thankful that I am going to finally receive some help.

I arrive at my doctor's appointment, which is at a prominent hospital, and think, *I am grateful to finally meet two good doctors.* I sit in the waiting room for over an hour, and they finally call me in for an examination. After I mention that my exposure occurred one year and one month ago, I carefully tell my exposure story and describe my symptoms. However, unknown to me, as I talk, and they write their report, they change and minimize several important facts.

In their three page Outpatient Progress Record written on June 15, 1989, by Dr. Bismarck and Dr. Moulage (Document #23) they state that I sustained a 5 minute exposure to gasoline fumes while at work.

They mention that I experienced an immediate headache, which resolved within seven days, and accurately state that I experienced *immediate* numbness and tingling in my arms and legs.

However, in their assessment of me they state that I was exposed to an unspecified refinery odor for 2.5 minutes and that I may have had a mild headache that lasted two weeks.

Their conclusion is that a 2.5 minute exposure to a chemical would not result in immediate, asymmetric neurological problems.

My comments regarding this report:

1. I told them that I was exposed to an unknown gas, but they wrote that I was exposed to gasoline.
2. The doctors correctly state that the odor is unspecified.
3. The doctors correctly state that my exposure time was 5 minutes long. However, later in that very same report they reduce my exposure time to 2.5 minutes.
4. The doctors minimize my headache by stating that I may have had a mild headache.
5. The doctors change a vital, important fact when they state that my symptoms are asymmetric which means only on one side of my body,

not on both sides. The symptoms they are now stating would not result from a chemical exposure.

A month later on August 16, 1989, Dr. Bismarck and Dr. Moulage provide a six-page typed report, (Document #24) which is an excerpt from the original report of June 15, 1989, to my attorney and to the judge of the Worker's Compensation Court. In this report, they describe my symptoms correctly only one time as numbness and tingling in my arms and legs. On other pages of this report, they describe my symptoms as only on one side of my body.

Note to reader: It is important to state correctly that my symptoms are on both sides of my body because a chemical exposure will affect both sides.

Mara and I are unaware of the changes in both doctors' reports. So when our attorney informs us that my doctor had filed his medical report with Workers' Compensation, we are so thankful and can hardly wait for the Workers' Compensation judge to render a good decision for us.

One year and three months after my exposure, on August 25, 1989, I am scheduled for a deposition with attorneys from both sides. Mara and I can hardly believe it! I will have an opportunity to explain and describe my harmful exposure and symptoms.

During this five hour deposition the interviewer asked me if I had asked anyone at work what particular gas or chemical I was exposed to on May 6, 1988? I clearly stated that right after the exposer I asked four times, what was I exposed too, and all I was told was don't worry about it you'll be okay. A short time later I was told that somebody below me had been washing out a vessel with a chemical and that I was exposed to that chemical. I was also told that there was another gas leak from another place that was far enough away that I likely did not inhale those fumes. However, months later I was told that I was exposed to raw gas, a harmless gasoline. (Document #25)

Many times during the deposition, I describe my exposure symptoms as in both of my legs and arms.

September 1989

Mara is scheduled to give a formal legal statement about my exposure. We are so very thankful that a solid lawsuit is developing. Mara's statement of September 27, 1989 clearly describes how my exposure has affected our lives.

She states that my injury has damaged our sexual relationship because of the pain, numbness, and strange nerve sensations throughout my groin and upper leg areas, that often prevent us from having sex, and that my injury has made me exhausted, irritated and grouchy.

And equally as important, the injury has dealt a blow to our procreative enthusiasm. That as a result of my exposure to the toxic chemical fumes, there is the fear that my reproductive genes have been damaged. Since we did not know whether our youngest child was conceived before or after my exposure, we experienced sheer terror as we anticipated the possibility that our baby may be born deformed. The memory of this experience has led us to consider not having any more children.

She further explains that my injury has also diminished my ability to perform other important functions of our marriage. That up until the time of my injury, we were regularly complimented by landlords, friends, relatives and church members on how clean and inviting we kept our home because I took pride and found joy in maintaining a pleasant home for our family. I had easily accomplished all of the heavy cleaning and more than my share of other household tasks. But since the injury, I do not have the energy to do any of the heavy cleaning, and am only able to contribute minimally to other chores.

She explains how our primary source of enjoyment used to be the whole family spending time together; whether just relaxing at home, playing with the kids, or going out for ice cream. About how I especially enjoyed helping take care of our three small children, but now I am unable to look after them. She was forced to drop out of the church softball league and other church, social, and recreational activities because I am unable to watch over the kids while she is gone.

She notates how my injury has deteriorated our sense of financial security. About how she once had absolute confidence in my ability to provide for our family's needs because I had the stamina for routinely working 60 or more hours per week, and never missing a day of work, and that now I collapse from exhaustion while working only 40 hours. How she lives in fear that I am going to lose my job, and that she must keep her part time job because we now need the stable, supplemental income.

She mentions that my injury has resulted in the degradation our companionship, and has caused both of us to become very irritated with each other. Although she realizes that I am suffering terribly from this injury, she cannot help but get angry and frustrated with me when night after night my insomnia wakes me at all hours of the night and keeps me awake, and all I can do during the day is sink into the couch. The frustration and tension of this situation has fueled several serious arguments that we had never experienced prior to the injury. She says that she is frightened that this injury is pushing us further and further apart.

Because of my poor health, I did not read this statement until sometime after 1992.

Mara and I do not understand all that is occurring with our lawsuit. However, we are happy to know that we have an attorney who will establish justice for us, and we can hardly believe that our long ordeal is almost over. Through our long delay of justice, many emotions have tried our patience, and my exposure symptoms have exhausted me. Yet we have not lost hope, because we have no reason not to trust Bashan Oil and Og Construction. We believe that they will do what is right for us, especially now that we have an attorney. We look forward to the enjoyment of justice, and eagerly await the call from our attorney with good news. Then finally, it happens, Mara answers the phone, and says to me, "James! It's our attorney! He wants to talk with you!"

I cannot get to the phone quick enough. After Mara hands the phone to me, she stays close by to hear the good news. However, our attorney says to me, "Your doctors are reporting that your injury is not work related."

Mara sees on my face the confusion of my heart, which causes her to step closer to me. As frustration builds within my heart, and feelings of confusion flood my brain, I feel insulted and offended and say, "That's wrong. My injuries are work related. I was very healthy prior to my exposure, and now I have something wrong with me from head to toe."

Mr. Gap then says, "Well, that's what your doctor is stating, and the Bashan Oil attorneys have said that they are coming after you with a lawsuit. They're going to—"

With passion, I interrupt and say, "What?"

Mr. Gap then stuns me when he says, "They're going to sue you for forty thousand dollars because of the trouble that you have caused. However, they are willing to settle for twenty-two hundred dollars."

I say, "We have already spent over five thousand of our own money on medical expenses."

A lump begins to form in my throat, and confusion staggers my heart as Mr. Gap says, "If you sign a Compromise and Release Form, they'll leave you alone."

I ask him, "What is a Compromise and Release Form?" Mr. Gap explains, "If you sign a CRF, that means that you release Bashan Oil and Og Construction and all other involved parties from liability."

As I remain silent, Mr. Gap asks, "Do you have private health insurance?" I say that we do. And I am surprised to hear him say, "If you have any more medical bills, turn them in to your insurance company."

For a moment, I am silent as I consider that my attorney is no longer supporting me and that I have lost him. However, and even more importantly, is the question, *Why did my doctors say that my injury is not work related?*

I know for sure that I have lost my attorney when he says, "And besides, I'm changing my law practice to airplane crashes."

I just cannot take any more of this! I have suffered exposure symptoms for twenty thousand, two hundred and eighty hours, and now it seems as if everyone I have trusted has turned against me. I have no idea what to do, so I sign a CRF. I do not want the pressure on my family anymore, and I just want to get away from all of this confusing heartache. I also believe that I will eventually recover my health. The signing of this CRF is a monumental, great disappointment. This turn of events truly sickens my heart.

The hope that *is* deferred, *is* the fainting of the heart, but when the desire cometh, *it is* as a tree of life.
PROVERBS 13:12

In the morning when I awake, and through each hour of the day, and through the next night, I consider, *Why did my doctors say that my injury is not work related?*

One day after work, I say to Mara, "Let's sell the property, (where we were going to build our dream house) and get rid of everything in our lives that is adding stress to us. Let's simplify our lives, and strengthen our family."

Even though I have been working long and hard drafting blueprints for this mountain dream home, I am surprised when she only says, "Okay."

So, we put our property up for sale, and within a short time, some fortunate family purchased it.

CHAPTER 10

Our Memorable Christmas Eve and Christmas Morning

_͜ϭ_

Behold, children are the inheritance of the Lord, _and_ the fruit of the womb _his_ reward. As are the arrows in the hand of the strong man; so are the children of youth. Blessed is the man that hath his quiver full of them:...

PSALM 127:3–5

...blessings and not burdens...

MATTHEW HENRY

A joyful heart maketh a cheerful countenance:...

PROVERBS 15:13

CHRISTMAS EVE 1990

TWO YEARS, AND SEVEN MONTHS after my exposure. I am thirty four years old; Mara is twenty seven; Lauren is six; Maribelle is four, and Madeline is almost one year old.

Mara is back in Madeline's bedroom tucking her into bed. While Lauren and Maribelle play in the family room, I say from the kitchen, "Who wants eggnog and brownies?"

Both of them scream, "I do! I do! I do!"

As they run into the kitchen I say, "Get up to the table, and I'll get two glasses of eggnog and a plate of brownies for you."

While they enjoy their first bites, I say, "Okay girls, I'm going to the shower."

They say, "Okay Daddy!"

As I leave the kitchen, the smells and sounds of this evening enlarge my heart with Christmas Eve joy.

After I enter our bedroom and shut the door, I quickly undress and slip into a Santa suit. I then turn the shower on and open the window next to the shower, but only a few inches. I climb out through the bedroom window, and very quietly crawl over to the kitchen window. As I kneel under the kitchen window, I can hear the girls enjoying their Christmas Eve treats. When I seated them at the table I made sure that they faced this window so that they would see what I am about to do. I carefully rise until my head is right at the bottom of the window, then spring up for only a second. And as I run to the bathroom window I can hear the girls scream, as they run down the hallway to our bedroom, "Daddy! Daddy! We saw Santa! We saw Santa!"

Through the partially open bathroom window I say, "What? I can't hear you! I'll be out in a minute. Go back to the kitchen."

I smile as I think, *Perfect. They think that I am in the shower!*

When I go back to the bedroom window and open it, I can hear them waiting for me on the other side of our closed bedroom door. I am not surprised that they did not go back to the kitchen. So as they wait for me, I quietly climb in through our bedroom window, and quickly shower. After my shower I open the bedroom door and find two little girls breathing so hard that they can barely say, "Daddy, Daddy, we saw Santa!"

I smile and say, "No you didn't. It's too early!"

"We did Daddy! We saw him! We saw Santa look in the kitchen window!"

With a serious look I say, "You saw someone look in the kitchen window? There must be someone in the backyard. I better go take a look!"

As I head for the back door, they follow close behind, and say, "Daddy, it was Santa!"

As I pass through the kitchen, I grab a flashlight, and when I arrive at the patio door, they stand close to me as I slowly open the door. But before I venture out, I lower my voice and say to them, "You girls stay here."

They do not say a word, but I can hear the fast beat of their hearts as I step out. I turn the flashlight on and begin my supposed search for footprints. As I carefully look around, I glance at them and see that they are staring at me. I slowly move the light around the yard, and then finally stop and kneel. For a few seconds I pretend to study the dirt, and then I say to them, "Boot prints."

I then pretend to follow the boot prints to the kitchen window and kneel right under the window. For a few seconds I study the dirt, and say, "You're right. He was here."

When I meet them at the door, they say, "Daddy we told you that we saw Santa!"

I say, "You were right! Well, I'm thinking that if Santa is in our neighborhood, then you girls should get in bed."

It is amazing how they so quickly agree. As they pull me toward their bedroom, I say, "Wait a minute! Eggnog and brownies! We haven't put eggnog and brownies out for Santa!"

So we stop in the kitchen, and all three of us put eggnog and brownies on a little table near the Christmas tree. I tuck them into bed, and ask them to tell me again about Santa's peek through our kitchen window. This is so funny, their little hearts can barley handle all of this excitement. After they tell a very passionate story, I give them a Christmas Eve kiss, and smile as I say, "Well, I hope that Santa leaves some toys for you girls. Merry Christmas, good night girls."

A few moments later when I am in our bedroom preparing for bed, the girls run into our room crying, because, as I knew they would, they had gone back to the family room.

"Mommy, Daddy ate Santa's brownies and drank his eggnog!"

I look at them and say, "What! What do you mean I ate Santa's brownies and drank his eggnog?"

With much passion, they say to Mara, "He did Mommy! Daddy ate Santa's brownies and drank his eggnog!"

So I say, "Okay, let's go look at the eggnog and brownies."

Mara and I follow them into our family room, and with only Christmas tree lights lighting the room, they point to the half-eaten brownies and half-glass of eggnog, and say, "See? You ate Santa's brownies and drank his eggnog!"

I look to the floor next to the little table, and as I bend over, I say, "What is this on the floor?"

As I slowly pick up a wide black belt, they become silent, as I say, "This is Santa's belt! He must have been here eating brownies, and then after he drank some eggnog, he must have taken his belt off so that he could eat more brownies. He must have heard you girls coming down the hallway so he ran out so fast that he left his belt. He must be outside waiting for you girls to go to sleep."

They are silent as I say, "Well, I'm thinking that you girls should go get in bed."

I start to laugh as I go to my knees to give them a big loving hug, and think, *I hope they don't smell my brownie breath!*

I then tuck them into bed, and they quickly fall into a deep Christmas Eve sleep.

Mara and I go out to the family room, and after we put the girls toys on the floor, and I carefully put the bottom of my boots into the ashes of the fireplace. Then I make a few ashy boot prints on the carpet in front of the fireplace and laugh to myself as I hurry off to bed.

Christmas morning is just as much fun. After a yummy breakfast, I pick up one of the girls new Christmas toys and say to them, "Let's go outside and play!"

So in the front yard, as we begin to play, one of the girls says, "Daddy what's that up on the roof?"

All of us turn to look, and I say, "I don't know. I'll get my ladder and take a look."

Finally, after I climb up the ladder and walk across the roof I arrive at a red bag. As I bend over to pick it up, I glance down at the girls. They look so cute just standing there like statues with strong deep stares. I say, "It looks like Santa's bag! It must have fallen out of his sleigh last night!"

They are silent as I look into the bag and say, "There's something in this bag!"

I reach in and pull out a nice little doll, and hold it up so the girls can see it. While their stares are fixed on me, I look back into the bag and say, "There's another doll in this bag!"

I pull that doll out and then another, and say, "My my, there is a cute little doll for each of you girls."

[Gold Statement 4: In 1990, the low for gold is $345.85 per ounce, and the high is $423.75 per ounce.]

CHAPTER 11

My Sorrow, Suffering, and Loss in a Wheelchair

⤺

REMEMBERING A PREVIOUS WARNING

A prudent *man* foreseeth the evil, and hideth himself; but the simple pass on, and are punished. (King James Bible)
PROVERBS 22:3

Noah foresaw the deluge, Joseph the years of famine, and provided accordingly.
MATTHEW HENRY

But Job answered and said, Oh that my grief were well weighed, and my miseries were laid together in the balance! For it would be now heavier than the sand of the sea: therefore my words are swallowed up.
JOB 6:1–3

And God shall wipe away all tears from their eyes, and there shall be no more death, neither sorrow, neither crying, neither shall there be any more pain: for the first things are passed. And he that sat upon the throne, said, Behold, I make all things new,...
REVELATION 21:4–5

FEBRUARY 1991

I DEVELOP STRONGER ELECTRICAL-LIKE FEELINGS in my feet, legs, and groin. It feels as if I have 110 volts of electricity hooked up to each toe, which is very irritating! The combination of increasing strong, sharp pains gradually consumes my body. It is more and more difficult for me to sleep, and I am becoming so very weary and numb from the lack of sleep. Many nights I am grateful for even a few hours of sleep. I often think about Gary's encouragement to me the night of my exposure: "Your symptoms will pass. Don't worry about it."

One day while I am at my desk studying my Bible, I rise and go to the book self. As I search for a book, the Spirit of truth says to my heart, "In twenty years you will lose the US Constitution."

I am surprised, but also aware of God's grace, enabling me to accept his visit, and warning. As my mind sobers, I begin to consider how the loss of our Constitution will affect my family and our country. And because I always try to provide security for my family, I consider, *In twenty years it will be 2011. Wow! That seems so far away. Many bad changes will have to happen before we lose our Constitution.*

I studied the Constitution and world history for six and a half years before Lauren was born, for two reasons. One reason was so that I could teach the public how to judge politicians according to the Constitution, and the other reason was so that I could publicly debate constitutional matters. My goal was to put spurs to the minds of many, and inspire politicians to make better choices. So with that education, and this new insight from the Spirit of truth, I understand that before we lose our Constitution we will suffer a large-scale disaster, and great economic problems. After a moment of serious thought, I realize that I should tell Mara. I could go to her, but I am inclined to call her to me, here where this insight was given to me.

"Mara!"

From our kitchen she says, "Yes James?"

With a hint of soberness I say, "Will you please come here?"

There before my bookshelf, as I mention to her the insight given to me, I incorrectly say, "In eighteen years…"

Before I finish my sentence, the Spirit of truth corrects me and says, "Twenty years."

I correct myself and say, "In twenty years we will lose our Constitution, and before we lose our Constitution, a large-scale disaster will occur, and we will suffer great financial problems."

After I finish telling Mara about the warning, and the insight given to me, she looks at me as if I am stupid, which is a great surprise to me, because she has never looked at me like this before.

A few days later when we pass by a large church, I say, "These large churches are a bad idea. Because before we lose our Constitution many in the congregations all across America will not be able to pay for their church because many will not be able to pay for their own houses."

Mara's silence strongly suggests to me that she thinks I am an idiot, and that I should not mention my foolish thought ever again.

A few months later, in April, I am no longer able to work because my exposure symptoms are so bad. My income has stopped, which greatly concerns Mara. This morning I mention to her, "Don't worry. All I need is a week or two of rest, and I will be as good as new, ready to go back to work."

I spoke to Mara's sister by phone, and she mentioned that she was searching all over America for a chemical detoxification clinic. I am pleased to hear that she found one only an hour away from us. I call the clinic and describe my exposure and my symptoms, and they suggest that I come to the clinic and speak with them about chemical detoxification.

Mara and I drive to the clinic, and as we speak with one of the staff, we realize that if I enter their eighteen-to-twenty-one-day program, I will be as good as new. I am encouraged to learn that the majority of the people who enter their program recover their health.

So back at home, we decide to pay the $4,500 for this detoxification program, with great hope that I will soon recover and be able to go back to work.

Very early in the program I begin to feel better. However, after twenty-one days, my body indicates that I need more detoxification. Our only problem is that we are low on money. I mention to Mara that it is silly for us to pay so much money for me to stay in a hotel.

She says, "That's true, but where will you stay?"

"I'll buy a tent and a sleeping bag, and sleep in a campsite."

One evening, about three weeks later as I am in my tent, I become very weak and ill. I expected this, because the staff at the clinic had mentioned to me that the detoxification process would make me sick. After I go to the park bathroom a few times, on my third trip I become so weak that I am not able to go back to my tent. For a moment, I stand outside the bathroom and ponder my dilemma.

Oh great, it's late! What will I do now? My only option is to rest in my truck.

As I slowly walk about forty feet to my truck, I become so weak that when I open the truck door I just fall into the truck and lie on the seat.

Through the next hour, I feel increasingly worse, so I decide that I had better go to the hospital.

The problem is that I do not know where the hospital is. All I can do is look to heaven and say, "Father, what is wrong with me? I have no idea where the hospital is, or if I can even drive to the hospital. Will you please help me drive to a hospital?"

I grab the steering wheel, and as I pull myself up, I think, *I'm too weak, there's no way that I can drive to the hospital, or even remember directions if I ask anyone for them. Well, I can remain here and possibly die or...*

I start my truck, and as I turn and look at my tent, I think, *Great. There's about two thousand dollars' worth of gear there!*

So I ask my Father, "Please don't let anyone take my gear."

I slowly drive to, well, I don't really know where. I drive for a few minutes, and pull into a gas station and ask for directions to the hospital. I feel so weak and ill that it is difficult for me to follow the directions. Thankfully, I finally arrive at the hospital at around nine o'clock.

By now, I am so weak that walking in to the hospital is very difficult. When I finally step through the door, the hospital staff quickly puts me on a gurney. A few moments later, I begin to shake, and convulse so badly that the nurses raise the sides of my gurney so that I will not fall to the floor. After my body stops shaking, I realize that I have wet my pants, so they give me hospital clothes to wear.

I tell the nurses about my exposure and the detoxification program. They do not seem to understand, or maybe they just do not believe me. Whatever the case, they do take good care of me until I feel well enough to leave at about 4:00 am. I put my wet clothes into a bag, and leave wearing hospital garb.

I don't feel strong enough to drive back to my camp, so as I walk across the street toward a small hotel, I have full confidence that God knows that I need to stay at this hotel. I ring the bell, and a moment later, an elderly woman appears at the window. I know that I must look questionable because I am wearing hospital clothes. However, as I tell her about my long, difficult night and that I am too weak to drive home, I see compassion for me on her face. I mention that I do not have my wallet, and ask if she will please allow me to stay in a room, and later today, I will go home and get my wallet and come back and pay for my room. Thankfully, she says yes, and hands me a key.

Later in the day, when I return to my camp, I am thankful, but not surprised, to find all of my gear still there. *Oh, I thank you Father.*

Due to the severity of toxins in my body, the detoxification program for me is extended beyond the usual twenty-one days, and I am now at day forty-three. I feel bad for staying for so long because Mara has called me a few times telling me that we are almost out of money. Each of those times, when I prepared to leave the program so that I could try to go back to work, the clinic staff told me that I must not leave until my detoxification is finished, because a sudden stop would be very hard on my body. So Mara and I agreed that I should continue with the detoxification program because we have invested so much money and time thus far for my hopeful recovery. We also agreed that it is silly for me to leave since I am so close to completing the program.

At day fifty-five in the program, Mara calls and says, "We are completely out of money. What are we going to do?"

I tell her, "Don't worry. I'll leave the program today, and try to go back to work."

I quietly gather my things and put them in my truck, and then inform the staff why I must go home. I thank them for their kind help, and leave.

During the one-hour drive home, I try not to worry about what might happen to me because I have left the program before finishing my detoxification.

When I finally arrive at home, I feel that I must look for work. However, after two days of searching, I painfully realize that my poor health will not allow me to continue to look for work. My only option is to sell my possessions. We need a lot of money, so that means that I must sell almost all of my things. That's okay, because I am happy to give up my possessions for my dear family. However, I am grieved to lose the enjoyments of my life, because this loss is the result of the exposure, and the injustice from doctors. As I walk through our home considering all that I must sell, I feel as if a large wave is about to sweep everything from me, which forms a lump in my throat. However, my heart becomes calm when I hear the happy sounds of my family. With deep gratitude I consider, *I still have them! I have so much with them! This time will pass. We are going to be all right.*

I put an ad in the paper regarding my possessions, and a few days later, when I am in the kitchen looking for a snack, Mara walks in, and as she begins to complain about a small matter, I say, "Mara, I don't feel good. May we talk about this later?"

She continues with a little more passion. So I say, "Mara, please stop. I don't feel good."

She increases her passion, and I say again, "Mara, please stop. I don't feel good."

She then increases the speed of her talk, so I plead, "Mara, please stop."

She surprises me when she says, "Why don't you shut me up?"

I say, "Mara, please stop!"

I then realize that she is trying to start an argument, and in this moment, I realize the many hardships that she has purposely caused for me through the past year. She again boldly says, "Why don't you shut me up?" A serious argument develops.

I realize then how bad and weak my condition has become, and how low I have fallen. Through the past three years my exposure symptoms, and the heavy intake of various pharmaceuticals, have not only deteriorated my health but also my character.

Later, I sincerely apologize for my ungodly manner.

A few days later, I hear Mara and the girls getting ready to go to the store. When Mara walks up to me, I think that she is going to invite me to go with her. However, while Madeline is in her arms, and Maribelle and Lauren are at her feet, she looks into my eyes, and says, "I'm leaving you."

As I look at her with disbelief, I begin to feel numb, and tears form in my eyes. With the little strength that I have left, I stop my tears, because I truly do not believe that she will leave me. Thirteen years ago, she brought happiness to me, and now, with our daughters present, she severely wounds my heart.

I remain calm because I believe that my exposure problems have exhausted her too, and maybe she just needs a break from all of the stress and confusion in our lives. So I say, "This is not a proper time to talk, may we talk tomorrow?"

She says, "Yes. I'm going to your mother's house, we can talk there tomorrow."

This is just what I thought! I have been wondering if Mom is somehow influencing Mara's change of character. Ever since Mom attended a psychology course about two years ago, she changed and became a problem to everyone in the family.

I follow my girls out to the driveway, and try so hard not to cry as I watch them get into our car. Through the past three years I have struggled with a lot of sorrow, because of the increasing loss of what I thought is my greatest possession, my health. However, in this moment I feel a new depth of sorrow in my heart. When they back out of our driveway, a large lump forms in my throat, and as I watch my four girls drive away, I feel like I will fall into a most pitiful cry.

I quickly go into what was our home, but now feels like only four walls and a roof. As I stand in our kitchen and look at our things, tears flood my eyes. When I begin to think about life without my daughters, and the life-long bruise that divorce will leave on them, my heart breaks, and I fall to the floor and weep.

Through the night, my pounding heart will not allow me to sleep, and by sunrise, my pillow is wet from my night of tears.

Through this long, lonely day I become hopeful for our marriage, because I believe, *God will help us with our marriage. Mara knows what the Bible says about divorce. She won't divorce me, and she knows that divorce will damage our girls for life. She just needs a little more time to think.*

Later in the day, as I drive to Mom's house it seems very odd that I need to go somewhere to talk with my wife.

At four o' clock, I arrive at Mom's house. When I knock on her front door, the lump in my throat grows bigger, as hope in my heart becomes greater. Mom opens the door, and as I step in, she leaves the room, as Mara walks into the room. I am confused, but encouraged by Mara's appearance, because she is wearing her "signal" nightgown. There were many evenings when Mara was in the kitchen preparing dinner while the girls and I played in the family room, she would leave the kitchen and return a moment later wearing her "signal" nightgown. The "signal" to me then was to make the girls tired, so that we might put them to bed early and then enjoy the evening together.

However, as Mara and I talk, I am confused about her "signal" nightgown, because she is distant and rebellious. I then realize that she is wearing the nightgown to hurt me, and my heart breaks when I realize that she wishes to follow through with divorce.

On my way back to the house, I remember a warning that God gave to me a year and a half ago. I was in our bedroom, and when Mara walked in, the Spirit of truth said to my heart, "Look at the shoes."

Mara was holding a new pair of tennis shoes. When I looked at the shoes, I noticed that they were not her usual style. They were very different. As I looked at the shoes, the Spirit of truth said to my heart, "In a year and a half she will make a major change in life."

At that time, when I told Mara what God had said to me, she became very angry. I was so ill that I could not give much thought about that warning, until now.

Later, when I climb into bed, I feel very tired because all of my sorrows, sufferings and losses have exhausted me. When I awake the next morning, I am even more exhausted, because through the night I thought about Mara's threat of divorce.

Through the next night, sad voices in my heart keep me awake. However, I am up early this Saturday morning because today is our yard sale. After breakfast I begin to carry my things out to the front yard, and by nine o'clock, 95 percent of my things are there in the grass that I once cared for.

Mara finally arrives, and surprises me because she will not put any of *her* things out in the yard. It is very difficult for me to watch people purchase my things at a third of their value, and then take them away. Other people will now enjoy my fishing boat, compound bow, guitar, and the gun that once belonged to my grandpa. Others will now enjoy my large tool collection that took me twelve years to acquire, and the majority of my large library that took me eight years to collect. I sold many other cherished possessions. However, there are two things that I refuse to sell; my little antique wood stove, and my Lionel train, given to me for Christmas when I was in second grade.

After the yard sale, I pull two thousand dollars out of my pocket and give it to Mara. I then say to her, "Oh wait a minute, I don't have any money."

After she hands the money back to me, I take $150.00 for myself and give the rest back to her.

She then goes back to Mom's, and through the evening I cannot believe how empty, and cold this rental house feels. I can only stay here for a few more days before I must leave, to I do not know where. The many happy memories in this house are now painful memories. This evening I have another sorrow in my heart, because tomorrow I will betray our dog when I take him to the pound.

Three days later Mara goes to Social Services and mentions our separation, telling them that I will not provide any money for her and our children. So they give her $1,542, and then a few days later I receive a bill from Social Services, requiring me to repay the money they gave to Mara. This angers me for a few reasons, one is because Mara earns a good salary working for Mom, and lives rent-free with Mom.

Thankfully, my sister and brother-in-law invite me to stay at their house.

It seems like all that is valuable or precious to me is continually slipping away, as I often need to sell another possession of mine so that I may have money for food.

I am especially hurt to learn that Mara no longer goes to church, and I cannot believe that she has turned from all of our Christian friends. Our friends and I are very troubled to learn that Mara has returned to Scientology. From a Christian perspective, her Scientology involvement devastates me, especially when I consider that she might teach our girls Scientology. Mara's many changes deeply grieve me, and I am very sad to learn that Mara now goes to western-type bars no less than four nights a week, staying out very late. Each evening and through each night, my heart is full of pain when I consider the lustful men in those bars drooling over her, my daughters' mother.

Month after month, I suffer with great confusion caused by my illness, and great sorrow caused by Mara's betrayal of us.

Six months after our separation, Mara and I meet on the front porch of my brother-in-law's house so that she can give me divorce papers. However, before I sign the papers I hand her a piece of paper that says, "God hates divorce."

Note to reader: In Ruth 1:20, Naomi changed her name to Mara, to express her "bitterness and sadness." I named my daughter's biological birth person "Mara" to express the bitterness, and sadness that she inflicted upon us.

My sad heart painfully knows the following proverbs:

A virtuous woman *is* the crown of her husband: but she that maketh *him* ashamed, *is* as corruption in his bones.
PROVERBS 12:4

A wise woman buildeth her house: but the foolish destroyeth it with her own hands.

PROVERBS 14:1

Mara's different nature deeply hurts me. I recognize her appearance, but her spirit is different, and it feels very odd that I do not know her anymore. The deep pain from our divorce feels like a piece of paper slowly ripped apart. How long can my heart bleed before I die? I often wipe away tears because my life-long dreams are dying.

Because of my nerve disease, good rest and a proper diet are especially important. However, after I move out of my brother-in-law's house I stay in a friend's garage for a night, in another friend's backyard for a few more days and then live in my truck.

I am very concerned because I have sold almost all of my possessions. However, today my emotions are like the changing tide when I receive a one-time payment of $2,200 from the Carpenters Disability Fund. I qualify for this payment because I have applied for Social Security Disability benefits.

Though I am not under court order to give Mara any money, I give her $1,670, which is a significant portion of all that I have. With the remaining money, I rent a small one-bedroom cottage on the poor side of town. Soon after, I begin to receive monthly payments of $850 a month from my Carpenters Disability Fund.

The exposure symptoms that I described to Dr. Bismarck and Dr. Moulage, are now verified by a nerve conduction study, performed by Dr. Definite on November 1, 1991. The test reveals both denervation in my feet, and that my right foot is eighteen degrees colder than normal. My diagnosis is chronic distal denervation in the feet consistent with chronic axonal polyneuropathy.

I do not understand what the test means, but I feel very confident that this test will convince the Workers' Compensation judge that my symptoms are work related. I desperately need a Workers' Compensation settlement so that I can purchase some things for my cottage and buy a truck that runs better. I am so anxious to make a home for my girls and me.

The other day I asked the Father what I should think about Mara's different spirit. And this morning during my bible time, as I read about Korah's rebellion in Numbers 16:1–50, I begin to understand that Mara has become insolent like Korah. So I turn to Jude:11 and read Jude's comment about Korah. Now I understand that Mara has cast off all accountability to God, and man, so that she may enjoy unbridled selfish ambition.

I also understand why she has become so unreasonable, and I realize that before she hardened her heart against the girls, and me, she must have hardened her heart against God. I am sickened to consider that she now loves her selfish ambition more than our daughters, God and me. Tears flood my eyes when I consider, *If she repeatedly says no to what is best and right, her conscience will become dull and insensitive. Like an alcoholic, she will slowly ruin herself. She will lose her honor as a mother, and probably tell the girls lies about me, which will ruin my honor as a father.*

The anguish in my heart is so great that I cannot sit here and think about our divorce anymore. However, as I rise, I know that there is no escape from these very sad thoughts. Through each hour of this day, I try to occupy my mind with activities so that I will not think about Mara's damage to our lives. However, there is no escape from the heavy sorrow in my heart, especially when I think about how our divorce must hurt the girls. My absence must be confusing and painful to them, and the thought of another man raising my daughters breaks my heart. Because of these voices in my heart, I always have a lump in my throat and tears in my eyes. The wound upon my daughter's hearts and mine is severe, so I must make every effort to minimize further confusion and pain, especially for the girls.

Every day I search God's word so that I may at least be right with God. However, I am not right with many of my friends and family because they have seen me give Mara almost all our possessions. They are also confused because I have given so much money to her. God sees that I am trying to relieve stress on Mara so that hopefully she will cause less stress on the girls. And it seems to me that the girls will be comforted if they see my things in their house, because part of me is still with them. No doubt, I will do my best to keep my little antique wood stove, and my Lionel train.

Another way that I can relieve stress on Mara is too not speak about her in a negative manner to anyone. Because negative talk, or should I say, the truth about her, will be like adding wood to the fire she started. If more wood is put on the fire, my girls will feel that heat. Though it pains me to not tell the truth about Mara, I am comforted when I consider that my Father is watching.

I have also decided to hide the severity of my exposure symptoms from the girls so that they will have peace and security with at least one of their parents. That means that I must also hide the severity of my symptoms from my family. Now, because I cannot tell my family about all of my afflictions, I talk much more with God about my trials.

My exposure symptoms are confusing because they change from day to day. I am also pained because my girls complain to me about their mother's different life. Mara has allowed me to see the girls only two or three times through the past four or five months. I have no idea why she limits my visits with them. My thought is not to argue with her because that will cause more stress for our daughters, and I should just be patient and give her some time to think.

The few times that Mara has brought the girls to me, I have noticed that all three of them were dressed in black from head to toe, which broke my heart. A moment ago, Mara brought the girls to me and after she leaves,

Lauren says to me, "Daddy, why is Mommy dressing us in black clothes? Some of our friends make fun of us."

When Maribelle hears Lauren's complaint, she says, "Yeah Daddy. Why is Mommy dressing us like this?"

I then learn from the girls that Mara has dressed them in black every day for the past four or five months. It seems that every day something new about our divorce grieves my heart.

On Sunday when Mara arrives to pick up the girls, she shows me a restraining order and says, "I have filled a restraining order against you." I am stunned and humiliated. I know nothing about restraining orders. So after I speak with my sister about the restraining order, she mentions that one of the restrictions in the order is that I must remain at a considerable distance from the girls' school when I go to pick them up. Through the next month, I am humiliated everyday when I park a considerable distance from the school and wait for the girls to walk to my truck. Until one day when I complain to my sister about the restraining order, she asks, "Did anyone from law enforcement serve you with a restraining order?" When I say no, my sister says, "James, that means that there is no restraining order against you."

My grief is much greater when I consider that Mara lied to me, and because of my desire to keep our family together, I am not willing to acknowledge all of the truth about who she has become. I later learn from my sister that the reason Mara dressed the girls in black, and would not allow me to see them, was to anger me, so that she could obtain an actual restraining order against me.

I do not talk to Mara about her ploy because I am trying to minimize frustration between us. I am comforted when I consider that my Father is watching.

My anguish increases now that I realize that Mara will use the girls to anger me. As fire reveals the true nature of metal, so a trial reveals the true nature of a heart.

Today as I wait for the girls in front of their Christian school, the vice principal asks me to step into her office so that she may talk with me.

As I step from my truck, I say to her, "May I ask why you need to speak with me?"

She says, "I need to speak with you about Mara."

As we begin to walk, I say, "Mara?"

She says, "I'll tell you when we are in my office."

Embarrassment stings my heart as I consider that I cannot take another negative thing about Mara.

Sorrow also fills my heart because before Mara changed, everyone spoke honorably about her. However, the attitude of the vice principle seems to be negative, so as we step through the office door I try to prepare myself for more embarrassment and sorrow. When the vice principle closes the office door she says to me, "We have watched Mara for a long time, and have written notes about how she dresses your daughters, the type of lunches she provides for them, and how often she brings them late to school."

Her words are like molten metal thrown onto my heart. After I take a deep breath, I say, "May I see the notes?"

She says, "The notes are so serious that we will not give them to you unless you first contact an attorney."

I say, "An attorney! I do not have enough money to hire an attorney because my only income is from a disability fund."

I again ask if I may see the notes. However, she again tells me that I must first contact an attorney. I thank the vice principal for her concern for my daughters, and tell her that I will do my best to correct the problem.

My family and others are well aware of Mara's neglect of our girls, and everyone is aware that Mara is not neglecting herself.

A few weeks before Thanksgiving, I ask Mara again if I may have the girls on Thanksgiving. And just as I thought, she says no. I am completely crushed. I cannot take any more of this. I cannot believe that I will not be with my daughters on Thanksgiving. I try to comfort myself with the thought that hopefully by Christmas, Mara will come to her senses and be more reasonable. I am beginning to realize more clearly the following verses:

It is better to dwell in the wilderness, than with a contentious and angry woman.
PROVERBS 21:19

The wife of thy covenant is thy companion, and yet, if she be peevish and provoking, it is better to dwell in a solitary wilderness, exposed to wind and weather than in company with her.
MATTHEW HENRY

A continual dropping in the day of rain, and a contentious woman are alike.
PROVERBS 27:15

Thanksgiving Day food does not taste as good because I am not with my daughters. My heart is troubled with the thought that Mara may not let me enjoy Christmas with my girls.

I have wondered if Mom, Mara, and one of my other siblings, have joined against me. Now I believe that they have, because I often notice that they seem to be working some kind of scheme against me. The problem is that they hate my Christian convictions. So they use Mom's novice psychology skills as a weapon against me. The family knows that Mom records all of our phone calls when we call her, so that she may analyze them later. Mom has become a big problem to the family.

Tonight my body feels a little better as I climb into bed. Now that I am comfortable on my pillow, I am thankful to lie here, only slightly troubled by my exposure symptoms. However, at 2:31 a.m., I awake feeling terrible, and remain awake until sunrise. I finally roll out of bed because I feel so terrible, so bad that I do not feel like eating breakfast. Through the day, I feel very sick, but I give myself hope, thinking that I will feel better tomorrow. However, through the next few days, I feel increasingly worse, but on the fifth morning, I feel well enough to go visit Dad at his office. To my good surprise, as I dress and then eat breakfast I feel even better. When I walk into Dad's office, I appear to be a normal healthy man. As usual, my very busy Dad says, "Hi James, how about a cup of coffee?"

With a smile I say, "Yes, that sounds so good!"

While drinking our cups of coffee, Dad says, "James, do you want to go for a ride in my truck with me?" Dad is probably going to one of his job sites, so with a hint of affection, I say yes. As we step through the back door toward his truck, I say, "Dad, do you realize that I have ridden in your truck with you since I was in third grade? Sure is good to go for another ride with you."

During the first minute of our ride, the Spirit of truth says to my heart, "Your Dad is taking you to see a psychiatrist."

My heart rate rises because I know that many psychiatrists oppose Christianity. I then earnestly pray from my heart, *Thank you Father. What should I think, and what should I do?*

Feeling very confident in my Father's providential kindness to me, I take a deep breath to slow my heart rate, and then turn to Dad and say, "Dad, are you taking me to see a psychiatrist?"

For a moment, he intensely stares straight ahead with a very sober face. He then turns to me and says, "Yes, I am."

As my heart rate increases, he turns back and looks straight ahead with a very intense stare. A short moment later, he says to me, "When we get there, will you go in?"

I say, "Yes, I will."

I then pray from my heart, *Father, I sure need Your help.*

In the foyer of a known prominent psychiatrist's office, we meet the psychiatrist, and he takes me into his fancy office. When I put my caboose in his chair, I pray again, "Father, I sure need your help."

A moment later, the Spirit of truth inclines me to look at the psychiatrists numerous books. He then says to my heart, "Focus on his pride."

My heart laughs, because I understand that the help I have just received is the understanding that almost all men will gladly focus on their own pride. Therefore, I say to the doctor, "You sure have a nice collection of books."

He begins to talk about his impressive career until our one-hour session is over. *Amazing.* He then leads me out to the foyer and mentions a very fine compliment about me to Dad. A moment later when Dad and I step through the front door of the building, Dad says to me, "Well, James, your mother can't get you now."

I do not ask what he meant by that statement, because any trouble regarding Mom is usually a volatile matter, and therefore I do not ever mention my visit with the psychiatrist again.

I am not surprised that Dad deceived me when he took me to the psychiatrist, because he does not like my Christian convictions. Though he attends church, and talks like a Christian, I think his opposition to me is because of his drug and alcohol addictions. I am surprised though, that he will not offer any financial help to me. Especially when I consider that as a contractor engineer he earns thirty thousand dollars each month.

A few days later, I go to a medical facility because I have an appointment with a new doctor. I am hopeful that he will understand my chemical exposure symptoms and help me improve my health.

After a nurse takes me into an examination room, I sit on the table and wait. Moments later, when the doctor opens the door and enters the room, I say, "Well hi there."

His demeanor is confusing because he does not say hello or anything, or even look at me. When he quickly turns his back to me and begins to write something on a piece of paper, I consider that he must be very busy and in deep thought. I have a very important question to ask him, which I realized when I recently read a book written by Alice M. Ottoboni, called "The Dose Makes the Poison." I can hardly wait for the doctor to turn around so that I can ask my question. A moment later, while I am still looking at his back, it looks like he stops writing, so I go ahead and take this opportunity to ask my question. "Doctor, do you believe that a chemical exposure could cause the symptoms that I described on the form that your nurse gave me?"

He keeps his back to me while he answers, "No."

His quick, short answer surprises me, and the rude tone of voice concerns me. He should first at least talk with me about my symptoms. Something does not seem right, so I mention another thought from Mrs. Ottoboni's book. "Surely doctor, you are aware of individual bioaccumulation of toxins?"

He does not say a word, as he quickly turns and leaves the room, making me feel a little embarrassed, as if I had said something wrong. I remain on the table, wondering if he is ever coming back. As I think about this man's demeanor, I realize that my questions have revealed that something is not right about this doctor. This moment makes me think that there are likely other medical people like this questionable doctor, so I think that I will study more about my exposure symptoms so that I am better prepared to discern other doctors. I decide not to deal with this rude man anymore, and promptly leave the building. It is odd that I do not receive a letter from the clinic about my unusual visit.

CHAPTER 12

A Wayward, Formerly Righteous Virtuous Spouse

⟿

MY ENDLESS GRIEF

...one sinner destroyeth much good.
ECCLESIASTES 9:18

DECEMBER 1991: LAUREN IS SEVEN YEARS OLD, MARIBELLE IS FIVE, AND MADELINE IS TWENTY-ONE MONTHS OLD
EVERY DAY MY BIBLE READING and prayer strengthen me, giving me much hope, causing me to believe that God has a very good purpose in this confusing time of my life. Each day I also do things that will put a smile on my heart. Things like clean my home, watch birds, or show kindness to someone.

However, I cannot help but be very sad because I am missing family evenings and my daughter's birthday parties.

After the divorce, one of the reasons that my heart became very sick and sad is because of Mara's great and rapid change of character. Before our divorce, she lived as a conservative Christian, and now she gives herself over to many harmful pleasures without regard for her family or for God. It is very sad to know the true nature of her heart, which is evident by her consistent ungodly attitude and immodest dress. Recently she further corrupted her attitude and appearance when she gave herself to cosmetic surgery. Before her surgery, her breasts were a size that many women would envy, and now they are so big that someone in her family told her that she looks deformed. I am sick because of her influence on my daughters.

I am afflicted with so much sorrow, that I just cannot take any more disappointments. These times, these afflictions, make strong men cry. This evening after I climb into bed, grieved voices in my heart will not allow me to sleep. I am thankful when exhaustion eventually causes me to fall asleep, silencing the cruel voices. However, during the middle of the night when I awake, God says clearly to my heart that my former spouse has shared herself with another man. These painful thoughts cause me to roll back and forth in anguish. At 3:00 a.m. I get out of bed, dress, and drive to Mara's house. I knock on her door, and am so hurt when she answers the door naked, thinking that I was her new boyfriend. When she sees me at her door, she quickly turns and runs as fast as she can to her bedroom. After she dresses, and comes back to me, I fall to my knees, and as I put my heart-felt arms around her waist, I begin to sob, asking her to please think about what she is doing. She remains silent. After a moment, I rise so that we may talk. She is very distant with me. So, before I take my leave, I say to her, "If you do not stop what you are doing, years from now the girls will say to you, '*Who do you think you are.*' " I then leave.

Through the following weeks increasing sorrow, grief, and disbelief torment me, mainly because Mara is so cruel to me. I am trying with all of my heart to revive our dreams that are slowly dying. It seems like the people and things I trust, even my own body, betray me daily. Mom's gossip and slander about me is turning my family and friends against me. I cannot remember the last time someone was kind to me, until one day when I stop at a pay phone to call Mara, I hear a woman's kind voice request that I put money into the phone. I am so thankful to hear her gentle voice that I purposely do not put money into the phone so that I may listen to her recorded request a few more times. Eventually I put one coin into the phone and listen to her soft voice five or six times, and then put another coin into the phone. I am so happy to listen to a woman who will never hurt me. After I put the final coin into the phone, I dial Mara's number, and when she answers the phone, sorrow fills my heart again.

During the first week of December, the old-fashioned Christmas music deeply saddens my heart, because I am not with my family. My house is so quiet and empty this evening, so I climb into bed early. Here in bed, my heart and mind find even more reasons to be sad. Since Thanksgiving I have not slept very well, not only because of my nerve disease, but also because I did not spend the holiday with my girls, which makes me think that Mara may not let me enjoy Christmas with my daughters. I am almost afraid to ask her if I may have the girls on Christmas because I do not think that I can bear to hear "no" again. However, I cannot bear to spend another holiday without my girls, so in a few days I will ask Mara if I may have the girls for Christmas. I know this sounds silly, but as I lie here in bed, I cannot stop my thoughts about the fact that if I do not have Mara, I do not have my girls. Thinking about her makes me toss and turn, until eventually, exhaustion makes me fall asleep.

However, the continuous sad cry in my heart awakens me with the biggest lump in my throat, because I am not with my family. I realize that I can no longer stop the strong, deep cry that I have suppressed since the divorce. I know that if I give myself to strong deep crying I will release at least some of my sorrow. So, after I roll out of bed and fall to the floor, my heart breaks, and I begin a most sad, pitiful cry. Through the next hour, I cannot open my mouth wide enough for the heavy flow of pain pouring from my heart. During my loud cry, I wonder if my neighbors can hear my unearthly howls. However, I am comforted when the Spirit of truth reminds me that my Father hears my cry, and understands each sad tear. After an hour of sobbing, I feel so exhausted that I must stop my cry and catch my breath. After my breathing slows, I remain motionless for a few moments, considering that God *did* hear my cry, and the sad thoughts of my heart. I climb back into bed and begin to think about the glorious Seraphim angels above God's thrown, who always cover their faces because of their reverence for God. When I begin to feel a little of their great reverence for God, I put my hands over my face, and thank God for His tender help to me, and tell Him again that I am so stupid for not listening to Him when He warned me that Mara will turn from Him and me. I ask again what lessons I must learn so that I will not be such a stupid man.

During the second week of December, I ask Mara if I may spend Christmas with the girls. And as I feared she says no, which breaks my heart. I wish I at least had their Christmas gifts in my home, because that would bring a little Christmas cheer to my heart. I cannot play any Christmas music, because it will make me think about the lost time with my family. This is not an enjoyable Christmas season, and I wish it would quickly pass. It is very difficult for me to go anywhere because it pains my heart to see families together. As each passing day draws me closer to Christmas, the pain of missing my girls increases my sorrow. How much can a man suffer before he dies?

Then to my good surprise, three days before Christmas Mara calls and says, "I'm bringing the girls over to you. You can have them for Christmas."

I then learn why Mara is bringing them to me when she says, "They all have fevers of 101 degrees."

I am not surprised that Mara is giving up the girls because they are sick. However, I am as happy as can be because the girls and I will be together for Christmas. Within a short time, Mara brings the girls to me and she then leaves town to spend Christmas with her friends in the mountains.

For where your treasure is, there will your heart be also.
MATTHEW 6:21

I am so very happy to be with my treasures. However, I now have a huge problem. If I cannot lower their temperatures before Christmas Eve, we will not be able to go shopping for gifts, or even purchase a Christmas tree. So here we are, three days before Christmas. I only have $80, and it will be almost two weeks before I receive more money. We do not have a Christmas tree, decorations, or any gifts. That's okay, because we are together, and no doubt we will make the best of our Christmas. After we finish tender hugs with each other, I ask the Father to please help me lower their temperatures. I then give each of them some medicine, and put a cool cloth on each little forehead.

The next day the girls' temperatures are low enough that I think that it will be okay to take them out to buy a tree, a few gifts, and a little food. While they are busy in another part of the store, I pay $1.00 to $5.00 per gift, and then at home we make our own ornaments for our tree.

The evening of Christmas Eve, Santa's suit remains in its box because I do not know where it is. Christmas morning is very difficult for me because I remember how wonderful our Christmas morning was last year. Here it is, Christmas morning, and my heart aches because Mara is not with us. I completely hide my sad emotions from the girls and concentrate on creating happy moments for them so that they may later have happy Christmas memories.

I put their three best gifts aside and let them open their other gifts. Now with wrapping paper all over the floor I hand their last three best gifts to them. All three girls open their gifts at the same time and say with excitement, "Silly String! A can of Silly String!"

With equal excitement, I say, "I'll count down from three, and then you can spray your cans, so put your thumbs on your cans, and get ready."

As the girls place their little thumbs on their silly string cans, the room charges with added excitement. My count is very slow as I say, "Three...two...one!"

All three girls scream and laugh as silly string flies all over the room. And for a moment I am their target as they chase me around the room. Silly string covers us, and the walls, and the Christmas tree now has new decorations. And yes, the carpet is covered too. The house is a mess, but we are blessed. Through the rest of my time in this house, I leave some of the silly string hanging on my calendar to remember this happy moment, and not until I move do I carefully pick it off, and save it.

Note to Reader: Twenty-two years later, I still have that precious piece of silly string and the Christmas tree ornaments.

CHAPTER 13

Alone in a Shed with God

$\backsim$

THE ARREST OF JESUS CONFUSED His disciples, convincing them that God did not have control of the moment. However, before the arrest of Jesus, Jesus clearly told His disciples that His arrest was "appointed" by God, and the fact that Jesus told Peter hours before His arrest that "the cock shall not crow this day, before thou hast thrice denied that thou knowest me," forewarned the disciples that the "appointed" disorder among them was God's order for man.

Our sorrows, sufferings, and losses often appear to be out of God's control. However, God always has a purpose. It is to our great benefit to ignore logic and psychology; and by prayer and the study of God's word, understand God's mind and will for our lives, and by faith submit to His purpose.

Then took they him, [Jesus] and led him, and brought him to the high Priest's house. And Peter followed afar off. And when they had kindled a fire in the midst of the hall, and were set down together, Peter also sat down among them. And a certain maid beheld him as he sat by the fire, and having well looked on him, said, This man was also with him. But he denied him, saying, Woman, I know him not. And after a little while, another man saw him, and said, Thou art also of them. But Peter said, Man, I am not. And about the space of an hour after, a certain other affirmed, saying. Verily, even this man was with him: for he is

also a Galilean. And Peter said, Man, I know not what thou say-
est. And immediately while he yet spake, the cock crew. Then the
Lord turned back, and looked upon Peter: and Peter remembered
the word of the Lord, how he had said unto him, Before the cock
crow, thou shalt deny me thrice. And Peter went out, and wept
bitterly.

LUKE 22:54–62

Luke alone records that Jesus made eye contact with Peter. The verb
'looked' is used to suggest an intent, fixed look.

THE MACARTHUR STUDY BIBLE

JANUARY 1992

THE CHRISTMAS WEEKEND PASSES much too quickly, and my heart is troubled because Mara is on her way to pick up the girls.

I am troubled everyday as I consider, *Why did my doctors state that my
symptoms are not work related?* Because of this statement, I have lost my
Workers' Compensation claim. This statement has caused me to lose a lot of
time with my daughters, and needed medical care. My heart aches because I
know that my girls are hurt and offended by the divorce. I am also very sad as
I consider that through the years my daughters will not see my love or care for
their mother. They will see another man with her. I will not be there to bless
them with simple laughter, and nourish their hearts, minds, and consciences
with God's word and His love. When parents are tender and healthy with
each other, the hearts, minds, and consciences of their children are properly
nourished.

Another sad thought deep within my heart is that our marriage and the
births of our children began a special process of maturing me with honorable
attributes of matrimony and fatherhood, but now that process has stopped,
which is another reason why I often wipe tears from my eyes.

After a year of receiving Carpenters Disability payments, I am very surprise to learn that I will receive only one more payment. This means that my monthly income will stop in a few weeks, which also means that I must move again to, I do not know where. I have rested very well in my cottage for one year, and if I am not able to find another place to live, I have no choice but to live in my truck. However, after talking with God about a home for me, I wait for His provision.

A day later when I am at the store, I see my dear Christian friend John, and after I tell him about my plight, I am so grateful when he says that I may move in with him and his family, that is after he confirms his offer with his wife. John calls me later in the evening and says that I may live at their house. Thank you Father.

I am about to lose my income, so the next day I file for unemployment. However, my application is denied because I have already filed for Social Security payments. After I explain my dilemma to the woman at the unemployment office, she says that there is a way that I can qualify for unemployment payments. She explains what I should say to my doctor so that he can write a certain type of letter to the unemployment office that will justify unemployment payments for me. Her advice works, and shortly afterward I begin to receive unemployment payments.

Through the past eight years that I have known John and his family they have always treated me with kindness and love. However, as I move my things into my room I discern possible trouble with John's wife, and through the following months, I increasingly feel uncomfortable with her until she finally reveals her true heart when she tells me to leave. I later learn from John that his wife threw me out because my own mother encouraged her to change her character, as she did with Mara. My mother also encouraged John's wife to divorce John so that she may find new enjoyments at the western bars, as Mara does.

Well, I have lost my home and now my unemployment has ended. My only option is to live in my truck and bathe in the river. After I live in my truck for about a week, another friend says that I may live in the shed behind his house if I pay him $100 a month for rent. I humble myself, and go to the welfare office and explain my problems to a caseworker. Thankfully, they now provide me with $300 a month. I quickly meet with my friend, and when he shows the shed to me, I am stunned because it is a dusty old building without even a doorknob on the door. When we step inside, I realize that there is no insulation in the walls or ceiling, which means that this old shed will be very hot in the summer and very cold in the winter. That is okay, because I am thankful to have a roof over my head and a place where my daughters may visit me.

The only furniture I bring into this shed is a mat so that I may sleep on the floor. And since there is no light fixture, I hang a droplight on the wall above my pillow. I am determined to make this old building a nice home for us, so I start cleaning because the girls will be here in a few days.

After I finish cleaning I make two kitchen cabinets out of two cardboard boxes, and as I look at my new cabinets, my heart is heavy as I think about the many professional kitchen cabinets I made when I worked as a carpenter. Well that's okay, because I am thankful for these nice cardboard cabinets. As I take a deep breath, I slowly look around at our new home and think, *Wow! No furniture, refrigerator, stove, bathroom, TV, radio, or telephone.* However, as disappointment enters my heart the Spirit of truth reminds me, *there are many people around the world who would be envious of this home.* I then go to my knees and thank God for my home.

Later in the evening when I climb into bed, my mind becomes very busy thinking about the nice condominium that Mara and the girls live in. However, I know that there is disorder and sorrow there, so that means that they only live in a house, not really a home. My heart is grieved because my daughter's are so affected by my ordeal, and Mara's indifference toward them, God, and me.

I often sadly consider that I no longer enjoy many things, such as the recoil of my forty-five Long Colt revolver during target practice, or the enjoyment of fishing as I stand on a riverbank, and I especially miss sitting next to an early morning campfire.

As I wait for Mara to bring the girls over to me, I feel more and more embarrassed because of what Mara will think when she sees my new home, and I am especially anxious about what the girls will think when they see our new home. When Mara finally arrives, the girls and I are so happy to see each other. After hugs, I take them into our new home, and as they look around, one of them says, "Let's build a fort!" Which makes the other two say, "Yeah Daddy, let's build a fort!"

Oh, I am so happy to hear that. As Mara leaves, we begin to build our fort, which transforms this old shed into our dear home. After the structure is finished, we throw our sleeping bags over it, making it look like the very best fort ever.

Later, as I begin to fix dinner, my heart becomes heavy because all we have to eat is a can of cold vegetables, a can of chicken, and some dry noodles. However, because we are together, our dinner seems like the best dinner. And for dessert we enjoy peanut butter mixed with honey.

Later on, when it is time for bed, my heart swells with sorrow as I consider, *Where will we sleep in this old building? Well, the only place is there on the floor in the corner.*

As we put our sleeping bags on the floor, I fear that mice might climb on the girls during the night. So I offer a prayer from my heart, *"Father, please don't let any mice climb on us during the night."*

After all of us are nice and warm in our bags, I hear the sweet sound of a home when one of the girls says, "Daddy, tell us a story!"

The other two raise their voices and say, "Yeah Daddy, tell us a story!"

Suddenly I am as happy as can be. So, to create a good atmosphere for our story time, I turn on our light, light my little tent candle lantern, turn off the light and begin our story.

"Once upon a time there was a nice house. Well it was really a nice home where a happy family lived; a dad, a mom and three little girls."

All three girls scream, "Are their names Lauren, Maribelle and Madeline?"

I smile as if I am the most fortunate man, and say, "Why yes, those are their names."

I then say, "And in the backyard is a worm, a bird, a butterfly and a few ants who are all very good friends."

The girls quickly become quiet, waiting to hear my story. During the story, I realize that *we are alright. We are together, and we have a roof over our heads. Yes, we are alright.*

I continue to tell a story about the backyard friends, until all three are sound asleep.

The next evening when we are again back in our beds, I am so happy when one of the girls say, "Daddy, tell us the Worm Story!"

I say, "The Worm Story?"

All three raise their voice and say, "Yeah Daddy, tell us the Worm Story!"

So I make up another story about the worm and his friends, and the family inside, and as I tell the story, I wonder who enjoys this story more, the girls or me.

Each evening when the girls and I climb into bed, they ask me to tell them the "Worm Story."

Often, during the day, the girls and I sit close together on the floor as I read *Calvin and Hobbes* to them. We are learning that we do not need a TV or expensive toys to make us happy. All we need are simple, sincere hearts as we sit together and read Calvin and Hobbes, and the Bible. And yes, we need playful imaginations for building forts. The weekend passes, and Mara takes the girls back to her house.

Though I try to make the best of my circumstances, at times it is very difficult because I become severely weak. Sometimes the back of my head is painful and swollen making it difficult for me to think clearly, for one to three days at a time.

Every day I crave warm food, so I am very thankful when once a week my good friend John drives me to Taco Bell so that I may enjoy a nice warm burrito with him.

It was a little more than a year ago when I filed for Social Security Disability. I have no idea when they will approve my monthly payments. No doubt, I will be thankful to receive Social Security payments for many reasons; one is so that I can enjoy warm food each day.

Today I splurged and bought a book because it is very difficult for me to live without a TV or a radio. It is especially difficult since the sentiments of my heart and the thoughts of my mind are always about the loss of my family. Now all through the day I think about reading my new book after the sun sets and the birds fold their wings. Each evening when I slip into my sleeping bag, the adventures within my new book draw me across the broad expanse of the great Pacific Ocean to Cocos Island. After I am all tucked in and feeling just right, I open my book, *The Venturesome Voyages of J.C. Voss*. The true stories in this book begin in the late 1800s, describing Mr. Voss's sailing voyage around the world in a very small sailboat. After I finish reading, I lay the book aside, turn off my light, and sink into my warm sleeping bag, hoping for a good night's sleep.

However, during the night when I begin to open my eyes, I realize that God is present. The Spirit of truth then clearly says to my heart, "Mara and your mother are attempting to manipulate your life so that they can have you legally committed to a mental hospital."

My sudden rapid heart rate causes me to sit up and consider, *Mara and Mom hate my Christian convictions, so it would please them to have me put away and out of their lives.*

I then earnestly pray aloud, "Thank you Father. I do not doubt your warning. This is very serious, so please be patient with me. Since the warning is so severe, will you please confirm it?"

A week later, late in the evening, my friend in the main house calls me to the phone. On my way I think, *Who is calling me? No one ever calls me, because only a few people know where I live.*

When I put the phone to my ear, I am surprised to hear Mara's sister. I am mainly surprised because she lives in LA. After we greet each other, she mentions the reason for her call, by saying, "I heard Mara and your mother talk about manipulating your life so that they could have you legally committed."

Before she finishes her warning to me, I pray in my heart, *Amazing! Thank you Father.*

I am now very cautious about whom I mention my exposure symptoms to; because I fear that someone might mention my poor health to Mara or Mom, encouraging their ploy against me. However, a short time later my health further deteriorates, forcing me to use a wheelchair.

Each day I do something that will put a big smile on my heart, like clean my home, and go to the river and enjoy the sounds and sights.

Now I understand why Mara and I argued so much during the last two years of our marriage. She was designing our divorce. She purposely irritated me mentally by carefully choosing what she would say, and not say to me. She purposely irritated me physically by choosing what to do for me and what not to do for me, and she also purposely created extra work around the house for me to do. Toward the end of our marriage, she often purposely tried to anger me so that she might justify our divorce. Her long-term ploy and my illness are wearing me down. However, God's word keeps me going with good hope. I often read Job, considering that Job's sad ordeal ended when God ended his afflictions.

Then the Lord turned the captivity of Job,...
Job 42:10

So the Lord blessed the last days of Job more than the first:...
Job 42:12

CHAPTER 14

Love, Hugs and Laughter are Balm

_~c~_

FOR MY DAUGHTERS' WOUNDED HEARTS

But above all things have fervent love among you: for love shall cover the multitude of sins.

I Peter 4:8

He commendeth charity of one toward another, because it doth as it were bury a multitude of sins, and therefore preserveth and maintaineth peace and concord.

1599 Geneva Bible

And Zacchaeus stood forth, and said unto the Lord, Behold, Lord, the half of my goods I give to the poor: and if I have taken from any man by forged cavillation, I restore him fourfold.

Luke 19:8

1992: Lauren is seven, Maribelle is five, and Madeline is three
Summer finally arrives, which means the girls can stay with me for a week or more at a time.

Mara seems happy to bring the girls to me, I am sure, so that she can go and play. Well, I am as happy as can be because I am with my girls, my life-long dreams.

We have learned to be content and happy in our little, humble home. After breakfast, we enjoy Bible time, and then laugh as I read a few pages of *Calvin and Hobbes*. Afterward the girls go outside to play with the kids from the main house. As I clean our home, I find a surprise and think, *I cannot believe Madeline's doll is there on the floor.* I have never seen this doll anywhere but in Madeline's arms.

When I lean over and pick it up, I think of an idea. I quickly look outside to see what the girls are doing, and think, *Good deal! They're busy, and won't be in for a few minutes.*

I quickly pick up my fishing pole and pull off some line, *That'll do. This will be so funny!*

I find a few nails and go to where my sleeping mat is in the corner of the room. As I place a nail in the bottom corner of the wall, I also listen, making sure that the girls do not come in and see what I am doing. After the first nail is set, I place other nails up the wall in the corner until I place the last nail close to the ceiling. I then place nails across the wall next to the ceiling until I reach the other corner, and then place nails in the corner of the wall down to the floor, and think, *This will be so funny!*

I stretch fishing line from each nail, up the corner, across the ceiling, and down the other corner to the floor on the other side of the room, and quickly look out the window to see what the girls are doing, and think, *Good deal, they are still busy.*

I get Madeline's doll and put her on the floor, sitting near the corner, across the room from my mat, and quickly tie the fishing line around her chest under her arms. I fix the dolls dress, and make her look as if she is just sitting here waiting for Madeline. As I listen to the kids play, I hurry over to my mat and gently pull the fishing line, and think, *Perfect!*

As I step over to the door, I make sure not to smile, as I say, "Girls, I have a question for you and your friends."

As they run to the door, I quickly go sit on my mat, so they will sit on the floor in front of me. When all of them are on the floor before me, I think, *Perfect, Madeline can see her doll from the corner of her eye.*

I act a little serious, which sobers them. Now with all their eyes intently gazing at me, as I begin with my question, I slowly reach behind my back, and gently pull the fishing line, making Madeline's doll move just a little. Madeline continues to look at me, yet I can see the disbelief all over her face.

The look in her eyes is so funny that I can barely keep myself from laughing. Then as curiosity almost pushes her face out of shape, she turns to look at her doll, and then looks back to me. I have never seen such a funny look on anyone's face. As she stares at me, I know that she does not hear a word I say. I continue my comments, purposely pausing, so that Madeline's suspense will build. When I then pull the line and make her doll stand up, Madeline turns her head so quickly to look at her doll, I am just glad that our Creator put it on her as tight as He did. As Madeline and her doll stare at each other, I erupt with loud laughter, confusing the other kids, until they see Madeline's doll standing, staring at Madeline. Our laughter almost lifts the roof off our happy home.

A joyful heart causeth good health: but a sorrowful mind drieth the bones.

Proverbs 17:22

The best medicine is a merry heart, not a heart addicted to vain, carnal, sensual mirth…it is a great mercy that God gives us leave to be cheerful and cause to be cheerful, especially if by his grace he gives us hearts to be cheerful.

MATTHEW HENRY

In our simple home, we do not have the many distractions that are in many homes, the things that seem good, but actually disconnect family members from each other. We do not worry about someone stealing anything from our home, because about the only possessions in our home is a few Calvin and Hobbes books, a Bible, a hymnbook and simple love. And yes, God is here with us, making us feel as if we have the very best home.

However, because sorrows, sufferings and loses bare down so heavy on my heart, I sometimes lose my patience, not very often, but more than before my exposure. God is using my tender, little girls to teach me better patience, and even better than that, God is teaching me to consider that my words hurt more than a fist. He is also teaching me that a proper, tender apology is the very best balm for a wounded heart. This is one of many reasons as to why I am a most fortunate man.

Another reason that I am a most fortunate man is because every day God draws me into a more earnest read of His word, and heart-felt prayer with Him.

This morning during our Bible time, we read verses that emphasis God's providential guidance in our lives, (Ecclesiastes 3:14, 9:1; Proverbs 16:1, 9, 33, 21:1, 31, 28:26). Afterward I explain to the girls that God's providence has moved us into our little home for many good reasons. After I explain some of the lessons we are learning, such as simplicity, contentment, dependence on God and love, I emphasize how fortunate we are because of God's care for us. I then suggest that we call our home the "Grand Hotel." My suggestion seems right to them, so from now on we call this shed, our home, the Grand Hotel.

A few days later, after Mara takes the girls back to her house, I am confident that God will continue to teach the girls that no matter what their situation is, their happiness depends on their reading of God's word, obedience to God, and their fellowship with God.

My exposure symptoms fluctuate from day to day; there is no pattern or reason as to why they change. When my symptoms are mild, I feel like I have a mild flu, with some weakness. However, when my exposure symptoms are strong, I feel like I have severe flu, with great weakness. These symptoms, mild or strong, now last up to about five days at a time. Another irritating symptom is that I always feel exhausted because I am always very tense, as if I must constantly hold on to myself so that I do not slip away and die.

Driving my truck now causes a lot of pain in my legs, so I leave my truck parked in front of the main house and use a wheelchair, which was given to me.

About two weeks later, the man in the main house complains about my truck parked in front of his house, so I put it up for sale. That is okay, because I desperately need extra money.

Within a short time, a nice man offers to buy my truck. He says that he has only $200.00 in his wallet, and asks if he may take my truck and come back with the remainder of the money. After I say yes, he gives me $200.00 and his phone number, and drives away in my truck. I am very sad to lose my truck. However, I am very thankful for the extra money. Hours later, I become concerned when the nice man does not come back. I call his wife, and after I explain who I am, and why I desperately need the remainder of the money, I ask if she knows when her husband will bring me the money. I become more concerned when she says that she does not know. The next day I speak with the wife again, and again she tells me that she does not know when her husband will bring me the money. I now realize how much my illness is weakening my discernment and discipline. I never saw, or heard from that man again.

Now when I sit at bus stops in my wheelchair and see a truck pass by, I think about the painful lesson I have learned.

I also understand how weak my mind is becoming, because sometimes I cannot correctly read a simple bus map. When I realize that I have boarded the wrong bus, a big lump forms in my throat, because now my delayed plans will force me to sit in the hot sun, sometimes for almost an hour as I wait for a bus. The problem with me sitting in the sun is that the heat severely hurts me, making me feel very weak. I am also very disappointed when my daughters have to wait at bus stops with me. I wonder how it will be for us this winter when we sit at bus stops in the cold rain. However, I eventually realize a great blessing at the bus stops. And that is, many of the people at bus stops are simple, good people, who are now my friends.

This evening I am thankful when the sun sets because now my home begins to cool, making me feel much better. I am surprised when at about nine-o-clock the man in the main house calls me from his back porch. When I open the door of the Grand Hotel he says, "Mara is on the phone!"

I think, *Mara. Why is Mara calling me?*

When I answer the phone, Mara says, "What do you do to the girls?"

I think, *What do I do to the girls? Here it comes. I have no idea what she means!*

I say, "What do you mean?"

Mara says, "After the girls spend some time with you, they are obedient to me for the first two or three days, and they don't argue with each other. What do you do?"

I am stunned, and very sad to realize that she has lost the simple grace of her former motherhood. I briefly mention that I read the Bible to the girls and just love them. Mara's self-centered, wayward life style has stripped her of her former tender good sense. I so wish that I had a proper home and enough money, so I could keep my girls with me all of the time.

CHAPTER 15

Workers' Compensation Insider Fraud

_&_

STILL IN MY WHEELCHAIR

...but also we rejoice in tribulations, knowing that tribulation bringeth forth patience. And patience experience, and experience hope.

ROMANS 5:3–4

How come we to glory in tribulations? Why, because tribulations, by a chain of causes, greatly befriend hope, which he shows in the method of its influence. 1. *Tribulations, worketh patience,* not in and of itself, but the powerful grace of God working in and with the tribulation. It proves, and proving improves, patience, as parts and gifts increase by exercise. It is not the efficient cause, but yields the occasion, as steel is hardened by the fire.

MATTHEW HENRY

...though now for a season (if need require) ye are in heaviness, through manifold tentations, That the trial of your faith, being much more precious than gold that perisheth (though it be tried with fire) might be found unto *your* praise, and honor and glory at the appearing of Jesus Christ:

1 PETER 1:6–7

A *trial,* as the word signifies, is an experiment or search made upon a man, by some affliction, to prove the value and strength of his faith. This trial is made upon faith principally, rather than any other grace, because the trial of this is, in effect, the trial of all that is good in us....The trial of faith will be found to praise, and honour, and glory. Honour is properly that esteem and value which one has with another, and so God and man will honour the saints. Praise is the expression or declaration of that esteem; Christ will commend his people in the great day, *Come, you blessed of my Father,* etc. Glory is that luster wherewith a person, so honoured and praised, shines in heaven.

MATTHEW HENRY

LATE SUMMER 1992

THIS EVENING I FEEL MUCH too weak to read my book about Mr. Voss's sailing adventures. However, the stories in that book always lift my heart, so I think that I will read a few pages anyway, and then try to go to sleep. As I begin to read, I feel much weaker and ill throughout my entire body, so I put my book back in its spot and slide deeper into my sleeping bag. My weakness becomes so great and makes me feel very uncomfortable. I am very tired because I have averaged two or three hours of sleep each night for the last few months. I finally fall asleep, and then sometime during the middle of the night I awake a second before my heart beats incorrectly, making my back jerk about six inches up off of my mat. When I fall back to my mat, tears fall from my eyes, and I pray, "Father, please don't let me die in this old building!"

When God reminds me that a sparrow does not fall to the earth without His approval, I feel much better. I wipe away my tears and try to calm myself. However, I am not able to go to sleep because my heart is now beating so hard. The next day I call my doctor and tell him what had happened to me last night. He tells me that because my nerve disease is attacking my sensory motor functions my heart is receiving "mixed motor messages."

Well, my new problem with mixed motor messages to my heart causes me to be more aware of myself and God, inclining me to more earnestly read my Bible, and spend more heart-felt time in prayer, because my Bible and prayer time are the only two places where I feel healthy and strong. As a result, my faith is exercised, simplifying my trust in God.

Recently, I have thought a lot about my former strength and vigor, comparing my previous good health to my current poor health. Provoking me to go to Workers' Compensation and explain to the judge how my exposure has severely damaged me. My Workers' Compensation claim seems so simple. That is why I think I should just talk with the judge. Later, after I file for a hearing with Workers' Compensation, I am very encouraged.

The day of my hearing, I arrive early at the Workers' Compensation building, and when I step into the courtroom, I am surprised to see that the judge and I are the only ones here. After I greet the judge, he says to me, "There is something not right about your case." I say, "I am confused about my case, because I do not know why my doctors said that my injury is not work related." When we here someone walk into the room both of us turn and look, and as we look back to each other the judge says, "I need to go to my chamber."

The judge's comment greatly encourages me. However, after this hearing I receive a notice from the judge, which states that my claim is denied because of Dr. Bismarck's report. Now I am confused much more than before.

The voices in my heart constantly remind me that I have fallen to a low, low point in life, and that I have not yet reached the bottom. I constantly consider; *What if I become so ill that I am not able to use my wheelchair. How long can I stay in this old building? How long can I live on $200 a month? How long can I survive on my low-quality diet? I have only a few pieces of clothing. I have lost almost all of my possessions. Mara is ruining her life. She has taken the girls, and they are moving on without me. What am I going to do? There is no way that I can improve my life.* When I also consider that my thoughts are words to

God, I am concerned that my words might offend Him, revealing my lack of faith in Him. I then ponder the lesson I learned about when the Apostles were out to sea in the storm. So as usual I open my Bible, and as I strengthen myself before God, I silence the logical voices in my heart. After prayer, I confidently say aloud, "This time will pass, and Lord willing, God will restore my life."

I understand that I am up against a Goliath of a problem, so for encouragement I often read the story about David and Goliath in 1 Samuel 17:1–58. Before David stood before Goliath, he strengthened his faith in God, recalling how God had helped him to kill a lion and a bear. David's strengthened faith in God enabled him to face Goliath victoriously. I often look back and recall how God has helped me with many lion-and-bear problems in my life, and I realize that there is a reason, and a purpose, for all that has happened to me. God taught David many good lessons when David was out in the wilderness, so while I am in the wilderness of life, I must keep myself in God's word, and close to God, so that I may learn the lessons that God has for me.

Sometimes I remember when many years ago God told me, "Years ahead Mara is going to turn from you and Me."

I then realize how easily I can disregard what God says to me, and as I consider all that has happened to us because I did not listen to God, I understand that I deserve the pain and shame that I am suffering from our divorce. However, I am so sad that my daughters must also suffer because I did not listen to God.

Thankfully, this morning my exposure symptoms are mild. As I eat breakfast, I look across the room at the box that I put my Workers' Compensation papers in, and consider that I should look at some of those reports. As I stare at the box, I consider that the Spirit of truth is speaking to my conscience, my mind, inclining me to read the reports. After breakfast, I begin to look through the papers, and when I pick up Dr. Bismarck's report, my thought is that I should read his report. I look at his report with common interest. Until

I read on page six that my exposure symptoms are isolated to my right arm and right leg.

I then say aloud, "That's not right. I had exposure symptoms on both sides of my body."

As my common interest becomes a penetrating stare, my heart and mind unites for a thorough investigation. Before I begin my study, I pray and ask my Father for wisdom, knowledge, and understanding. As I read through the report I find an interesting comment which states that my complaints of pain and weakness in my right arm and right leg are not likely related to the named exposure incident. The doctors also state that they are not aware of a chemical exposure that would result in the immediate onset of asymmetric symptoms, isolated to my right arm and right leg.

I say aloud, "Right arm and right leg…asymmetric…isolated to my right side. This is a mistake! I had exposure symptoms on both sides of my body. The doctors have made a simple mistake. This is why my case was denied."

I slowly reread the paragraph and sit stunned and amazed at my discovery. I must call Dr. Bismarck and tell him about his error. And after he corrects his report, I should receive Workers' Compensation! Dr. Bismarck wrote this report almost three years ago. My Workers' Compensation paperwork is in such a mess because I have moved around so much, and because of my poor health, I have not been able to read more carefully the reports until just now.

My mind floods with thoughts about all that I have lost and suffered due to this one incorrect statement. I look around at the old building, and as I take a deep breath, I smile as I think, *My days in this place are numbered. Soon the girls and I will be together in a better home, and I will eat better food and get proper medical help!* I then look to heaven and say, "Thank you so much Father."

I feel like a highflying eagle out soaring early in the morning, and I have just spotted my first fish. I must carefully read this report again, so I turn to the first page and begin a most studious read. On page two Dr. Bismarck correctly states my symptoms as an immediate onset of pain, characterized by numbness and tingling in my arms and legs.

However, on four other pages he describes my symptoms as only on one side of my body. When I remember that Dr. Bismarck described my symptoms in his clinical notes, I quickly search through my box of papers until I find Dr. Bismarck's clinical notes, and discover that he did correctly state my symptoms in these notes as, immediate numbness and tingling in both arms and both legs.

I think that when Dr. Bismarck learns that his error has caused three long years of suffering for my daughters and me, he will quickly correct his report.

Before I call Dr. Bismarck, I open my dictionary and study a few words in his reports just to make sure that I correctly understand everything.

After a day of research, later when I climb into bed I feel so happy because of my discovery. I am sure that I slept with a big smile all through the night, until morning.

This morning I awake feeling just a little lively, so I roll out of bed and quickly fix breakfast.

During breakfast, I decide to call Dr. Bismarck from a payphone because the call is long distance. After I am ready to go, I comb my hair a little nicer for this most excellent phone call. However, when I first begin to roll down the sidewalk in my wheelchair, I do not feel so excellent, though I am thankful for my wheelchair. Two blocks later, I arrive at a payphone. Thankfully, I am able to speak with Dr. Bismarck directly. I carefully explain to him his error, and mention that his error caused the denial of my Workers' Compensation claim. I also mention my poor health and my poor living conditions, believing that my sad state will encourage him to correct his report quickly.

Dr. Bismarck says, "Send me the report, and I'll look at it."

Before we say good-bye, I say, "Dr. Bismarck, may I mention one more thing?"

He says yes, and I say, "About two years ago Dr. Definite preformed a nerve conduction study on me. His test documented denervation in both of my feet, which confirms your correct statements."

He says, "All right. Send me my report, and I'll look at it."

After we say our good-byes, I sit for a few moments, feeling so amazed and thankful to God for showing me this error. I think, *I can't believe that our ordeal is almost over, and I can't wait to tell the girls!*

After I call the girls, I head for the Grand Hotel, and before I arrive, I realize that I must study every piece of paper in my Workers' Compensation file to see if there are any other errors. I mail a copy of Dr. Bismarck's report to him along with Dr. Definite's report, and a cover letter, reiterating the information that I explained to him during our phone conversation. Through the day, I try my best to contain my happiness so that I will not look like a silly idiot. Through the next two weeks, my daughters and I often talk about the good changes coming to us.

During the third week, I begin to wonder why Dr. Bismarck has not mailed me a corrected report. He knows that I am desperate for my Workers' Compensation claim. In the middle of the fourth week, I feel sick with disappointment, because I have not received the doctor's report, and the girls are now so discouraged that they do not even ask about it anymore.

My patience is wearing thin, so I call Dr. Bismarck and mention that I have not received his corrected report. Dr. Bismarck says that he has not received the report. My heart almost fails. I take a deep breath, and take the opportunity to mention all that I explained to him during our first conversation, and he again says, "Okay, send me the report, and I'll look at it."

Before we say good-bye, I again check with Dr. Bismarck to make sure that I have his correct address, and he confirms that I do. I then quickly mail copies of both reports to him.

Through the next four weeks, I am increasingly concerned because again I do not receive Dr. Bismarck's corrected report. However, I give him the benefit of the doubt, thinking that he is very busy, and again mail him copies of his reports. A week later, I mail yet another set, and then wait for his response. After almost two weeks, it is now clear to me that Dr. Bismarck will not respond to me. My feelings are deeply hurt, because Thanksgiving is a few weeks away, and I had hoped that I would be out of this shed by Thanksgiving, and especially before Christmas.

However, there is still hope! I will just show the errors to the Workers' Compensation judge. I am sure that he will quickly correct the errors and grant me the deserved Workers' Compensation award. So with renewed hope, I call my divorce attorney and ask if I may stop by his office and show him something. He says yes, and I quickly gather my notes and head for his office. When Mr. Arnold looks at my notes, he is amazed at my discovery, and says that I have found something "really big." He then suggests that I obtain a Workers' Compensation attorney. However, when I mention that I am too ill to look for an attorney, Mr. Arnold says that about twenty-five years ago he had served as a Workers' Compensation attorney. He also tells me that he is a little rusty, but he will show my notes to the Workers' Compensation judge. Oh, I am as happy as can be!

Mr. Arnold and I drive to Workers' Compensation and schedule another hearing. A few weeks later, we appear before Judge Graft, and clearly explain the error and truth in Dr. Bismarck's report, and Dr. Definite's computer test. Mr. Arnold tells the judge that my Workers' Compensation claim was denied based on Dr. Bismarck's error. We are very pleased when we learn that Judge Graft has ordered Dr. Bismarck to write a new report. However, I am troubled when Dr. Bismarck does not call me in for another examination. This is disturbing, because my previous examination by Dr. Bismarck was three years ago.

My daughters and I wait with great anticipation for the corrected report, and our hope is high because we now see an end to our lengthy ordeal of sorrows, sufferings, and losses.

This evening I have a very irritating pressure and pain in my head, both arms, and both legs and therefore I am not reading my Jon Voss book. The pressure is so great that I can feel my pulse beating in my feet. Hour after hour, I relieve some of my pain by twisting my feet back and forth.

However, now I suffer even greater pain because, as I feared, Mara has met a man. Numerous people have mentioned to me their disgust for this man because of his arrogant, rude, self-centered attitude. Possibly, Mara's attraction for him is because of his great wealth. Whatever the reason, I am just crushed because Mara and my daughters now live at this arrogant man's house. I am greatly troubled about this man's ungodly involvement and influence in my daughter's lives.

The news about my daughters moving into this rich man's house makes me feel like Mara has stuck a knife into my heart; no it feels more like a spear in my heart. Then when I learn that Mara does not tell the girls when I call, or leave a message on her answering machine I feel as if my wounded heart will bleed to death. A lump forms in my throat when I consider that Mara is attempting to separate the girls from me.

Usually, the last week of each month I have only enough money to purchase minimum food. When Mara and the girls arrive, I am devastated because the girls look and smell like they have not bathed for a few days, and their hair is a mess, causing me to think that I need to obtain enough money so that I can properly care for the girls.

As I hug the girls, I decide to sell my antique woodstove and my Lionel train so that I can buy hairbrushes, combs, hair ties, scissors and anything else they need, and yes, a few weeks of better food.

The following weekend a friend takes us to the flea market, so that I can sell my stove and train; and then we go to the store, and purchase all that the girls need.

Every day the girls and I have a lot of hope that Dr. Bismarck will certainly provide a corrected report to the judge, and then before Thanksgiving we will receive just compensation.

However, as Thanksgiving approaches I realize that I will not receive compensation before this holiday, and it is very painful for me to watch busy shoppers prepare for Thanksgiving. The morning of Thanksgiving, I am very sad because I am not with my girls. However, I am thankful when Mom picks me up at about ten-thirty, and we go to my brother's house. The happy sounds of the day do not make me happy, and the good aroma of tasty food is not pleasing to me. Slowly and painfully, Thanksgiving passes, and I am now confronted with the possibility of not enjoying Christmas with my daughters. My heart resounds with endless echoes of sorrow, because I cannot stop thinking about that arrogant man. *That rich, arrogant man will enjoy time with my daughters all through December. That rich, arrogant man will enjoy my daughters on Christmas Eve and Christmas Day. That rich, arrogant man will enjoy my daughters, and I will not!* An animal caught in a trap feels less panic and pain than I do.

Last night my heart received another mixed motor message, and now through this day, it is beating as fast as if I had just run a fifty-yard dash. Though I am very concerned about my deteriorating health, I am thankful that the Workers' Compensation judge will soon receive Dr. Bismarck's corrected report.

CHAPTER 16

Some Doctors are Evening Wolves

⁓

Her princes in the midst thereof *are* like wolves, ravening the prey to shed blood, *and* to destroy souls for their own covetous lucre.

EZEKIEL 22:27

For such is power without justice and goodness to direct it.

MATTHEW HENRY

1992: FOUR YEARS AND SEVEN MONTHS AFTER MY EXPOSURE

WHEN I START TO BECOME anxious with questions as to why Dr. Bismarck is taking so long, I calm myself with the thought that Dr. Bismarck remembers my two phone conversations with him, and I am certain that Dr. Bismarck's office received my four sets of mailings regarding the truth about my symptoms.

After a number of months, Dr. Bismarck provides the requested report to Judge Graft. In his report, Dr. Bismarck states that he reviewed the clinical notes about my first computer test performed by Dr. Endorser four months after my exposure. He also states that he reviewed his clinical notes and his first report before he wrote this second report.

My good hope in Dr. Bismarck turns to anger when I read his following report, because he now states that I only have a complaint of my right leg.

In Dr. Bismarck's one page report written on December 15, 1992, (Document #42) he states that his records support his original impression that I have a structural or muscular injury that is likely responsible for my complaint of right leg pain. He further states that his records do not reveal a condition that may be attributable to the named chemical exposure on May 6, 1988. The doctor closes his report recommending that I consult a neurologist for further evaluation and possible treatment.

We previously read in two of his reports wherein he states that I have exposure symptoms in both my arms and legs. So the question is, why is this professional doctor changing his previous statements now?

My attorney tells me that my Workers' Compensation claim is denied because of Dr. Bismarck's report; I am confused and completely frustrated. How can Dr. Bismarck state that I only have a right leg complaint when Dr. Definites' computer test confirmed that both of my feet have denervation in process? This means that my Workers' Compensation claim is delayed for an undetermined amount of time until I am able to prove that I have symptoms on both sides of my body.

Why are they doing this to me? I am a simple two-pieces-of-pie man, who enjoys his walk on this earth, and would not harm them or anyone else. If I see a bug or an ant on the ground, I make sure to not step on it, so why do they step on me? It is because they are like evening wolves on an insatiable prowl for weak prey. As the wolf searches endlessly for meat, they greedily search for ways to prevent my just compensation. Though they know the law, they commit unpardonable crimes, because they lack a sense of shame. They do not fear punishment because they know that the judge will not condemn them.

God watched this doctor change words in my medical reports, and God saw that the changed words outraged me. Then God watched Workers' Compensation authorities support those changed words. As those changed words destroyed my Workers' Compensation claim, and so damaged my life, God heard my heart cry. God also heard me when I called out to Him as Samson did when he placed his hands upon the pillars.

...O Lord God, I pray thee, think upon me: O God, I beseech thee, strengthen me at this time only, that I may be at once avenged...
JUDGES 16:28

God enabled Samson, as He has now by His word enables me. As Samson pushed and brought the house down, I will now push and bring the evil authorities down. As we proceed through my story, the documents I cite will reveal both good and evil professionals. A line is drawn that will separate the good from the evil.

Note to the reader: I named this doctor "Dr. Bismarck" because he is so much like the German battleship *Bismarck*. The *Bismarck* was longer then our eminent battleship Missouri, and carried greater firepower. The mission of the *Bismarck* battleship was to attack all British ships from a great distance, keeping itself safe. Therefore, when the *Bismarck* patrolled, the crew believed that they were the invincible rulers of all of the oceans.

However, about nine months after the *Bismarck* was commissioned, aircraft from the *Ark Royal* scored a hit, jamming the rudder of the *Bismarck*. Unable to maneuver, the ship was forced to move only in a slow circle. The next morning two British battleships attacked the now inferior *Bismarck*. The vulnerable Germans were not able to defend themselves, so they "scuttled the ship to prevent its capture," meaning that they opened valves to flood the ship and sink it.

Dr. Bismarck is unaware that my Father is watching him. If he knew my Father, he would fear that my Father might scuttle him if he does not stop acting as evil as the crew of the Bismarck. However, for now Dr. Bismarck is allowed to attack me so that my Father's will for me may be accomplished in my life.

I can think of no way to stop or avoid the arrival of Christmas. I try to prepare myself for the first day of December, but the morning of December 1, I realize I have miscalculated how brokenhearted I feel. I am devastated because I am not with my family, and also because I do not have any money for Christmas. Day after day, I feel numb with disbelief. When I awake on Christmas Eve morning, I quickly sit up and stare at the undecorated Christmas tree leaning against the wall, which makes my heart pound very hard. However, my heart calms a little when I consider that my brother was kind enough to bring this simple Christmas tree to me last week. This morning, the Grand Hotel feels like a cold, old, empty building. Later in the evening, my brother picks me up, and I stay at his house through Christmas.

Winter is exceedingly cold in this old building because I only have a small electric heater. Every day I live inside my minus five degree rated sleeping bag. As first light begins another day, a deep winter chill on my face awakens me. The Grand Hotel feels very cold this morning, so I slip my arm out of my sleeping bag and turn on the small electric heater, quickly pulling my arm back into my nice warm bag. As I pull my bag up over my head, I am thankful to God, because He has fashioned my body so that it produces so much free heat for me. My sleepy brain is now heated with hot thoughts about the denial of my Workers' Compensation claim.

No doubt, when my room is warm enough I will slip out of my bag and read some of my Workers' Compensation reports. I am very curious to see how the other medical reports describe my exposure symptoms. A short while later when first sunlight begins to shine through my window; I sit up and remain in my bag as I eat breakfast. After breakfast, I continue to stay in my sleeping bag as I read my Bible, and after my Bible time the morning sun finally fills the Grand Hotel, making it nice and warm. A moment later, I slip out of my bag, and after I dress, I pull my Workers' Compensation box over to the window so that I may enjoy the warm sun as I sit on the floor and read reports.

As I look through the papers, I am surprised to find a legal interview with my partner Jack Sand, who was up on the platform with me during the exposure (May 9, 1989, Document #17). I am a little troubled when I see that the interview was given twelve months after our exposure. Jack and I were still working together, so it seems odd that he never mentioned anything to me about this interview. Now I am very curious to read what Jack said about the exposure.

During the interview with Jack he is asked if he recalls an incident that occurred on May 6, 1988. I am thankful that Jack honestly answers, that both of us got a little nauseous from the exposure.

I pick up my pace of reading and a few lines later I am most thankful to read that the interviewer asks Jack if I had complained of any problems at the time of the exposure. As I read Jack's answer I am as happy as can be when he says, that I became nauseous, and that my legs tingled. Jack is asked if I have mentioned anything about continuing problems since the exposure. My old partner responds, yes, that I have some problems with my legs, and that a doctor told me that the muscles in my legs are deteriorating.

Well, I am thankful that Jack told the truth about my symptoms. As I stare at the report the pace of my heart increases as I consider, *He didn't mention that we hid...Someone must have told him to not say anything about our hiding after the exposure.*

Now that I have discovered deceit I wonder if the other reports are corrupt. As I anxiously search through the numerous reports I am surprised to find the legal interview of Gary Betray. I quickly look at the date of this interview and realize that Jack and Gary met with the interviewer on the very same day. As I consider, *that's odd that neither one of them told me about their interviews.* I begin to feel as if my partners were deceptive.

As I begin to read Gary's interview of May of 1989 (Document #18) my trust in him fades. The interviewer asks Gary if after the exposure, did we go back up on the scaffold to work. Gary answers, no, because our job was not important enough to have us work in respirators so he assigned us another job. As my heart races, I say aloud, "What! Why did Gary say that?" My heart begins to pound so hard, and after I take a deep breath, I say aloud, "Gary knew that I had to lie on the ground, and why did he say that he assigned us…," I stop as I realize, *Someone told Gary to say what he said.*

As I consider the size and power of Og Construction, I realize that they have professional skilled liars who have already fixed many lies within my exposure story. After I take a deep breath, I ask the Father for wisdom, knowledge and understanding about these reports, and continue my read. I am very troubled to read that after the exposure Gary filed an incident report with Og's safety personal and after that the report cannot be found. My emotions heave as I read Gary's comment wherein months after the exposure I told him that I still have dizziness, nauseous feelings, and that I have developed a terrible sleep disorder. I am surprised that he stated what he said to me. Gary told me that there is a flu virus going around and that I might have the flu. As I read further, I am thankful that Gary said that I came back to him six months later and told him that I had gone to an outside doctor who informed me that the muscles in my legs are deteriorating as a result of the gas exposure. I am grateful for his honest statements. However, I have the feeling that Gary is not going to reveal all of the truth about the exposure. So I take another deep breath and continue my read. At the end of the interview Gary is asked if he has anything else to say, and he answers, no.

I can't believe it! After our exposure, Gary told us to get into a truck and hide. Well, he obviously cannot tell the truth about us hiding after the exposure because he has already lied, stating that he had assigned us another job. And why is his incident report now missing?

My heart is noisy with very troubling thoughts. While I ponder Dr. Bismarck's errors that caused the denial of my Workers' Compensation claim, I look in my box and gather Dr. Definites' report, regarding my computer test, Dr. Bismarck's clinical notes, his first report, and Jack's interview, and then I find my deposition. Holding all of these reports in my lap, I lift them up to God and say, "Father, all of these reports state that my exposure symptoms are on both sides of my body. Why are the doctors and the judge ignoring these facts? What shall I think?"

A few nights later, when I open my eyes at about 4:30 a.m., I understand that God has something for me, and a moment later, the thought enters my mind, *When an authority oppresses people, he does so because he is instructed to do it by the authorities above him.*

As the thought speeds up my heart, I say aloud, "That's in Ecclesiastes—I think chapter five!"

After I thank the Father, I sit up, turn on my light, and open my Bible to Ecclesiastes chapter five and find the thought in verse eight. I am amazed at this insight, and I am sure that there are other verses similar to this verse, so I begin to look for other verses that will help me better understand the motives of Dr. Bismarck and the judge. After a lengthy study, I clearly understand that the errors that caused the denial of my claim are not a mistake; they are deliberate! I am thankful to understand, but also angered, because the people opposing me are very powerful. However, I am comforted when I consider that my Father has given me the insight about these mere puppets, and if it is His will, He will enable me to prevail over them.

During my desperate search for a doctor who understands chemical exposures, I call a scientist who attributes his 90 percent recovery from plutonium exposure to a doctor, who is employed at the Los Alamos, New Mexico nuclear facility. I call the doctor at the Los Alamos facility and explain my exposure story, and after I finish she says that there is an excellent doctor where I live who understands chemical exposures. I can hardly believe the good chain of information. After our talk, I call the recommended doctor, Dr. Honor, and make an appointment.

I arrive at Dr. Honor's office and am quickly impressed with him because of his genuine attitude of heart, and professional conduct. I certainly believe that he is the very best doctor for me, and everyone else. During my examination, I explain my exposure story, and then describe Dr. Bismarck's altered reports, which conclude that I have a right leg complaint due to a bad back. Dr. Honor examines my back, and after he determines that there is nothing wrong with my back, he orders an MRI of my lower back. After his examination, Dr. Honor schedules another appointment for the next week. I understand that Dr. Honor wishes to improve my health, and I also believe that he desires to help me establish my Workers' Compensation claim. Before I leave, I say to Dr. Honor, "Your card states that you are an MPH. What does that mean?"

He says, "Master of Public Health." I say to him, "No doubt, I am in very good care!"

Dr. Honor writes an eight-page medical report describing my past and present medical history, and his evaluation of me, and mails copies of the report to the Workers' Compensation Court, my attorney, and to me.

I receive Dr. Honor's circumspect report accurately describing my exposure and my exposure symptoms, and am very pleased.

During my next visit with Dr. Honor, he performs more tests, and then schedules me for another appointment for the next week. He then mails his two-page medical report to the Workers' Compensation Court, my attorney, and to me.

My next visit with Dr. Honor is similar to my previous examination, but this time, I learn some very good news. My MRI test clearly reveals that I have no abnormalities with my spine. Dr. Honor mails this medical report to the Workers' Compensation Court, my attorney, and to me.

The result of this MRI is very encouraging because it proves to Judge Graft that Dr. Bismarck's reports are wrong; and should easily establish the correct reports as truth for me in court.

Then Dr. Honor schedules me for a neurology consultation with Dr. Preponderate.

I step into Dr. Preponderates office and my first impression of him is very good, because he seems to be a disciplined, highly educated man. During his evaluation of me, I feel confident that his great knowledge and vast experience with the nervous system will enable him to write a most excellent report for the Workers' Compensation judge. After he performs a few tests, he writes a five-page medical report and mails copies to the Workers' Compensation Court, my attorney, and to me.

A number of days later, when I pull mail from our mailbox and see an envelope from Dr. Preponderate, I quickly open it, and as I stand at the mailbox, I read all five pages. I am very pleased with his report, because it is circumspect, and accurately describes my exposure and my exposure symptoms. Gratitude inclines me to look up to God and say, "Thank you so much for the excellent reports of Dr. Honor, and Dr. Preponderate. I then hurry back to the Grand Hotel so that I may compare Dr. Preponderate's report with Dr. Honor's reports.

Dr. Preponderate's report was written on January 4, 1993, (Document #47). I am so pleased to read in his report, that there is nothing wrong with my back. Further into his report Dr. Preponderate makes a most excellent comment, when he says that he agrees with the conclusion of the second electromyographer study given by Dr. Definite who feels that I have a chronic distal denervation in my feet consistent with a chronic axonal polyneuropathy.

I am certain that these reports will establish the validity of my Workers' Compensation claim.

My days in the Grand Hotel are numbered, and soon the girls and I will be together in a better home.

A week passes, and I step into Dr. Honor's office for another evaluation. During this examination, Dr. Honor performs more tests, and then mails copies of his report to the Workers' Compensation Court, my attorney, and to me.

Through the next month, I feel very happy about the good improvement with my Workers' Compensation claim, that is until I receive an order from Judge Graft, written on March 1, 1993 (Document #51). The order is regarding the opposing attorneys, Mr. Goliath's, request to have Dr. Honor's reports stricken from the record. Judge Graft's decision angers me, and I have no idea why he would issue an order striking Dr. Honor's reports from the record because as he says, *they are duplicative.*

As I read further I learn that Judge Graft states that Dr. Honor's reports are duplicative because Dr. Bismarck and Dr. Moulage have already established that my injury is not work related. I can't believe it! Judge Graft knows that Dr. Bismarck's reports are both inaccurate and inconstant. As I read further I read a comment that I truly cannot believe. Judge Graft says, though my attorney and I have inferred that Dr. Bismarck's report is not accurate he does not agree.

Judge Graft also incorrectly states that I have not made any effort to provide information to Dr. Bismarck about the identity of the chemicals involved in my exposure. Really! After my exposure my attorney and I filed medical reports with the Workers' Compensation court after we received them. The following is a summation of those documents that were available for Judge Grafts review:

In Document #24, Dr. Bismarck's first report to Workers' Compensation court, the doctor states a few times that I told him that I was exposed to unspecified fumes that smelled like gasoline for five minutes.

In Document #25, my five-hour deposition describes my numerous attempts to learn the identification of the chemicals that I was exposed to. My deposition clearly states that my questions were not answered.

In Document #41, Dr. Honor's initial visit progress note states that after my exposure I asked four times, what were we exposed to, however, the identity of the fumes was not revealed to me. The report also mentions that I asked my foreman again six months after my exposure about the identity of the fumes, and was told that we were exposed to raw gasoline plus a solvent of some type.

In Document #46 Dr. Honor's progress notes, states that my employer would not tell me what the nature of the exposure was. However, after I repeatedly asked I was told vague descriptions.

Through November and December 1992, I called Bashan Oil five times and ask them if they would provide me the identity of the chemicals that I was exposed to, and I requested the identity of chemicals in the area in which I worked. I then wrote the following letter, summarizing our phone conversations, and mailed it, certified, to Mr. Ignore, a Bashan authority, on January 8, 1993. I then filed the letter with the Workers' Compensation Court on January 14, 1993:

Attention Mr. Ignore:

In November of 1992 my doctor sent a letter to me asking if I could get a list of the chemicals that I worked around from day to day while working at Bashan Oil. I called you on 11/23/92 explaining this to you.

I mentioned to you that I had done quite a bit of work in (*certain* areas I worked in), and that my doctor and I wanted a list of the chemicals that are in those areas. I also mentioned that my doctor stated in his note to me that by law this information should be given to me no later than fifteen days of my request. I called you again on 11/30/92 to see how the information was coming together.

I called you again on 12/8/92 and 12/11/92 both times leaving a message. I have not heard from you since our phone conversation on 11/30/92. You are not the first to hear my request at Bashan Oil. A week or so before our first phone conversation on 11/23/92, I had spoken with someone else regarding my request. It has been about 37 working days since my first request. Because of the 5/6/88 incident I have not only been left with a bad medical problem but my life has been greatly altered. The information that I am requesting would greatly help my situation. Would you please send me a list of the chemicals found in (the *areas* I worked in). ASAP PLEASE!

Thankfully,
James Landon

P.S. Whichever way you go with my request, please send me your decision in writing.

Mr. Ignore did not respond to me by either phone or letter.

In Document #50, Dr. Honor's progress note of January 23, 1993, states that I called Bashan Oil, and then sent a registered letter requesting information about my exposure. However, at this time I have not received a response. Dr. Honor also states that he will mail a letter to the Union requesting assistance in obtaining exposure data.

Dr. Honor mailed a letter to the Carpenters Health and Safety Fund in Washington, DC, on January 23, 1993 requesting chemical data information related to my exposure. Dr. Honor's letter was also filed with Workers' Compensation Court.

On February 2 1993, a Bashan Oil authority wrote a letter to an Og Construction attorney stating; that according to an *Applicant's Brief,* I contacted the Bashan Oil Company in late November 1992, to try to determine the identity of chemicals to which I was exposed.

So why does Judge Graft say that he cannot find any effort on my part to learn the identity of the chemicals regarding my exposure? Judge Graft has either not reviewed the important documents pertaining to my case that have been submitted to him, or he has been instructed by authorities above his bench to lie about my case.

A few days later, I go to Dr. Honor's office for another examination, and on my way back to the Grand Hotel I stop by Workers' Compensation and file the report from this examination. I know that Dr. Honor's reports are "stricken" by Judge Graft's Order, however, they are very important for my case, so I filed this recent report, making the judge more accountable. If I put the true facts about my case on one side of a scale of justice, and put Judge Graft's erroneous statements on the other side of the scale, my side would drop to the floor because of its moral and legal weight. I do not play games, especially his.

It was four weeks ago that I filed Dr. Honor's report with the Workers' Compensation Court, and I am now at Workers' Compensation again to file yet another recent report from Dr. Honor. This is called "push back."

Now, on April 27, 1993, during another Workers' Compensation Court hearing, and after so much confirmed evidence regarding my work-related injury, Mr. Goliath tries to take unfair advantage of my weak financial condition by offering me an unjust, low settlement. His offer is for $200, with the requirement that I will sign yet another Compromise and Release Form (CRF). I wonder what he would do if someone offered a similar cruel, unjust offer to one of his children?

I tell Mr. Goliath that I will consider accepting his offer, if he will describe in the CRF, all of my health problems resulting from my exposure. He seems pleased, as he asks the judge if he may be excused so that he can draft the CRF.

Mr. Goliath is happy about my acceptance of his offer, but my attorney, Mr. Arnold is not happy with me and asks, "What are you doing?"

More than an hour later, Mr. Goliath enters the room and hands the CRF to my attorney. After my attorney reviews it, he hands it to me. Since I am only interested in the description about my exposure symptoms, I turn to that page and read a very detailed, accurate description of my exposure symptoms. I then say to Mr. Goliath, "Thank you for the accurate description regarding my exposure symptoms. I reject your offer." I have now proven, and have documentation, that Mr. Goliath completely understands my exposure symptoms.

At the next hearing, I am surprised when Judge Graft offers me Mr. Goliath's previous $200 settlement. I explain to Judge Graft that I will not accept this settlement offer because my chemical detoxification cost me more than $4,500. I go on to say that, I have lost thousands of dollars in wages, and the greatest reason as to why I will not accept the offer is because I am not able to play with my daughters as I did before my exposure.

My attorney, Mr. Arnold, seated next to me says, "If you don't accept the judge's offer, I'm walking out on you."

As we fix determined eyes on each other, I wave my hand in front of his face and say, "Bye." Judge Graft tells us to go out into the hallway and talk about the matter. Out in the hallway nothing is concluded, and I do not fire Mr. Arnold. However, I am confused about Mr. Arnold's change of attitude. It seems as if he is hindering my pursuit of justice. I have rejected their settlement offer, and therefore their ploy to take unfair advantage of me will probably continue in a different form.

Dr. Honor requests another report from Dr. Preponderate, and thankfully, Dr. Preponderate writes an excellent report written on May 10, 1993, (Document #60). This report is then filed at Workers' Compensation. The report states that it is very clear that I had no prior symptoms of neuropathy before May 6, 1988. And that my symptoms began immediately after the exposure, increasing within the next 48 hours. I am very thankful that my doctor states that my polyneuropathy was confirmed by nerve conduction studies in August of 1988.

By now, my attorney and the opposing attorney have written many briefs for the court regarding my case, intensifying our debates.

[Gold Statement 5: In 1993, the low for gold is $326 per ounce, and the high for gold is $406 per ounce.]

CHAPTER 17

The Statute of Limitations

~~&~~

Many do seek the face of the ruler; but every man's judgment
cometh **from the Lord.**

PROVERBS 29:26

MY EXPOSURE OCCURRED FIVE YEARS ago on May 6, 1988. Today is the
last day of my five-year statute of limitations. After today, I will be barred
from reopening my Workers' Compensation claim. So, here I am at Workers'
Compensation, without my attorney, requesting another hearing.

Judge Graft then presents an order denying my request for another hearing, because he says that I am beyond my five-year limit. Though my exposure occurred on May 6, 1988, his order states that my exposure occurred on
April 1, 1988; and in the last part of this same paragraph, he states that my
exposure occurred on May 1, 1988.

Judge Graft is an aged, experienced judge, so it seems to me, based on his
fraudulent work with my case, that he incorrectly stated the dates of April 1,
and May 1, on purpose. This does appear to be "willful misconduct."

Six important documents were filed with Workers' Compensation court
prior to Judge Graft's Order Denying Applicant's Petition. These documents
state the date of my exposure as May 6, 1988 thirty-two times!

I am so upset. Why are they doing this to me? I am not a cow that can stand out in a storm all day. This exposure storm is dragging my anchor!

However, because of my hope in God, I file yet another report from Dr. Honor with Workers' Compensation.

When I show the incorrect dates to Mr. Arnold, he yells at me, telling me to "shut up!" However, I file my paperwork with the court.

A short time later, Judge Graft reverses his order because of the incorrect dates; which is Document #74: Judge Graft's order to reopen my case.

Mr. Goliath schedules me for an evaluation with a new doctor. I have no idea why they want me to see *their* new doctor. It is probably to somehow further strengthen their injustice against me. That is okay, because after Judge Graft ordered Dr. Honor's reports to be rejected, I told Mr. Arnold to file six more of Dr. Honor's reports, of which I confirmed he did.

Today when I am at Mr. Arnold's office, I give him another report from Dr. Honor, and say, "The next time that we are in court, put this on the judge's bench." Mr. Arnold says, "James, Judge Graft has ordered that Dr. Honor's reports are stricken."

I reply, "I'm not asking you to file this report, I'm asking you to put it on the judge's bench at the next hearing, before he comes out for court."

Mr. Arnold passionately says, "James you can't do that! You are going to get us in so much trouble!"

I reply, "If we put the report on his bench, he will have more accurate medical information about my exposure symptoms. If you don't do it, I will."

Mr. Arnold says, "You will? Okay, then I'll do it."

At the next hearing, when I am seated with a courtroom full of puppets, all of us waiting for Judge Graft to enter the courtroom, I ask Mr. Arnold if he is going to put Dr. Honor's report on Judge Graft's bench. When Mr. Arnold hesitates, I look at him as if I will take the report and put it in the judge's bench for him, which compels him to say, "Okay, I'll do it." Moments later when Judge Graft is seated at his bench he looks down at the new report lying there, and when he understands what it is, he looks up and says, "I ordered Dr. Honor's reports stricken from the record!"

I lean over to Mr. Arnold and say, "He is now more accountable for the truth about my case."

A few days later, when I arrive for my scheduled appointment with this new doctor, I am surprised to meet an elderly, kind-looking woman named Dr. Connive. Her appearance and character seem good. However, she is *their* doctor, so I do not trust her. My examination begins with her asking me to take off my boots and socks, and sit on her examination table with my legs stretched out. After I am on her table, she asks me to pull my jeans up to my knees. And as she stands next to the table, she looks at my legs for about five seconds, and says, "They look fine to me."

I say, "Doctor, I am sure that you are aware that a nerve conduction study has proven that my problem is within the nerves in both of my feet and lower legs. You can't see my nerves." She does not respond to my comment. However, she proceeds with the examination.

During my examination, I explain my exposure story and the accurate and inaccurate medical reports. I then ask Dr. Connive to comment, please, in her report, about Dr. Bismarck's errors, and the correct reports. She does not respond. Through my entire examination, I feel very uncomfortable. And after I leave, I am thankful to go as far away as I can from her!

I think much about my examination on my way back to the Grand Hotel, feeling as if a crime has just been committed against me.

Each day as I wait for a copy of Dr. Connive's report, I try to prepare myself for great disappointment.

When I finally receive her report, I am very upset, much more than I thought I would be, because…well, read a few of the following quotes from her report and you will understand why I was so upset.

Her report was written on March 28, 1994, (Document #103). Dr. Connive states on the first page of her report that she spent a little more than 9 hours in review of records and the writing of her report. She states that she reviewed Dr. Bismarck's first report, the interview of Jack Sand, the eleven reports written by Dr. Honor, Dr. Preponderate's report, and Dr. Definite's computer test.

And then she states that I "comport myself in a blatantly fraudulent manner simulating a religious cripple on crutches." She also says that I lost no time from work as a result of the exposure, and that I stopped working in 1991 because of my unpleasant divorce. She claims that my neurologic examination was normal, and therefore I comport myself as if I "have a serious and progressive neurologic disease." She deeply hurt me when she said that she firmly believes that my Workers' Compensation claim is driven by factors for secondary gain, the most obvious of which is to avoid child support payments for my three children.

She also claims that I have sought care from health care providers who are neither competent nor credible in order to substantiate my false claims. She continues her damage by stating that my exposure would not by any stretch of the imagination cause the symptoms which I claim to be suffering from the exposure.

She further reveals her bias when she warns my health care providers and me regarding Workers' Compensation fraud. And she further reveals her unprofessional stupidity by stating that I received several competent medical evaluations at the time of the incident. She is referring to Dr. Bismarck, and Dr. Moulage. The doctor ends her report by stating that there is no evidence of any injury to me as a result of the exposure, "emphasizing that my chemical exposure was trivial."

Dr. Connive's comment about my supposed neglect of child support payments is very hurtful. So I go to Mom's and mention to Mara what Dr. Connive stated about my neglect of child support payments. I ask Mara if she would please write a letter stating the truth. I do not mention or even hint to her as to what she should write; I left it up to God to influence her heart. Mara wrote a letter on February 12, 1995 (Document #128). This letter is filed with Workers' Compensation court. Mara states that Dr. Connive says that I have reported a claim of injury so that I may evade child support responsibilities. Mara emphatically says the opposite, emphasizing that her authority in deriving a conclusion on this matter is not based on biased conclusions such as those of Ms. Connive, who is an unqualified observer, but it is based upon knowing Mr. Landon for 17 years, both as a husband and as the father of her children.

Well, I must say that I am thankful that God used someone like Mara to state the truth for me. Thank you so much Mara.

After I read Dr. Connive's comment that it is well known by everyone who pumps their own gas that a brief exposure to a gasoline odor does not result in a disabling condition, I ask my sister to drive me to a Bashan Oil gas station so that I may see the warning label on the gas pump, which states that there is detectable amounts of chemicals in gasoline and it's vapors that may cause cancer, birth defects, or other reproductive harm.

I am certain that Dr. Connive is aware that the very toxic MTBE (Methyl tert-butyl ether) was present in the fumes during my exposure. She is well aware that two nights after my exposure I was suffering a lot of pain and went to the hospital for an evaluation. And that the treating physician understood that I was suffering severe pain, and therefore he gave me a prescription for Vicodin. If I was prescribed Vicodin for severe pain, then why did Dr. Connive say, that I received medical attention and was found to be completely normal?

Dr. Connive asked specific questions about the exact location of my home. After I answered her questions, I understood that there was a strong possibility that Dr. Connive was going to establish some sort of surveillance on me. And I was correct in my discernment, because a short time later, I notice an individual who parks near my home every day. I often see him looking at me through binoculars. The first time that I spoke to him, I was rude. The second time that I spoke to him I apologized for my first rude encounter. And now the third time that I speak to him we talk about the injustice against me, which seems to humble him.

When Dr. Connive concluded her Workers' Compensation report, she was unaware that the Social Security Administration was also concluding their report regarding my injury. Four months after Dr. Connive files her report with Workers' Compensation, I receive a report from Social Security. Thankfully, the Social Security Administration judge honored his bench by acknowledging the truths in my doctor's reports. I must mention that this judge's calm, professional demeanor while seated on his bench filled my heart with peace, and confidence.

Six years and two months after my exposure, and three years after I filed for Social Security, I receive the judges Notice of Decision, which was written on July 29, 1994, and is Document #107. This report is filled with Workers' Compensation. When I look at the first page I stare for the longest time at, "Notice of Decision - Fully Favorable" As I begin to read the report a rare good feeling flows through my damaged body and into my sad heart. The judge states that after a thorough evaluation of the entire record, he concludes that I have been disabled since April 10, 1991, and that my impairment is considered to be "severe." The judge describes my problems as, loss of strength and motion in both legs and feet, with chronic pain secondary to toxic neuropathy. As I read this report the judges words sound like a trumpet announcing good news in my heart. He also states that my impairment prevents me from performing even a full range of sedentary work. I am amazed to read that I was exposed to toxic fumes in 1988, and that my employer either does not know the exact combination of chemicals or declines to disclose the information, if it is known.

This next comment is for Dr. Connive. The Social Security judge understands that my condition has slowly worsened over the years, causing me to stop work in April 1991, because I could no longer carry, walk and stand as required. And I so wish that Dr. Connive could read that the Social Security judge says that I cannot put weight on my lower legs or feet without great pain. I am surprised to read in his report that while I am at home I walk on my knees, and outside I use crutches or a wheelchair. All of this true, I'm just surprised that the judge mentioned this comment. The honest, honorable judge also states that my complaints are supported by nerve conduction studies and the opinion of both examining and treating physicians. His next statement says that he agrees with the conclusions of the doctors.

The judge makes another very interesting comment, stating that my limitations are consistent with the record when considered in its entirety, and closes his report by stating that my allegations are found to be credible.

Truth and justice are satisfying and sweet, like a pretty melody in my heart.

After the Workers' Compensation corruption, I am very thankful for the integrity, truth, and accuracy of the Social Security Administration.

I have waited so long for some sort of relief of my sorrows, sufferings, and losses. I now feel as if I have a crown of happiness on my head. My hope is high because I feel certain that the reports of Dr. Preponderate and Social Security will strongly influence the Workers' Compensation judge for my benefit.

Social Security rated my disability as 100 percent. However, a long-time past employer did not pay into Social Security on my behalf, so my monthly Social Security check is reduced by $400 per month. Social Security payments should start in about two months.

I am continuously saddened, because each hour, day, and evening I am not with my daughters.

However, Social Security is going to pay me for the three long years that I waited for my Social Security approval, which means that I will receive a big check. So now I will be able to move into a nice home, and hopefully enjoy more time with the girls. But then I consider that I do not have a vehicle, so I'm not sure how I will gather things for a house.

I decide I will just keep things simple and purchase a sailboat, for several good reasons. I will be able to move about my entire home with only a few steps. A sailboat is inexpensive to live aboard and already has furniture. And besides, I think that the girls and I will have so much fun living aboard a sailboat. Even if there were no benefits to living aboard a sailboat, I will still buy one because owning a sailboat will make me a captain!

I feel like a most fortunate man because of the good changes coming into my life. For the first time in a long, long time I have a constant good feeling flowing from my heart throughout my body. That is, until an unjust problem develops between me and the owner of the shed and he says in anger, "Get out!" My friend Jim was present when this problem occurred, and he knows that I am innocent in this matter. This is a serious problem for me because the owner then said that I must leave within a week or two. His cruel words almost paralyzed my heart. And now because of my limits, my heart is weak and fearful as I consider, *how am I going to find another place to live in such a short time?* My heart begins to pound harder when more unanswerable questions confront me, *why is this happening? If I could only stay here for two or three more months I'll receive money from Social Security, then I could buy a sailboat.* And when the thought enters my heart, *my truck, I've lost everything, even my truck. I wish I still had my old truck so I could look for another place to live. I don't even have a phone.* The logic of this problem, now linked to so many previous problems, begins to form a lump in my throat. As the speed of my thoughts increase, making my heart labor because of heavy stress, I sense the presence of God, and am truly amazed at the rapid change within my heart and mind. As my fears retreat, hope advances right into my heart, restoring strength to my mind. The Holy Spirit, the Comforter, gives me the understanding that nothing happens to me unless my Father allows it. I then understand that God has a very good reason, a purpose, for moving me out of the Grand Hotel. I also understand that my Father is again exercising my faith, which means that I must earnestly apply myself to this lesson as I applied myself to my training with John Alacrity. John's hard demanding training blessed me with carnal benefits. My Father's hard demanding training will bless me with eternal benefits, as long as I conform to His Word, and offer myself acceptable to Him.

So after time in prayer, as I open my Bible I honestly consider my frailty as a man and my inabilities as a Christian, which truly humbles me before God. As I read, I realize a greater appreciation for God's word, because through the Bible I am able to build true God honoring faith and hope for any situation.

I search through the Bible, reading scripture that will encourage and strengthen my faith, and stop at Isaiah 40 and begin to read. As I read verses twelve to thirty-one I am absolutely astonished at the incomprehensible awesomeness of God, which makes my problem seem so very small. After I confess my sin of weak, wavering faith I am grateful for the exercising of my faith and confident to talk with God about a new home for me.

Two days later I mention to a friend that I am looking for a new home, and he mentions that there is a couple at church who might rent their basement bedroom to me. The next Sunday before church, as I explain my need to the couple, I discern that they are simple, good people. As we talk they mention that they live on an island, which makes me wonder if maybe I am dreaming a most wonderful dream. Thankfully, they say that I can move into their basement room as long as I pay rent after I receive my Social Security check. I must say, that during church service it is difficult for me to pay attention to the Pastors message because my grateful heart inclines me to open my Bible to Isaiah 40 and reverently gaze at our unapproachable (Isaiah 6:3-4 filled with smoke; Revelation 1:17) Creator who lovingly cares for me.

After church I call my sister, and after I explain why I must move out of the Grand Hotel she offers to help me move to my hew home.

A few days later she arrives at the Grand Hotel, and after we put my things into her car, I mention that I should go back in and make sure that I'm not leaving anything behind. I quickly go to the shed, and as I stand in the doorway for a quick look into the empty room, the Holy Spirit begins to remind me about the intimacy I enjoyed with my Father while I lived here. My quick look becomes a soft heart-felt stare, filling my eyes with tears. As cherished moments with God tenderly enter my heart, I follow my tears to the floor. Down on my knees, devout gratitude bows my head for prayer. However, my heart lifts my head for another look, so that the eyes of my mind may behold the past memories with God. While I stare, looking through the treasury of my memories, I realize how fortunate I am to have lost my possessions and health, because in this shed I learned that as long as I have God and His Word, I have all I need to make me happy and content. To my amazement, I further realize that though my heart was often sad, it was my soul that was happy and content.

Feeling as if I have opened a new treasure chest, with tamed passion I begin to analyze this new thought. As my thoughts link together, I consider that when I was born my soul was spiritually dead, and the moment I became a Christian, God gave spiritual life to my spiritually dead soul. And now that my soul is spiritually alive, though my heart is often very sad, I can be happy and content if my soul is properly nourished with the Word of God. Amazing, though I often had a lump in my throat because of my sad-fast beating heart, it was my soul that was happy and content, because of God's Word and His presence. Now I can clearly see that there were many times when my happy soul influenced my heart with happiness.

Well, now I am eager to find other lessons that I must learn. So my mind, heart and soul unite, and as they begin their search, holiness comes to my mind. As I consider holiness (removal from that which is common, unclean and unfit for Heaven) I think I understand why God has removed common carnal distractions from my life. For now, I realize that because so many common carnal things are removed from my life I rarely grieve the Holy Spirit, (Ephesians 4:30) and that is one reason why through the past year I experienced my greatest fellowship with God. I now understand that the Grand Hotel was God's special classroom for me.

I feel profoundly fortunate, and while I offer my most sincere thankfulness to God, I realize that I want to be in a similar Grand Hotel way of life when it is my time to die and go to God. So I ask the Father if He would please be merciful and gracious to me and put me back into a Grand Hotel way of life during my final days in this life. Because a greater degree of hardship and pain, creates a deeper, more earnest heart for God.

As I rise, the thought of Isaiah 2 and Ezekiel 40 enter my mind. So when I turn and walk toward my sister, I say, "Thank you Father. That is so true. Please help me to faithfully climb the mountain and the steps."

Isaiah 2:2-3 states that during the last days (after the seven years of tribulation, during the thousand years when Jesus is on the earth) the temple of the Lord will be on top of the highest mountain in Jerusalem. And many people will zealously go to that temple. I agree with Mr. Henry that the required climb up that mountain symbolizes the various difficulties of our Christian walk. As an assent up that mountain would be against the heart, so it is that sometimes a proper Christian walk is against the heart. There are times when the struggles of our Christian walk seem as if we are climbing the steepest part of that mountain.

In Ezekiel 40 we have a detailed description of that temple on top of the mountain. After the guard at the temple gate gives approval to enter the court yard, there are six sets of stairs (:6, 22, 26, 31, 34 and 37) to climb as a person advances toward the worship of Jesus. The Bible does not mention how many steps comprise the first set of stairs. However, we read that the second set of stairs has seven steps, as does the third set of stairs. The fifth set of stairs has eight steps, as does the sixth set of stairs. The six sets of stairs have a similar symbolism as the mountain. However, it seems to me that the last two sets of stairs have an extra step, suggesting to us, that as we draw closer to worshiping Jesus, we must consider that our walk, or effort, is to change; imposing extra effort against the heart; requiring greater caution in thought and conduct.

Regarding our degree of effort, all of us Christians must consider how God measures each of us, and determines divine favor for us.

Measured: 2 Kings 14:3, 15:3, 16:2, 17:2, 18:3, 21:2, 22:2; 1 Kings 21:25-26; 2 Chronicles 29:34; Acts 17:11; Revelation 2-3; 2 Corinthians 5:10-11

Divine Favor: Genesis 4:4-7, 6:8-12; 1 Samuel 2:26; Proverbs 3:1-4, 8:33-35, 12:2; Luke 1:30, 2:52; Acts 7:46; Hebrews 11:1-40

CHAPTER 18

Living Aboard a Sailboat

~&~

GOD TURNS A PERSON THIS WAY OR THAT WAY
ACCORDING TO HIS WILL.

> The king's heart *is* in the hand of the Lord, *as* the rivers of waters:
> he turneth it whithersoever it pleaseth him.
>
> PROVERBS 21:1

AUGUST 1994: LAUREN IS TEN, MARIBELLE IS EIGHT, AND MADELINE IS SIX
I MENTION MY SAILBOAT IDEA to the girls, and they think that it would be
great. I think it is a short-term fun idea, because I believe that I will receive
a Workers' Compensation award within six to twelve months. After I receive
my Workers' Compensation award, I hope to buy a new truck and move into
an actual brick-and-mortar home.

I find a twenty-eight-foot sailboat that looks just right, so I buy it, inspiring many mariner dreams. It is not intended to be a live-aboard sailboat, but
that's okay, because we will only enjoy it for a short time until I receive my
Workers' Compensation award.

The heavy medication I am taking has dulled my thinking, which
decreases my ability to make choices that are more appropriate. If my
mind were clearer, I would likely purchase a more appropriate live-aboard
sailboat.

For reasons unknown to me, Dr. Honor is no longer my doctor, so he has referred me to Dr. Joust.

When I meet Dr. Joust, his young age disappoints me. No doubt, my Workers' Compensation battle is very difficult, so I need a more mature, experienced warrior. However, during my examination I realize that Dr. Joust is truly a knight, with his lance firmly in his hand, ready to joust with the Workers' Compensation Court. During my first evaluation by Dr. Joust, I learn about his vast experience helping the victims of the Bhopal chemical release.

In the following letter to my attorney, Dr. Joust makes an excellent declaration regarding my previous MRI study, and the three previous nerve conduction studies. My attorney received Dr. Joust's letter on August 11, 1994, six years and three months after my exposure. This letter is Document #109.

Dr. Joust states that he reviewed Dr. Bismarck's medical reports in which Dr. Bismarck describes my medical complaints as the result of structural, muscle, or disc herniation. Dr. Joust emphasizes that I have subsequently had several studies that do not support such a hypothesis. My doctor refers to the nerve conduction studies and the MRI test as proof that Dr. Bismarck's conclusions are erroneous. Dr. Joust then expounds on those studies, verifying more directly that Dr. Bismarck's conclusion is wrong.

Dr. Joust states that these studies strongly verify my diagnosis as chronic axonal sensory polyneuropathy. And to more strongly enforce the conclusive diagnosis of the test, Dr. Joust mentions that this diagnosis was initially made by the neurologist Dr. Preponderate and now again by the neurologist Dr. Data. When Dr. Joust spoke with Dr. Data via telephone, Dr. Data said that he believes that it is unlikely that structural or muscle-skeletal injury is responsible for my condition. Dr. Joust strongly enforces my verified computer diagnosis by stating that axonal neuropathy may result from other medical causes. However, both Dr. Connive as well as Dr. Honor thoroughly tested me for common medical and toxic conditions that cause such neuropathies, and could not find a specific etiology. Meaning that there is only one possible cause of my nerve disease, and that would be the chemical exposure. Dr. Joust establishes his comment by stating that it is well known that gasoline and many of its hydrocarbon constituents cause nervous system damage.

Thank you, Dr. Joust. I have waited for this truth! The judge will certainly acknowledge this letter.

On August 11, 1994, Dr. Joust wrote another letter (Document #110) exposing Dr. Connive's report as erroneous, and by sound medical evidence proving my medical complaints as related to the exposure. Dr. Joust letter was mailed to my attorney, and filled with court.

Dr. Joust's report is based on his evaluation of me on July 11, 1994, and before he wrote this report he reviewed the reports of Dr. Honor, Dr. Preponderate, and Dr. Connive.

Dr. Joust states again that my previous computer tests have confirmed nerve impairment in both of my legs. He also mentions that my MRI test proves that I do not have a bad back, and that a likely cause for my medical complaints is a toxic etiology. He emphasizes again a most excellent point by stating that other causes of a chronic neuropathy would include alcohol, diabetes, thyroid abnormalities, or a vitamin or nutritional deficiency, diagnoses which have also been eliminated in this case. Later in the report Dr. Joust repeats his last comment so that his point is clearly understood.

Further defending me, Dr. Joust explains that the vapor of Naptha, a gasoline constituent, is readily absorbed by inhalation, and is a central nervous system depressant, and may manifest as damage to the peripheral nerves in some cases. My doctor establishes greater evidence on my behalf by stating that I was told that I was exposed to 'raw gasoline.' N-hexane, also present in gasoline, is a known neurotoxin. And the fact that gasoline has many chemical components which have been associated with nervous system disease, lends evidence to my medical complaints.

Dr. Joust exposes an error of Dr. Connive by stating that when she wrote her report, she referred to my first computer test that showed nerve impairment only in my right foot, and did not refer to my second computer test that showed nerve impairment in both legs.

My doctor's final comment expresses that he is troubled because Dr. Connive said that I comport myself as a blatant fraud simulating a religious cripple on crutches, and that my motivation for my disability is to avoid child support payments. He advises that these matters are complex issues which require more than one evaluation.

I am amazed and grateful because of the excellent reports written by my doctors.

On August 12, 1994, I acquire another Nerve Conduction EMG test, which proves again, that I have nerve impairment on both sides of my body, and it proves again that Dr. Bismarck's diagnosis of me is wrong. I am very hopeful that this test will convince the Workers' Compensation judge that he must acknowledge the truth about my exposure symptoms.

Through the past year because of my deteriorating health, I have not been as active with my case. But that's okay, because Mr. Arnold has filed many briefs for me with the court. However, it does concern me that I have not received any mail from Workers' Compensation. So as my hope weakens, because it seems as if I might remain aboard this boat much longer then I thought, I begin to remodel my sailboat so that living aboard will be much easier.

Often in the evenings, I suffer from a lot of pain and feel very weak. Therefore, there are many evenings that I do not feel like going all the way up to the men's bathroom in the parking lot for a shower. During these evenings, my only option for bathing is for me to wait until it is dark so that no one will see me when I go out on the dock wearing only cut-off jeans. Down on my knees, I hold the hose above my head and quickly bathe.

During the winter, the wind blows hard through this marina, making it very cold, causing me to debate with myself about bathing out on the dock. I have learned that the best way to silence my debate is to rub soap all over me before I go out on the dock, which commits me to bathing. I usually bathe at about 9:00 p.m., and quickly climb back into my boat where it is nice and warm.

One evening in January, when I was out on the dock bathing, two fellow boaters were very surprised when they walked to the end of the dock and found me out there bathing.

However, during summer or winter, I am very thankful that I am still able to either bathe up in the shower, or out on the dock.

This Friday evening I am very happy when the girls arrive for the weekend. After hugs and kisses, we begin to talk as if we have not seen each other for a very long time. As we stand before each other, I feel like a most fortunate father, because the expressions of our love and gratitude for each other ebb and flow, uniting our hearts as one.

During our talk, Madeline stutters with one of her words, making me think that her little mistake sounds so cute. However, when she begins to stutter with another word, I notice that her face shows a hint of struggle, which draws all of my attention to her. As Lauren and Maribelle continue their talk with me, I look at Madeline and wonder what has happened to her to make her stutter. When she stutters again, I pull her into my arms and say, "Honey, why are you stuttering?"

Before Madeline answers, Lauren and Maribelle say, "Daddy, when we are with Mommy, Madeline stutters all the time. And when we are with you she stops stuttering!"

I then remember that the last time the girls were with me I had heard Madeline stutter a few times. But now she stutters with almost every sentence. Through the evening, Madeline's stuttering troubles me.

However, in the late evening before I tuck her into bed, I notice that she is not stuttering as much, and by lunch the next day, her stuttering stops. My conclusion is that she desperately needs my hugs, love, and prayers.

My doctors have written numerous reports in which they state, by clear and convincing evidence, that my symptoms are the result of my chemical exposure at Bashan Oil Refinery. In the following report, it is evident that Dr. Connive deliberately conceals these important facts, as she offers her fraudulent reports for the benefit of an organized scheme within Workers' Compensation.

In Dr. Connive's report written on October 25, 1994 (Document #115), she mentions at the opening of her report that her contention is that I am malingering, and avoiding child support payments.

Then she goes on to say that because of the complicated issues of my case she spent seven hours of painstaking preparation for her report. Well, it is well known that liars must take great pains to keep their lies harmonious.

She states that she reviewed reports written by my doctors: (Document #109: Evidence of computer tests, August 11, 1994; Document #110: Summary and assessment, August 11, 1994; Document #113: Neurologist's confirmation, August 22, 1994; Document #114: Lack of other medical explanation, September 26, 1994; Document #111: Electromyography laboratory, electrodiagnostic studies, August 12, 1994; and Document #107, Social Security Administration: Notice of a Fully Favorable Decision, July 29, 1994).

In these reports, the authorities agree and confirm the polyneuropathy in both of my legs and feet.

From the list of reports that Dr. Connive states that she reviewed, Dr. Joust's 8/11/94 report, refutes Dr. Bismarck's diagnosis of me, which says that my right leg pain is due to a bad back or a previous foot injury. Dr. Joust also affirms that my symptoms are the result of my polyneuropathy, and emphasizes that my several medical tests do not support the conclusions of Dr. Bismarck or Dr. Connive. My doctor stresses again that my nerve conduction studies and the MRI study is strong evidence that the conclusions of Dr. Bismarck and Dr. Connive are wrong,   and that these test are evidence that I have a chronic axonal sensory polyneuropathy. My doctor strengthens his conclusion by adding that this diagnosis is also concluded as true by the neurologist Dr. Preponderate, and the neurologist Dr. Data.

In Document #107, the Social Security Judge states that I have an impairment which is "considered to be severe," which is loss of strength and motion in both legs and feet and that my complaints are supported by nerve conduction studies, and the opinion of both examining and treating physicians.

Dr. Connive reviewed these reports, so why does she conclude that she found no physical findings to support a diagnosis of polyneuropathy? She states again that my symptoms might be the result of diabetes. However, Dr. Honor and Dr. Connive have already tested me for diabetes, and concluded that I do not have diabetes.

Dr. Connive attributes my foot pain to a number of procedures and surgeries on both of my feet. However, the *only* procedure or surgery on my feet occurred when I was in my early thirties when *one* small bunion was removed from each foot. After my bunion removal, I did not feel any problems.

She also states that she has never encountered a case of peripheral neuropathy from workplace exposures due to solvents, and that any reference to workplace exposures resulting in peripheral neuropathy is rare.

Dr. Connive made a similar comment in her first report, Document #103, on March 28, 1994, wherein she says that the incident which I describe, the May 6, 1988 exposure, would not by any stretch of the imagination result in any of the symptoms I describe.

However, isn't it interesting that in 1991, three years before Dr. Connive wrote this report, she published a book about chemical exposures in the workplace? In her book, she states the opposite of what she says in this report. Her book states that a single chemical exposure of irritants or solvents may produce acute symptoms.

It is evident that Dr. Connive works in concert of action with a secret party within Workers' Compensation, who through my case show a continuous pattern of racketeering activity.

Before my next hearing, the Workers' Compensation judge reads all of the above reports, and yet still he denies my case, because his decision is solely based on the corrupt reports. By now, I clearly see that this judge is also part of the "collusion" faction within Workers' Compensation, who by design intentionally misrepresents my case for the purpose of fraudulent profit.

My daughters and I are very upset because of the denial of my case. I think that it is best that I do not talk with them anymore about my case. The rejection of my claim means that I will remain aboard this sailboat through the approaching cold winter.

Living aboard this sailboat is difficult because the small floor space, which is about thirty inches wide and seventy-two inches long, with a couch on each side of the floor. There is very little storage area, and the galley is very tiny. The low ceiling in the bathroom will not allow me to stand up, and my closet is only twenty inches wide. When my daughters are with me, we are very crowded. However, we make the best of our time together. Each Saturday morning after breakfast, and Bible time, we turn on the TV and watch Bob Ross and Lawrence Welk. We then turn off the TV, and while I wash dishes, the girls go out to the dock and play with two boys who live with their Christian parents, aboard a beautiful sailboat three slips down. After I finish washing dishes, I pour a cup of hot coffee and go topside, and make myself comfortable as I recline on the boom of my sailboat, watching the children play. I enjoy good fellowship with the family who lives aboard the beautiful sailboat.

Often, when the girls are here with me aboard the sailboat, they ask me to tell them the worm story.

A few days later, after my girls have left, I learn from my neurologist that my nerve disease mimics the most severe form of multiple sclerosis. I am thankful that I now have a better understanding about the nature of my illness. When my symptoms are strong, they now last up to three or four weeks.

This evening I feel a little weak as I crawl into my bunk. However, in the middle of the night when I awake, I feel severe weakness and great pain from head to toe, and when I realize that I have wet the bed, a big lump forms in my throat. This severe weakness makes it very difficult for me to crawl out of my wet bed. This is a great problem because I do not have a shower, a washer, or a dryer. As I struggle to leave my bunk, I pull my wet sleeping bag and sheets onto the floor and fall onto the couch. Because I feel so weak and ill, I do not care about cleaning myself.

A few hours later when I wake up, I am stunned at how horrible and weak I feel. I am too weak to eat breakfast, so I remain on the couch and listen to talk radio. At eight o'clock, I usually enjoy listening to John MacArthur. However, due to this severe weakness, I am forced to listen to a radio program that I usually avoid, because I am not able to lift my arms to change the station.

During the middle of the day, I eat a little food and then fall back on to the couch. Through each hour I try to encourage myself, thinking that I will feel better in a day or two.

In the late evening, I do feel a little better, so I crawl out to the dock and bathe.

Two nights later, while I am asleep on the couch, I awake and learn that I have wet the bed again, so now there are two wet sleeping bags on the floor. The second wet sleeping bag was the cushion on my couch, so now I lie on hard wood, which through each day and night develops pain in my hips, causing me to roll back and forth. The back of my head and neck are usually so swollen and painful that I am not able to turn my head or lay the back of my head on my pillow. And because I am so very fatigued I do not care that I am so uncomfortable.

During the next few days, I try my best to build hope within my heart by again thinking that I will feel better in a day or two. Usually the movement of my boat, and the sound of the wind blowing through the rigging, appeals to me, but not now.

I am so weak that eating, brushing my teeth, combing my hair, and washing my sleeping bags are unimportant to me. During my fourth week of this struggle, time becomes meaningless.

These severe symptoms continue to crush me. During the fifth week, I encourage myself once again by clinging to the hope that I will soon feel better. Because I am not eating enough I am losing a lot of weight. Physically, mentally, and emotionally I am wasting away. I completely understand why suicide is frequent among MS sufferers, but I am certain that I will never commit suicide. I must wait for my Father to change my time of deep sorrow.

Finally, during the sixth week, I begin to feel better! However, my weight has dropped from 195 to 170 pounds, and my size thirty-two waistline is the same as before; all of my weight loss is in my upper body.

When my sister learns about my poor health, she comes to my boat, gathers a few of my things, and takes me to Mom's. I remain there for four months until I am well enough to return to my little sailboat.

About a year before this time, I began to experience feelings like electrical shocks in the back of my head. Now these shocks occur multiple times a day. When I turn my head, it sounds as if someone is waving their hand past my ear. And recently a new problem developed. Sometimes when I talk I feel an electrical shock in my tongue that makes it jerk, causing me to mispronounce words, which completely humiliates me.

Another big problem is that my eyes are always very red and painful, so I no longer talk with people when I am out in public.

Mom took me to an urologist to determine why I am wetting the bed. His conclusion is that my body has become so weak that I am losing muscle control.

I often remind myself that this time will pass, and someday I will understand why my Father has allowed my sorrows, sufferings, and losses. So often I encourage myself with the following verse:

> **...all things work together for the best unto them that love God, even to them that are called of *his* purpose.**
> Romans 8:28

I confuse a few people in the marina when I rename my sailboat "Fortunate Man."

My desire to be with my daughters is so very strong! Last month I missed another Thanksgiving with my daughters, and this Christmas will be my third Christmas without them. I am certain that Dr. Bismarck, Mr. Goliath, Judge Graft, and the others who have betrayed me will enjoy a very good Christmas with their families.

Shortly before Christmas, six years and seven months after my exposure, I go to another appointment with Dr. Joust.

After the examination he writes a report of his findings in a letter to Mr. Arnold (Document #116) which adds greater clarity and weight to my case.

In this report he points out that Dr. Data, who performed the most recent nerve conduction study in August 1994, is a neurological specialist practicing at both the Veteran and the Community Hospitals. He documents that Dr. Data's findings show evidence of a neuropathy in both the right arm and right leg, and that impairments in two limbs suggest a poly-neuropathy.

Dr. Joust states that most non-work related causes of a neuropathy have been excluded by previous relevant tests, and that Dr. Connive's suggestion to consider diabetes had been already heeded by my other medical providers.

He adds that he is personally loath to come to such a conclusion as "*malingering*," which is a strong contention; without the benefit of a full psychological evaluation, or without stronger evidence than that which Dr. Connive has previously presented.

I believe that Dr. Joust's excellent report will prevail in court, and that long before next Christmas my girls and I will enjoy a comfortable, warm home together.

In addition, I should no longer miss any time with my daughters because all of my doctor's, including a Social Security administrative law judge, have well defined my symptoms as related to the exposure at my workplace.

Furthermore, in Dr. Connive's published book about chemical exposures in the workplace, she states that a chemical exposure should cause symptoms that actually can be defined.

Dr. Connive knows that my toxic work injury is *well* defined, and that my symptoms *are* related to the exposure at my workplace, which again, has been proven by my two doctors, two neurologists, and three computer diagnostic tests.

Recently I hired a new attorney to work alongside Mr. Arnold, because it seems as though Mr. Arnold has changed his attitude toward me, and sometimes I wonder if he is more of a help to Bashan Oil than he is to me. As I do not have the heart to fire him, he now works alongside my new attorney, Mr. Dull-Sword.

Note to reader: Although the following documents are lengthy, as you read them you will see both the art of lying, and the art of exposing lies. This information is also very important so that you will understand my actions later in the story.

On November 2, 1995, seven years and six months after my exposure, Workers' Compensation Court requires that Dr. Connive submit to a deposition (Document #131) in which she lies about my toxic injury. However, during her deposition she is forced to tell the truth.

During the deposition the interviewer asks Dr. Connive to briefly describe an axonal sensory polyneuropathy. Dr. Connive answers that when chemicals cause a peripheral neuropathy, an electro diagnostic study, which is an EMG, will document the malady as an axonal neuropathy. She then emphasizes that there is a delayed proximal latency when there is an axonal neuropathy.

Thank you Dr. Connive! Toxic substances did cause my "axonal neuropathy" which is established by numerous EMG studies, and I also did experience delayed proximal latency.

The definition from the *Webster's Dictionary* for the words *delay, proximal, and latent* are: Delay: To put off to a later time; Proximal: Situated toward the point of origin or attachment as of a limb or bone; and Latent: Present but not visible, apparent, or actualized; existing as potential.

On the day of my exposure, my symptoms were present but not visible, existing as a potential nerve disease, and put off to a later time of development. And my symptoms progressed, fully manifesting themselves during the three years following my exposure, disabling me 100 percent. The Social Security judge noted in his report that the development of my diseased condition has slowly worsened over the years, which again confirms the *delayed proximal latency.*

Continuing with Dr. Connive's Deposition: The interviewer asks if there is any other way, other than computer test, to diagnosis an axonal polymotor polyneuropathy? Dr. Connive answers that there is; by a clinical exam or an account of the symptoms. Well, I did mention an account of my symptoms every time that I spoke with each doctor. Later, numerous computer tests confirmed my accounts.

Dr. Connive is asked if she found any fault with my EMG tests. Remaining true to her errors she emphasizes my first computer test which showed disease only in my right foot, and does not mention the other two tests. The interviewer asks the doctor about the other two tests performed by Dr. Definite and Dr. Data, and asks if she found any fault with those tests. And again, Dr. Connive emphasizes my first test, and does not mention the other two tests. The interviewer then asks again, if she found any fault with those two tests? Dr. Connive answers, no, however; she would rely on the first test.

This is the first time that Dr. Connive gives due credit to the nerve conduction study performed by Dr. Definite (Document #32, 1991) and to the electro-diagnostic study performed by Dr. Data (Document #111, 1994). Both of these computer studies prove that I have a disease in both feet and both legs. However, she nullifies the credit she gives to these studies when she says that she would rely on Dr. Endorser's interpretation. Dr. Endorser performed his computer test on me in 1988, four months after my exposure, when my disease was in its early stages of development. Therefore, his study showed disease only in my right foot.

One year and two months prior to Dr. Connive's deposition, Dr. Joust stated in his report (Document #110, 1994) that in Dr. Connive's report she only referred to the first study of 1988 in which she explained unilateral impairment as due to previous trauma. And that she did not comment on the second study of 1991 in which nerves in both legs were found to be impaired.

Three months after Dr. Joust mentioned Dr. Connive's omission of the second study, Dr. Connive wrote another report (Document #115, 1994), in which she states that she has now read this document. However, under her sworn oath in this deposition, Dr. Connive again attempts to avoid the important study of 1991, and again chooses to establish the first study as conclusive fact. It is so obvious that Dr. Connive is attempting to establish Dr. Bismarck's incorrect diagnosis of me as fact.

Dr. Connive's deposition continues: The interviewer asked, do you agree that different people have different susceptibilities to a polyneuropathy or to central nervous system disorders. The doctor answers yes. The next question is, do different exposures affect different people differently? Dr. Connive answers, yes. The question is asked, what is toxic to one person may not be toxic to another person? The doctor answers, yes.

In Dr. Connive's book, she makes a similar statement about how different exposures affect people differently. Her book states that the evaluation of each person must be as an individual in regards to chemical exposures. It seems that Dr. Connive's evaluation of me is not as an individual, but is biased in favor of Bashan Oil.

Dr. Connive is asked if polyneuropathy progresses and spreads to other parts of the body. The doctor answers that polyneuropathy could progress. The interviewer asks if by progressive, that means that nerve dysfunction would develop in other parts of the body? Dr. Connive answers that the nerve disease usually presents at more or less the same time in multiple extremities, so not necessarily; that it may become more severe as it develops. Then the interviewer asks how such a disease is documented; by computer test or clinical findings? The doctor answers that either by test or clinical findings; but that it depends on the instinct of the doctor, the patient's report, and symptoms.

I believe that the "instinct" of Dr. Bismarck and Dr. Connive is to falsify my reports.

The interviewer asks her if I complained about symptoms in both lower extremities shortly after my exposure, and if I had also complained about symptoms in my upper extremities, and she answers yes.

The interviewer asks if it is correct that the industrial hygienist, Mrs. Taint, stated in her report regarding the exposure, that there was a high concentration of almost finished gasoline for a minute, and she answers, yes. However, Dr. Connive does not recall if this report stated how high the concentration was.

The interviewer states that the exposure occurred as a result of the heating or steaming of an exchanger. Dr. Connive says that two different things happened, and that she is not a hundred percent clear, but one was an odor.

Then a great question is asked by the interviewer, if it is correct that the industrial hygienist stated that the fumes were a high concentration because it was more than a normal vapor order? Dr. Connive becomes a little agitated as she answers yes it was more than a normal vapor order.

The interviewer appears to strengthen my defense by asking if it is true that it was more than a perception of an odor, and that something serious occurred. Dr. Connive answers yes, the workers were evacuated from the area. Dr. Connive then states that one could drink gasoline until it killed you, but it wouldn't cause a peripheral neuropathy.

The interviewer's questions just get better when she asks if it is correct that there is no report that states what the composition of the fumes were. The doctor answers that eventually we must use common sense, and that we know what gasoline is made of. The faithful interviewer points out that there is no record that states if other chemicals were mixed with the gasoline or not.

Dr. Connive finally tells the truth when she says, I'm not a hundred percent clear on it, but there was an odor. She states, that it was more than a normal vapor odor, and was present at a high concentration. This answer clearly conflicts with her March 28, 1994 report (Document #103) which states that my exposure was a trivial incident in which I perceived a gasoline-like odor that did not cause temporary nor permanent disability.

As the deposition continues, and through a series of questions, the interviewer confirms that the hygienist's report, the refinery report, and Gary Betray's report are now missing! And also confirms that my four story climb up the ladder caused me to breathe deeply during the exposure, and therefore I ingested the vapors at a higher rate. The interviewer also established that my need to lie down after the exposure is an indication of my chemical intoxication.

Dr. Connive's deposition statements reveal that she actually does understand the truth about my toxic exposure and the resulting symptoms. Her comments clearly define my chemical exposure as work related. However, in her previous reports she denies the facts about my chemical exposure. She is a liar and has an evil heart. She chooses to be a wolf in sheep's clothing for the corrupt benefit of opposing counsel.

Dr. Connive's book proves that she has a very good understanding about chemical exposures. I am certain that she knows very well that all of my medical reports are harmonious with what she states in her book.

On the last page of each of Dr. Connive's reports, she states that she declares that under penalty of perjury, that the information contained in her report and its attachments, if any, are true and correct to the best of her knowledge and belief.

Dr. Connive, you foolish woman, you purposely declared many lies about me in your reports. I contend that you have of long history of perjury, lying about many injured workers, for the benefit of corrupt people, associated with Workers' Compensation. I believe that I am the first one to document that you are a liar. And, may I say, that I have well documented your many lies. You said in one of your reports that my doctors and I should be advised of the regulations concerning Workers' Compensation fraud. I now say to you, that you should be advised of a book in Heaven wherein all of your lies are recorded (Revelation 20:11-15). You must seriously consider the sober warning in the following verse.

And there shall enter into it [heaven] **none unclean thing, neither whatsoever worketh abomination or lies: but they which are written in the Lamb's book of life.**
REVELATION 21:27

This serious warning about lying is for those who make it a practice to lie. I have thoroughly proven that Dr. Connive makes it her practice to lie. This is very sobering when we consider that Satan is the father of lies (John 8:44). His nature is to lie, and so the nature of his children is to lie. Satan's nature is to malign Christians, and so the nature of his children is to malign Christians. Consider Dr. Connive's comment in her March 28, 1994 report that states that I comport myself in a blatantly fraudulent manner, simulating a religious cripple on crutches.

Weeks later, I take an enjoyable twenty minute train ride to the grocery store. When the train arrives and stops at my destination, I step from the train, and as I pass through the station I am inclined to stop at a newspaper stand and buy a paper, which is unusual for me to consider buying a newspaper. However, I believe that God wants me to buy a paper. After I pay for the paper, I board a bus, and as we roll along I find a very interesting article in the paper which gives me insight about "insider" Workers' Compensation corruption.

Now, based on an excerpt from the newspaper article, consider the nature of many within the Workers' Compensation system who make it a practice to commit crimes. By this example, we clearly understand why Dr. Bismarck, Dr. Connive, and Mr. Goliath are not afraid to commit crimes. It is because they are certain that Judge Graft and other Workers' Compensation judges make it a practice to protect those who commit crimes. We see how Workers' Compensation judges use Satan's gavel for the promotion of Satan's work.

In the newspaper article, written in a well-known newspaper in 1991 (Document #5), it describes how a State Board of Equalization Official was charged with 23 felony counts for filing false expense reports, which carried a maximum penalty of six years in jail and $230,000.00 in fines.

However, the State Board Official negotiated a plea bargain with prosecutors, and the judge reduced his many crimes to a single misdemeanor charge. He pleaded no contest and was sentenced to pay only $5,500.00 in restitution, a $1,000.00 fine, perform just 200 hours of community service, and only spend one year on probation.

The Worker's Compensation Judge then gave this felon an undetermined amount of reimbursement for medical expenses, and awarded this criminal more than $90,000.00 in Workers' Compensation stress benefits, plus a lifetime pension increase for the two decades he spent on the board.

Another reason that corruption is so prevalent is because of tolerance of corruption. Consider the following verse.

Because sentence against an evil work is not executed speedily, therefore the heart of the children of men is fully set in them to do evil.
Ecclesiastes 8:11

When corrupt rulers defy the laws of our land, or when they do not properly execute punishment for crimes, they encourage crimes and greatly hinder justice and truth. That is why Dr. Joust's first report did not prevail for me, and I wonder if his next report will benefit me.

Dr. Joust writes another excellent four-page report (January 10, 1996, Document #135). In his report, he refutes Dr. Connive's last report, and states many valid reasons why my injury is work related. Dr. Joust provides two additional pages that state his education at three honorable universities, and mentions his service at two highly respected hospitals. He also lists nine references regarding his impressive eleven-year work history, his three board certifications and licensures, and four of his publications.

An honorable doctor at the Los Alamos nuclear energy facility recommended the honorable Dr. Honor to me, and Dr. Honor recommended the honorable Dr. Joust to me. However, dishonorable people rejected the work of honorable people. Thus is the reason as to why the corrupt Workers' Compensation people will not honor the honorable reports that so well prove that my injury is work related.

The following verses help us to understand what God thinks when He watches my two *honored* doctors write their *honest* reports. By these verses we also know what my Father thinks when He watches Dr. Connive write her offensive, evil, inaccurate reports.

The tongue of the wise useth knowledge aright: but the mouth of fools babbleth out foolishness. The eyes of the Lord in every place behold the evil and the good.
PROVERBS 15:2–3

The evil man is snared by the wickedness of *his* lips,…
PROVERBS 12:13

The wicked entangle themselves in trouble by their folly, when God in justice leaves them to themselves. They are often *snared by the transgression of their lips* and their throats are cut with their own tongues.
MATTHEW HENRY

Dr. Connive then wrote yet another report on March 19, 1996 (Document #136) which shows the injustice in my case, and speaks for itself. My Father has already read it. In this report she states that there is no evidence that I had any exposure, or that I sustained either a short term or long term exposure. And then, she classifies my exposure as a nuisance odor episode, and says that I was evaluated by competent doctors. She also emphasizes that the pain in my feet is due to my orthopedic problems.

The so-called *competent doctors* of which she refers to are Dr. Bismarck and Dr. Moulage. And as their reports have proven, they were the instigators of the fraudulent activity in my case. I did not have any orthopedic problems as she again states. As I have already stated, I had developed very slight occasional pain from wearing a new pair of stiff hiking boots resulting in a bunion on each foot, and during a brief time when I was not working I had them both removed.

CHAPTER 19

Putting It All Together

~⤸~

EXERCISE STRENGTHENS MUSCLES, JUST AS TRIBULATIONS STRENGTHEN GOOD ATTRIBUTES.

...but also we rejoice in tribulations, knowing that tribulation bringeth forth patience. And patience experience, and experience hope. And hope maketh not ashamed,...
ROMANS 5:3–5

Patience does us more good than tribulation can do us hurt.
MATTHEW HENRY

SUMMER 1996

BY NOW, MY ATTORNEYS HAVE filed many trial briefs with the Workers' Compensation court, clearly stating the truths within my doctors' reports, and the errors within the reports of Drs. Bismarck and Connive. My reports contain great clarity, and legal weight of which should easily provide justice for me.

However, I am very disappointed when I receive another denial from Judge Graft, as stated in the judge's Findings of Fact and Orders he wrote on August 23, 1996 (Document #142). In the order he states that the burden of proving my industrial injury is my responsibility, of which must be proved by preponderance of the evidence. The judge states that after reviewing the testimony at trial, and the exhibits that we have filed with the court, he concludes that I have not met my burden to prove that the named exposure caused or contributed to my condition.

Well, with this order it seems clear to me that Judge Graft is biased against me, because if he were an honest judge he would acknowledge the preponderance of the evidence stated by my doctors.

The American Dictionary of the English Language defines preponderance as: to exceed in weight; to incline or descend, as the scale of a balance; and to exceed in influence or power. Now judge for yourself if my doctor's reports exceed in influence or power.

This recent denial is very upsetting, and again I have no idea what to do. This confirms again that I cannot trust anyone associated with Workers' Compensation, and I wonder if I should even trust Mr. Arnold, Benedict Arnold. He seems to, yet again, to hinder my efforts in court. My frustration with my case motivates me to collect more reports from Workers' Compensation and thoroughly study them.

Through the following year and a half, I gather numerous Workers' Compensation medical and legal reports, and from them I document many errors.

[Gold Statement 6: In 1998 the low for gold is $273.40 per ounce, and the high for gold is $313.15 per ounce.]

FEBRUARY 1998

LAST NIGHT I SLEPT AT MOM'S, (I excuse the hurtful things she does to me, and enjoy many very good moments with her, because of our unbreakable mother - son bond) and during breakfast, I mention to her that I have collected many Workers' Compensation documents, and have discovered widespread fraud within my case. She seems to doubt that I have discovered fraud, so I reach into my duffel bag for my notes, and as I pull them out, I say, "Mom, take a look at these notes."

As I show the fraud to her, she becomes very serious and says, "James, it looks like they have done this to you on purpose."

I say, "They have Mom."

She says, "Let's go to the computer."

Amazing, she has much work to do with her home-based business. So while her employees work she offers to help me. We sit down at her computer, and after we discuss a few thoughts, she starts typing. Hour after hour and week after week, we sit together typing. I am grateful, and Mom is more and more amazed as she learns about the fraud that caused the denial of my claim. Mom clearly sees the "willful misconduct" in my case, so she mentions a friend of hers who is a former multimillion-dollar Workers' Compensation fraud investigator. Mom stops typing, calls her friend, and mentions our documentation of Workers' Compensation fraud. After they finish their talk, Mom mentions to me that her friend is happy to come over and look at our documentation. However, he did suggest that we first finish our work on summarizing this fraudulent activity, and then he will come over and look at our paperwork. This is very encouraging to me.

Finally, after three long months of sifting through a massive amount of reports, organizing, and editing, we complete a twenty-five-page document that so well proves insider fraudulent activity in my case, (Document #153: Summation of Fraudulent Activity).

Mom invites her friend over for dinner, and my first impression of Mr. Scout is very good because his appearance and character make him seem like he would be a great undercover investigator.

During dinner, I explain my exposure story, and then after dinner Mr. Scout looks at our documents. As he reads, he becomes increasingly sober, and moments later he says, "There's fraudulent activity in your case. The judge, attorneys, and doctors are guilty of fraud. I highly suspect that Bashan Oil has spoken to the judge and your attorney. Get a different judge, and fire your attorney."

I say, "How do I do that?"

As Mr. Scout offers advice, Mom and I realize that we are dealing with a problem of extreme seriousness. Mr. Scout makes it clear to us that because of the nature of my case; I am dealing with "Bashan Oil's Big Boys." After he mentions more advice and a few warnings, he asks me, "What type of a man were you at work?"

I am surprised at his question, but I say, "All of the men respected me because I was a hard working, trustworthy, moral man. And because of my playful nature, many of the men often teased me." After I mention other thoughts, Mr. Scout responds,

"That's your problem. They know you are too patient and nice. They know they can take advantage of you, because you are just too patient."

He tells me that my biggest problem is that I am correcting a judge. He says that I should never attempt to correct a judge, and if I do, no one will help me.

I tell him that in a street fight if more than one man is involved, I would focus on the biggest man, because if I bring him down, everyone else will back off.

He says, "James, you are not listening to me. You must never correct a judge."

Mr. Scout cautions me about surveillance, and also mentions that because of the seriousness of my documentation they will stay one step ahead of me. Thankfully, he offers to come back and talk with us again.

After Mr. Scout is gone, I discern that something is troubling Mom, so I ask, "Mom, what are you thinking about?" She says, "You asked Mr. Scout two times if there was a possibility that someone might hurt you because of your documentation." The stress in Mom's voice adds weight to her words when she says, "He wouldn't answer you; all he said is that you are dealing with Bashan's Big Boys."

I calm my heart for her, and say, "Yes, that concerns me. However, do you remember the time when Mara and I were in a park and someone tried to start a fight with me?" Mom's eyes brighten as she says, "I do. I do remember that. God helped you." I say, "Now I understand why the Father helped me. He taught me then that He is able to protect me." She says, "I know James, but I am still afraid for you."

Through the remainder of the evening, we talk about Mr. Scouts' advice and warnings to us. Both of us are concerned about the warnings, and very hopeful that our documentation will gain justice for me. We then go upstairs, and as Mom climbs into bed, I fix my bed on the floor at the far end of her large room.

The next morning after breakfast Mom reminds me that Mr. Scout advised that I should call Workers' Compensation Information and Assistance and tell them about our documentation. I sit up a little taller and say, "That's right; he did suggest that I call them. Good deal Mom! I have no doubt that they will respond to our documentation the same as Mr. Scout responded."

When I call Workers' Compensation, I am surprised when a Workers' Compensation attorney answers the phone.

I explain my exposure and the history of my case, and then describe our documentation. I am shocked by how rude the attorney is as she says with a raised voice, "You don't have altered medical reports."

As I try to talk, she becomes increasingly argumentative. Our talk ends, and I sit stunned with disbelief.

After I explain to Mom what this attorney said, Mom tells one of her employees to drive me to the Workers' Compensation office. After we arrive, I step into the Workers' Compensation attorney's office, and speak with the same person that I spoke with on the phone. As I explain who I am, I put my documentation on her desk, and as I open to page nine of the altered report section, I point to a sentence and say, "Read this."

For a brief moment, she reads, and then looks up at me and says, "You have a criminal case here. Take your paperwork to the district attorney and show your documents to him."

I am as hopeful and happy as can be! After our brief talk, I feel that I must go to the district attorney as soon as possible.

We arrive back at Mom's and I take a deep breath and explain the good news to her. I then call my daughters and tell them the very good news.

I then call the DA and tell him that a Workers' Compensation attorney advised that I call him and explain my exposure story and documentation to him. After I finish my talk he says, "Bring your paperwork to my office, and I'll look at it."

Before we end our talk, I explain to him that because of my nerve disease I use crutches, and do not have a vehicle, so it will take me about two hours to get to his office, because I will travel on a few buses and a train. Therefore, I will make the trip tomorrow. He says, "Okay."

The next day a friend goes with me to the DA's office, and when we step through the front door of the building, the DA that I had spoken with on the phone says to me, from the second-floor balcony, "I'm not going to look at your paperwork."

I say, "Yesterday you said that you would look at my paperwork." He rudely says, "I'm not going to look at your paperwork unless someone in a position of authority requests that I look at it."

I say to him, "I mentioned to you yesterday that a Workers' Compensation attorney told me to contact you."

With district attorney authority he says, "I'm not going to look at your paperwork."

I remind him that I was exposed to chemicals at Bashan Oil, and that tests prove that the exposure caused me to develop a nerve disease. I also tell him that two doctors purposely altered one word in two of my medical reports, which caused the denial of my Workers' Compensation claim. I remind him that I have these altered reports. Again, he firmly says, "I'm not going to look at your paperwork."

The look on his face convinces me that he is absolutely not going to look at my paperwork. So with great confusion and disappointment, I turn and make the long trip back to Mom's.

The stress to my nervous system caused by this trip to the district attorney, forces me to rest for a few days, after which I go back to the same Workers' Compensation attorney who had told me to contact the DA. She is surprised when I tell her how the DA responded. She suggests that I show my documents to the Workers' Compensation Information and Assistance

Officer, and warns me that when Workers' Compensation reads my paperwork, things are going to heat up.

I walk up to the Information and Assistance office, and when I step up to the receptionist's desk, I ask for a complaint form. The receptionist asks, "What is the nature of your complaint?"

I say, "Fraud against a Workers' Compensation judge."

She nervously points to an adjoining room and says, "Go talk to that man."

When I look to my right into the office where she is pointing, I am stunned when I see a man looking at me with a very serious, unwelcome stare. As I step toward him, I offer a smile, hoping to soften his spirit. However, when I introduce myself, he refuses to shake my hand.

I feel like I am out on the streets standing before a violent person. However, I encourage myself by keeping in mind that he will be very surprised when he sees my documentation.

As I explain my exposure story and the history of my case, he becomes more defiant with me.

However, I become very hopeful as I open my paperwork to page nine, thinking that he will be as amazed as Mr. Arnold, Mom, Mr. Scout and the Workers' Compensation attorney were when they first saw the comment on page nine.

So with a hint of enthusiasm I confidently lay my paperwork on his desk, and ask him to read the same comment that the Workers' Compensation attorney read.

As he reads, I remain silent, waiting for him to look up at me with amazement. However, when he looks up to me I am discouraged by his stern look; and especially discouraged when he says, "I need to go and talk to someone about your document." He then quickly leaves the room.

I should be encouraged, but become confused when I pick up one of his business cards that reads: Mr. Delay, Head of Information and Assistance. If he *were* the Head of Information and Assistance, why would he need to speak with anyone else? He should know exactly what to do!

When he returns, he is more negative than before, and when I try to talk with him about my documentation, it is clear to me that he is not willing to talk with me about the matter. However, I am encouraged when he suggests that I contact Judge Short, and talk with him about my documentation. Mr. Delay mentions that Judge Short is the presiding judge of [our state] Workers' Compensation. With great thankfulness, I shake his hand and say good-bye.

I arrive back at Mom's and tell her about my conversation with Mr. Delay. She is confused about how he handled my documentation, but very encouraged when I mention that Mr. Delay suggest that I contact the presiding judge of the state Workers' Compensation, Judge Short. Mom and I become very enthusiastic as we prepare a copy of our Summation of Fraudulent Activity to mail to Judge Short. After we send it by certified mail, we can hardly wait for a likely quick response.

Day after day, we wait with great anticipation for the judge's response. However, after more than a month of waiting, we are very disappointed to realize that his response is taking so very long, and eventually we are upset when we realize that he is not going to respond to us at all.

I begin to request help from all departments within Workers' Compensation. Each department shows interest when I first begin to mention my documentation. That is, until I mention that a Workers' Compensation judge is involved. When I mention Judge Graft's involvement, they rudely turn from me and go back to other work. Similar subsequent experiences with each of the departments increase my frustration.

The only Workers' Compensation person who has listened to my complaints, and has offered good advice, is the Workers' Compensation attorney who suggested that I go to the DA. So because of her honesty and helpfulness, I return to her office. When we first meet, I am calmed when I realize that she understands my frustration with Workers' Compensation, and I am increasingly thankful, because she listens to me with great sincerity. As we talk more about my frustration with the Workers' Compensation departments, she rises from her desk and asks me to follow her. After a short walk down a hallway, we enter a room, and when she closes the door, I realize that we are completely alone. She lowers her voice and says, "James, no one will help you because of the seriousness of your documentation. What you have documented is *very* serious, especially since a judge is involved. All involved parties know that you have an incurable disease, so they are waiting for you to die, because after you die, they will make sure that your documents disappear. You should file your new twenty-five page document with the Workers' Compensation court. When you do, things will heat up."

She then tells me that in two weeks she is moving to another city, and kindly says that she is happy to help me until then. I thank her for her earnest concern for my daughters and me, and as I turn to leave, I mention that I will probably come back at least one more time.

I am disappointed that she is moving, however, I am very encouraged, because if she says that I have a criminal case, that likely means that I should not have to do any more documentation of criminal activity to gain justice.

I research all possible authorities who prosecute Workers' Compensation fraud, and are encouraged to find an Insurance Fraud Division in our state, in a different city.

I contact them by phone and explain my documentation, and am hopeful because they seem to be thankful that I am reporting Workers' Compensation fraud. That is until they learn that I am reporting the fraudulent activities of a Workers' Compensation judge. I am stunned when the representative says, "We don't deal with that type of fraud. We only deal with employee fraud."

We end our talk, and I sit for the longest time in disbelief, very upset with this entire ordeal. My activities, thoughts, and frustrations with my Workers' Compensation case cause so much pain throughout my damaged nervous system, and make me feel so ill, that I do not work on this dilemma for many weeks.

Eventually, the Workers' Compensation noise in my heart stirs me back to work on my documentation, so I head for Mr. Delay's office. Each time that I speak with him, he increases his opposition toward me, and purposely misdirects me. I now think that it is wise to have a witness with me when I talk with Mr. Delay. During my next two visits with him, I take a special witness with me, and they conclude, as I do, that he is a big waste of my time.

I am also very disappointed with Mr. Arnold and Mr. Dull-Sword because of their lack of success with my case. Through the next couple of weeks, I contact five more attorneys, hoping that at least one of them will help me. Each one of them is interested in my Workers' Compensation problem until they learn that a judge is involved in fraudulent activities.

EARLY 1999

FOR THE PAST FEW YEARS, a local hospital has provided services for my work injury. The hospital filed my medical bills under their Workers' Compensation category. However, since Workers' Compensation refuses to pay my hospital visit bills, my nurse practioner tells me that, although she understands my deteriorating health, and Workers' Compensation case; and that I need continued medical services; the hospital will no longer provide these services for me. I believe a Workers' Compensation settlement will soon occur and pay my bills, so I go to a hospital in an-other city. My round-trip bus ride is four hours long.

During my talk with a friend about my Workers' Compensation prob-lem, he recommends that I join a prepaid legal service. He explains that if I pay a monthly fee, I can call them at any time and speak with an attorney about my Workers' Compensation problems. Although I cannot really afford the twenty-five dollars a month, I figure that they might resolve my Workers' Compensation problem, so I have no choice but to pay for this service.

Though I now have a legal service, I am still looking for another attorney. This week, three more lawyers decline to help me.

A year later medical services are stopped at the second hospital for the same reason services were stopped at the first hospital. My prescription intake is up to twenty-one pills per day, which is also stopped. The sudden withdraw-al from medications is very difficult. I now struggle with a greater severity in symptoms, which limits my pursuit of justice.

The side effect of at least two of my prescriptions is an increased sugar appetite. For some time now, I have consumed a tremendous amount of candy and cookies every day, and at my worst, I eat two sixty-four ounce bags of candy each day, in addition to many other sweets.

The withdrawal of all medical services provokes me to a more earnest pur-suit for justice. So as often as I am able, I study my Workers' Compensation paperwork.

During the past eleven months, I have called the legal service numerous times, and have noticed a definite pattern with them. Each time I call for advice their talk sounds impressive, yet either nothing, or very little, is ac-complished. I consider the status of my Workers' Compensation case before I joined, and after I joined this legal service, and deduce that this service is of zero benefit to me.

I quickly estimate how much money they have automatically deducted from my checking account. The two hundred and seventy five dollars is a great amount! So I call the legal service, and cancel my membership. Customer service requests that I send a letter confirming termination.

I am irritated that I must first write a letter to the legal service, board a bus, and deliver the letter to a mailbox. But I am motivated to write the letter when I consider that in about three weeks it will be time for them to deduct another twenty-five dollars from my account.

Later that day I drop the letter into a mailbox, and as the door shuts I say, "Good deal! The door with the legal service is also closed."

Through the following months, my exposure symptoms feel much worse due to the lack of medications, and because of the summer heat, which I must endure when I go to the library to study about my Workers' Compensation case. However, the results of my studies at the library increase my hope as I gain a better understanding about what I must do. There are times when my library activity causes a lot of pain and swelling in the back of my head, my neck, and down my spine. When this swelling occurs, I am not able to turn my head, and my vision becomes blurred. Often when I return to my boat I have to lie down for the remainder of the day, and sometimes for several days, until the pain and swelling have somewhat subsided. But I must continue my study of this Workers' Compensation case, because I do not think that anyone else will truly try to win justice for me.

I am beginning to realize that when my head, neck, and spine are painful and swollen I lose track of all time. A week or two may pass, and to me it seems like only three or four days.

I am able to accept the fact that my trials have separated me from my possessions. However, it is very difficult for me to accept the fact that willful injustice has separated me from my three darling daughters.

CHAPTER 20

The Next Few Years

—⌀—

SOMETIMES GOD WISELY PERMITS HARDSHIPS so that the bounty that we live in will not make us soft and unappreciative. From some hardships, we must learn the art of war so that we might be useful to God.

> **These now are the nations which the Lord left, that he might prove Israel by them (*even* as many of *Israel* as had not known all the wars of Canaan, Only to make the generations of the children of Israel to know, and to teach them war, which doubtless their predecessors knew not.)**
>
> JUDGES 3:1–2

1999 TO 2001

As I STAND IN THE galley of my sailboat washing breakfast dishes, Lauren is lying in the forward bunk, reading the *Readers Digest*. Moments later I hear her close the book, and as she crawls from her bunk, she begins to tell me about the story that she has just read. She is a happy sound coming toward me, so I reach for the towel, and as I dry my hands, I turn around so that I may listen to her. As she describes the story that she just read, I lean against the galley and listen. During her talk, God says to my heart, "Your daughter will meet her husband in another state."

With a hint of animation, I interrupt her and say, "God just said to my heart that you are going to meet your husband in another state."

With more than a hint of animation, she says, "No I'm not, because I am never leaving this state!"

When she said that, I remember the Bible verse that says:

The heart of man purposeth his way: but the Lord doth direct his steps.
PROVERBS 16:9

I confidently smile and say, "God has just told us what His plans are for you."

Lauren replies with passion, "Daddy, I love this state. I'm never leaving."

I say, "Okay daughter, I will ask God to talk to you about moving to another state."

Through each hour of this day, I grow more and more curious about Lauren's future husband, my son-in-law, and I am certain that he must be a simple, good Christian man. No doubt at sometime in the future God will move Lauren to another state, so I think that I will start asking my Father if He will please send me with her.

A few years before my chemical exposure I had sprained my lower back at work, which caused me to visit a chiropractor.

You may recall that in 1989 I went to a chiropractor, Dr. Faithful, who recommended that I consult an attorney. It is unknown to me that Mr. Goliath has asked this chiropractor to give a deposition statement regarding my case.

I have just returned from yet another trip to Workers' Compensation to gather more reports and am surprised to see Dr. Faithful's deposition.

In her fifty-six page deposition, (Document #147) given on February 22, 1999, Dr. Faithful correctly describes the onset of my exposure symptoms, and the resulting deterioration of my health. She emphasizes that my chemical exposure symptoms showed up as totally different symptoms compared to my back symptoms.

During my chiropractor visits with Dr. Faithful, I had told her about my exposure symptoms because I was very concerned about them, and no one else would listen to me. I did not realize at the time that she had listened so well. Thank you, Dr. Faithful, for your accurate honest answers about my exposure symptoms.

Many honest authorities have contributed sound medical proof confirming my Workers' Compensation claim. All of their reports are consistent, harmonious, and accurate. And now, without my knowledge, Dr. Faithful's statements strengthen my medical file. She makes more certain the validity of my testimony regarding my chemical exposure. I am now wondering about Mr. Goliath's thoughts regarding Dr. Faithful's statements, as he is a trained lawyer.

I am certain that Mr. Goliath is aware of a statement written in the Medical Evidence of Injury section of a state *Workers' Compensation Handbook*. This section states that at every opportunity we must consider that the heart of a claim or defense of a claim is the medical file. A good medical file will prove that a condition or disability has resulted from activity while in the course of employment. A proper medical report contains facts and is not based on surmise. Our state Supreme Court has determined that a medical opinion based on an incomplete history is mere hearsay. Therefore, a "hearsay" opinion is not entitled to credibility if other medical evidence contains a correct medical history. It is especially significant if the injured workers' testimony of the matter is corroborated by other evidence.

The reports written by Bashan Oil doctors are not consistent, harmonious, or accurate. They are not entitled to credibility because they are clearly a self-willed opinion, in conflict with my accredited testimony and my substantial medical file. However, Mr. Goliath will support and defend them, even if it ruins my life. Mr. Goliath should fear my Father, because many years ago, He used a young shepherd boy to bring down the fearsome giant Goliath.

On September 5, 2000, I again write a letter to Dr. Bismarck explaining the correct and incorrect statements in his two reports. I also note my EMG studies that confirm his correct statements and ask him if he would please correct his reports.

On October 2, 2000, I make a phone call to Dr. Bismarck's office and speak with his assistant, who tells me that he has been out of the country and is just now returning to the office, so he has not had a chance to look over my paperwork. She says that she will return my call. However, she never returns my call.

Six months later another EMG study, performed by Dr. Moore on April 16, 2001, written twelve years, eleven months after my exposure (Document #160), confirms disease in both of my feet and legs, and verifies that I have chronic axonal motor-sensory neuropathy in my legs.

After many months of researching Labor Code, on November 6, 2001, I go to the Office of the District Attorney and speak with the Senior Inspector. After I explain my exposure story, I show him the accurate and inaccurate reports, and ask him if he would please help me in resolving this matter. He makes me feel as if I am bothering him with a trivial complaint and does not offer any help. Before I leave, I ask him if I may have his notes from our meeting. He surprises me when he actually hands me he his notes.

Recently when I stayed with Mom because my nerve disease symptoms were so very severe, she did not allow me to purchase any food, so I was able to save $500. To me this is a lot of money. I know that I should put all of it into my piggybank, but I don't, because I refuse to let my dream of owning a nice rifle slip away. So I call a gun business in Colorado. I speak with the owner about ordering a custom-made rifle and he says that I need to send him $450, which will start my order. After the owner receives my check, he tells me to give him a little time to finish working on another rifle order, and then he will call me so that we may talk about the details of my order.

After about two weeks, the owner calls me and says that he has made the barrel for my gun. This is a surprise to me because he was supposed to call me first so that we might talk about different options for the barrel and other parts of the gun. When I begin to tell him about the barrel that I wish to order, he interrupts me and says that he has already made the barrel. I ask him if he would please return my money. However, he responds that he will keep my money to cover the cost of the barrel that he made, and he then hangs up. I mail him a letter, and also send him a number of emails, hoping to recover my money. He responds to two of my emails in which he avoids my complaints, but then does not answer any other communications from me. I am too weak to work on either my Workers' Compensation case or the problem with this gun, so that means that I have just lost $450.

When after my exposure Bashan Oil and Og Construction betrayed me, it felt as if they had thrown me off a cliff. Since my exposure, judicial injustice makes me feel as if I have been in a downward spiral for the past 1,634 days. I do not know which is more foolish, the Workers' Compensation corruption or my long patience with Workers' Compensation. The former Workers' Compensation fraud investigator was right when he said that I am too patient. Now that I realize that, in this matter, my long patience is a fault. I understand that I must look at some examples in the Bible of how men of God dealt with trouble in their lives.

I grab my Bible and sit at my table. Before I begin to read, I talk with my Father about my downward spiral and ask what lessons I should learn, and what I must do to stop my free fall. Before I finish reading in my Bible, I understand that I must take control. The question is how do I gain control over trained legal authorities?

CHAPTER 21

Taking Control

⤴

WHEN THE UNRIGHTEOUS PROMOTE UNGODLINESS, THE RIGHTEOUS MUST DO A GOOD SERVICE FOR GOD AGAINST THE UNRIGHTEOUSNESS.

Curse ye Meroz: (said the angel of the Lord) curse the inhabitants thereof, because they came not to help the Lord, to help the Lord against the mighty.

JUDGES 5:23

NOVEMBER 2001: FOURTEEN YEARS AND SIX MONTHS AFTER MY EXPOSURE

THIS MORNING I AWAKE FEELING sad, because a few days ago I missed another Thanksgiving with my girls. A few days later, I feel even worse, because tomorrow is the first day of December. A month ago, I tried to prepare myself for another Christmas holiday without my daughters, but there was no way to soften that hard blow. My last Christmas with my girls was nine years ago, and this December I know that my sorrow will be as deep as it was on that first Christmas without them.

Through December, injustice encourages me to go back to court so that my Attorneys can explain again the errors in Dr. Bismarck's reports, the many lies in Dr. Connive's reports, and the truth stated in my doctors' reports. As I pray about going back to court, I am reminded about Mr. Scout's comment, "You are too patient. Fire your Attorneys and get a different judge." When I begin to consider how fraudulent reports have prevailed over me, I realize that Mr. Scout was right. As I sit before God, listening to my own thoughts, and to Him, I become very sober and realize that I must seize control of my case, and our lives. I do not tell my attorney's about my decision to file for another hearing, because they seem to allow injustice for me. Through all of my court hearings, they have not allowed me to stand up in court and challenge the false reports, as a man would challenge another man on the street. Their limits have constrained me, allowing fraudulent reports to gain victory over me. As I ponder going into court without my attorney's, and sitting in my attorney's chair, I am encouraged, because the court will then hear from me and me alone. I am especially encouraged after I carefully consider Bible verses about various benefits of diligences (Proverbs 10:4, 12:24, 27, 13:4, 21:5 and 1 Timothy 4:15).

I know the history of my case, and I have studied a lot of Workers' Compensation labor code, so I feel confident enough to speak to the bench about my case.

When I begin to ask the Father about going into court alone, He reminds me that He has listened to my thoughts, which gives me more confidence. As I ask God if he would please give me wisdom, knowledge, and understanding about speaking to the court, I am reminded about the time when the Apostle Paul stood before a judge; or at least someone who Paul thought was a judge. I quickly turn to Acts 23:1–10 and read the story about Paul's day in court. This court was comprised of seventy-one religious members called the Sanhedrin. One part of this assembly was the legalist Pharisees, the other part was the liberal Sadducees, and the head of this council was a corrupt high priest. This ruling body was the Supreme Court of Israel.

I am certain that before Paul stood before this court, he considered the following. In Matthew 3:7 John the Baptist called these Pharisees and Sadducees a "generation of vipers." In Matthew 23:13–29 Jesus called these Pharisees and Sadducees "hypocrites," "blind guides," "fools," "serpents," and a "generation of vipers." And no doubt Paul remembered that it was this Sanhedrin that condemned Jesus to death (Matthew 26:59–66). Paul must have also considered that the righteous, innocent Stephen stood before this Sanhedrin and said to them,

> **Ye stiff-necked and of uncircumcised hearts and ears, ye have always resisted the Holy Ghost: as your fathers *did*, so do you.**
> ACTS 7:51

After which this religious group stoned Stephen to death.

Before Jesus' death, He said one of the most revealing statements about the true nature of this Sanhedrin in His following verse:

> **Woe *be* to you, Scribes and Pharisees, hypocrites: for ye are like unto whited tombs, which appear beautiful outward, but are within full of dead men's bones, and all filthiness.**
> MATTHEW 23:27

However, I am certain that Paul was not intimidated by the pomp, power, and cruelty of this worldly Supreme Court, because the Supreme Court of Heaven entrusted him with full authority. And because Paul's daily concern was his accountability to the Supreme Judge in heaven, when he stood before the men who were "full" of "all filthiness" he looked upon them with unwavering courage. Paul's resolute valor must have offended the high priest, because when Paul said,

> **...Men *and* brethren, I have in all good conscience served God until this day.**
> ACTS 23:1

The high priest "commanded them that stood by, to smite him on the mouth."

Then said Paul to him,

...God will smite thee, thou whited wall: for thou sittest to judge me according to the Law, and transgressing the Law, command-est thou me to be smitten?

ACTS 23:3

The priest truly deserved to be called a "whited wall." He understood that Paul had called him a hypocrite because mud walls were painted white, meaning that they looked clean on the outside; however, on the inside they were very dirty.

And they that stood by, said, Revilest thou God's high Priest? Then said Paul, I knew not brethren, that he was the high Priest: for it is written, Thou shalt not speak evil of the ruler of thy people.

ACTS 23: 4-5

Paul did not ask the high priest to pardon his comment. However, he asked the men, who were offended by his statement, to pardon his comment. Some think that Paul did not ask the priest to pardon his comment because Paul did not consider the priest to be God's high priest.

I begin to ask the Father how Paul's attitude and actions in court should influence my attitude and actions at my next hearing. After prayer, I understand what I must do. So to strengthen my decision, each day I read various scriptures to encourage myself. I more clearly understand that Jesus and the eleven disciples would understand my decision, because all of them were courageous, strong, straightforward and impulsive men. However, I am sure that the bold Apostles were very surprised when they saw Jesus on two occasions violently cleanse the temple courtyard of corrupt moneychangers and sellers of animals (John 2:14–17; Matthew 21:12–13).

As I also consider that Jesus and the Apostles were meek and submissive to the Father, I also understand that they were not always meek and submissive to ungodly men. That is why men often responded violently to them. The Apostles and Jesus feared God, not men. I am greatly encouraged about my decision.

Workers' Compensation hearings are usually scheduled for thirty minutes, and on rare occasions for one hour. So I am a little apprehensive when I learn that my next hearing is scheduled for eight hours. Some of my apprehension is because I know that my diseased nervous system cannot endure stress for even an hour.

My confidence begins to weaken when I learn that ten attorneys from the opposing side will be at the next hearing. As I weaken, thoughts echo in my heart, *Why have they scheduled my hearing for eight hours? It's probably because they know that I will be in court without my attorney. They must think that at the next hearing they will have a great opportunity to hold me in court all day and skillfully nullify my documentation of their fraud. And why is there a new judge? That's okay, because God is with me. They have no idea that I talk with God about their fraud and our next hearing. None of them would appear at the next hearing if they understood that God is going in with me.*

After much prayer, and encouragement from the Bible, I feel confident, and ready to speak to the court.

JANUARY 8, 2002

AS I RIDE THE BUS TO MY HEARING, my mind is busy thinking about the authoritative-looking people who will sit in court with me. Their clothing will make them look honorable, and trustworthy. However, I know their wicked hearts, because of their fraudulent activity with my case. They are very cruel people who have deeply hurt my daughters and me.

When the bus arrives at the Worker's Compensation building, I step off, and as I walk toward the building, I feel bold, and ready to confront the honorable-looking people. As I approach the courtroom doors, I am very curious to see the new judge. I hope that this judge is a good one, and not another puppet. I will know within the first few minutes of the hearing if she is a puppet.

When I open the door and step into the courtroom, everyone turns to look at me, making my boldness fade before the courtroom doors close behind me. However, some of my boldness comes back when I see my attorney's empty chair, next to Mr. Goliath. During all of my past hearings, I have wished to sit in that chair, so that I might say all that should have been said at my second hearing twelve years ago. As I walk to my chair, I just hope that no one can hear my pounding heart, especially the many opposing attorneys, seated to my right. The judge looks as if she is in her early sixties, so that means that she likely has a lot of experience. I hope that will be to my benefit.

As I pull my attorney's chair out, I say to Mr. Goliath, "Good morning Mr. Goliath."

I am not surprised that he will not look at me when he says, "Good morning James."

That's okay, at this moment I must not let him bother me, because I must try to gain control of my pounding heart. As I look down at my notes I quietly take a deep breath, and try to gather my thoughts, but I cannot, because of the ungodly presence next to me.

It feels odd, but very good to sit in my attorney's chair, because today everyone in this courtroom is going to hear from me. However, my heart is beating too hard for me to talk, so I try to hide my nervousness by staring at my papers. The pressure of this moment is already beginning to exhaust my damaged nervous system.

Before I developed this nerve disease, strength and courage defined my nervous system and heart. It must now be some of that old strength and courage remaining in me, that causes me to look over at the attorneys, and then to the judge. Well, I should not have looked at them, because now my heart is beating even faster, and a lump is beginning to form in my throat. Great, I should not have looked at them, because my diseased nervous system cannot handle the pressure of this moment. The only way to hide my out-of-control fear is to again look down at my notes. As I pretend to read my paperwork, I begin to think about my long-term sorrows, sufferings, and losses that the people in this courtroom designed for me.

Thankfully, my Father is watching me and listening to the thoughts in my heart. Because of His love for me, He begins to encourage me. As usual when He begins to encourage my timid heart, I meet Him there in my heart and commune with Him, *Father I sure need your help.*

After my prayer, I clearly understand that the people in this courtroom are like the wind and the waves that frightened Peter when he stepped out of the boat, and walked on the ocean toward Jesus (Matthew 14:22–33). I am greatly encouraged when the Spirit of truth reminds me that when Peter became frightened, he began to sink until he reached out for Jesus' hand. I now feel very strong and courageous because I am harmonious with God. I now by faith, feel my hand in Jesus' hand. And as great confidence and boldness well defines me in this moment, I look at the attorneys and think, *You are only wind and waves that no longer frighten me.* As I behold them, my resolute heart turns my head for a look at the judge. While she looks at her notes I think, *You look important sitting there in your robe. I will respect you if you convince me that you are a good judge. And if I learn that you are not a good judge, you are going to hear from me.* With authority, I look to my left at Mr. Goliath, and as he looks at his notes, I think, *Today we are going to talk.*

As I look back at the judge, and then at the attorneys, I think, *Filthy Workers' Compensation puppets are all around me! I am a man of God, and you are only wind and waves.*

When the judge lifts her head, everyone looks to her. She then opens court, and a few minutes later, she says to me, "I understand your twenty-five page documentation. However, Judge Graft has already ruled on that."

She has no idea how she has just sobered me, causing me to think, *Now I know who you are. You are another Workers' Compensation puppet!*

I look harmless as I sit here with both of my hands resting on the table. And the wolves around me probably think that I look like easy prey. I should wait to hear her next sentence before I act. However, I make a serious tight fist with my right hand, and consider how quiet the courtroom is.

The judge says, "And besides, it's too complicated."

That is what I thought. She is another puppet. So as I powerfully rise from my chair, I hit the table as hard as I can, and as I point at the judge, I say with authority, "Woman! Now I know who you are. You are another Workers' Compensation puppet!"

The echo from my blow to the table is still heard in the ears of all who are present when Judge Sock-Puppet says with judicial authority, "Sit down!"

However, with authority from Heaven's Court I respond, "Puppets have no authority over me. I will not sit down! If you are not going to rule properly, then get your caboose out of my way because I am after justice!"

She slightly lowers her voice and says, "I don't like it when you call me a name."

With a hint of authority I say, "Then earn my respect. This room is not yours. The legislature has provided this room for its citizens, and you are mandated by Labor Code to render justice. It is your duty to enforce the Labor Code. The legislature has granted authority and power to you to amend the erroneous decisions of a previous judge. But I see that you are going to ignore your oath, and allow fraudulent reports to stand as fact."

Before she has a chance to speak, I describe the history of my case, the details of the altered reports, and my vast preponderance of evidence. When I finish the judge surprises me by saying, "I have no authority or jurisdiction under Workers' Compensation to deal with a felony."

Thank you Judge Sock-Puppet, you have just confirmed that there is fraudulent and felonious activity in my case, so I say, "The legislature has given you the power and the authority to re-weigh an erroneous decision rendered by a previous judge."

Before I entered this courtroom I had read a portion of the Labor Code from the selected provisions of this State's Constitution regarding the *Duty to Report Misconduct, Article XIV Labor Relations;* which states that when circumstances warrant, a referee (judge) shall take or initiate appropriate disciplinary measures against a referee, lawyer, party, witness, or other person who participates in the Workers' Compensation process for unprofessional fraudulent or other improper conduct of which the referee becomes aware.

Labor Code obligates Judge Sock-Puppet to initiate appropriate disciplinary measures against Dr. Bismarck, Dr. Connive, Mr. Goliath, and all others who are guilty of fraudulent activity, which includes Judge Graft.

I then turn to the attorneys and say, "All of you understand the fraudulent activity in my case. I have communicated very well with you, and you are now fully accountable. You have no excuse. You are no longer going to quietly ruin our lives within the walls of this little room. If you do not do what is right, I will take this story to the national media and call you to account before the nation."

Mr. Goliath tries to sound authoritative when he says, "James, sit down."

I turn and fix a serious eye on him and say, "You clearly understand what I'm talking about."

He does not say another word, or even look at me.

I discern that the judge is not going to rule properly. I would like to remain and say more to the attorneys, however, I feel as if I am going to faint, so as I turn to walk out, I see the stenographer and bailiff enter the courtroom. It is interesting that this judge opened this court hearing without the presence of the stenographer or a bailiff. The judge says, "Stay here so we can record what you said."

I reply, "You heard all that I said, I have nothing more to say."

I turn and leave the courtroom, and as I walk down the hallway, I begin to feel very weak, and stop two times to steady myself by placing my hand against the wall.

When I step out of the building, I feel extremely weak, which forces me to put my right knee on the grass. However, to my regret I realize, *Oh great. The grass is wet!*

I walk about twenty feet to a tree and lie down, not caring if the grass is wet. When I awake three hours later, I feel horrible and very embarrassed for lying here for so long. I sit for a while until I feel well enough to stand up, and head for the bus stop.

I had two motives for my attitude and actions in court: 1) Direct communication so that full accountability would be established; and 2) I hoped that the judge would charge me with contempt, which would have involved other authorities. I then would have had the opportunity to reveal the injustices of my case to those other authorities. However, I was not charged with contempt, nor was the court session recorded.

After the hearing, on January 8, 2002, I receive Judge Sock-Puppet's minutes of the hearing, (Document #164). I am pleased to read that she stated that during court hearing I told everyone present that if they do not properly rule according to court law, I will expose their unjust actions to the national media. I am very surprised and thankful that she stated that she told me that she "had no authority or jurisdiction under Workers' Compensation to deal with a felony."

She refuses to punish the crimes committed against me. However, if *I* was to commit a felony, I am certain that she would punish me.

Judge Sock-Puppet also states in her minutes that during court, I became very angry and starting pounding on the table, yelling, with language that she cannot quote.

She is obviously lying and trying to make me look bad. I only hit the table one time, and I did not use any bad language. However, I did speak with a slightly raised, authoritative voice.

Judge-Sock Puppet concludes her statements in the minutes by stating that the matter is taken off of the calendar until I advise the court on how I wish to proceed.

I feel that I accomplished much good at my hearing. However, the judge should not put the responsibility on me to proceed with further action. Because of my poor health, I don't think I can get back up anymore to take any further action. The judge and the attorneys should proceed with my case and render a proper judgment for me. As it is, none of the authorities who were present at my hearing takes any further action with my case.

A judge should serve as an exalted attorney, invested with authority to hear and determine the merits of an agreement or a disagreement between opposed parties, and therefore must distinguish truth from falsehood, rendering a lawful judgment.

I am not a trained attorney, or a judge. However, even with my novice degree of skills, I can clearly distinguish truth from falsehood. And I think to myself, *Who has influenced Judge Sock- Puppet, causing her to ignore my preponderance of evidence and favor fraudulent reports.*

Okay, let's just say for a moment, that Mrs. Sock-Puppet is an employee who has been exposed to chemicals while at work. And, let's just say that I am her Workers' Compensation judge. If I discovered that doctors had altered her medical reports, and that attorneys had allowed the fraudulent reports to stand against her, I would call all of the involved attorneys to my bench, and warn them about my unquestionable court authority, and also remind them about our promised adherence to legal ethics, which must be evident by our candor to the court. I would implore them to seriously consider our oaths, and obligation regarding our critical role in the honest administration of justice. I would charge them that if they have knowledge that their clients' intend to promote unjust reports to my bench, they must correct the error, or withdraw from their client.

And let's just say that after I remind the attorneys about their code of ethics, I then call Judge Sock-Puppet to my bench, and give the following settlement formula to her. And although insurance companies prefer that the public not be aware of this formula, I am going to give it to you. And then I would read it to all present before my bench:

Insurance companies and lawyers use a formula to calculate a settlement amount for an injury. This formula is called "Range of Compensation." The formula may vary; however, it includes the following aspects for a basis for negotiating a settlement:

1) Medical care
2) Loss of income and related fringe benefits

3) Permanent pain and other physical discomfort
4) Loss of family and property
5) Loss of social and educational experiences
6) Increased risk of future functional impairment
7) Embarrassment, humiliation and inconvenience
8) Fraud, misrepresentation, long-term willful misconduct and breach of an obligation

I would then say to everyone in the courtroom, "Now let us proceed with the best settlement terms for Mrs. Sock-Puppet."

If this scenario actually took place, my judicial conscience would be clear of any guilt throughout the day and into the evening, and later when I am on my pillow I would slip into guilt free, very sound sleep.

Proper compensation is a fundamental principle of American Tort Law, but a dishonest judge dishonors this principle.

The doctors, attorneys, and judges involved in my case will not heed my warnings about their fraudulent activities. However, they should seriously consider the following warning from my Father:

He that justifieth the wicked, and he that condemneth the just, even they both are abomination to the Lord.
PROVERBS 17:15

Thankfully my sister considers my great need, and today she gave me her 1982 Toyota truck. Although it has 222,001 miles on the odometer, that is not a problem, because Toyota's confidently smile at high mileage.

Today I am elated because I am headed for a visit with my daughters. It sure feels good to drive a truck again. When I pass by bus stops, I thank my Father for this truck.

I have gained a truck; however, I am losing my life. Every day my disease makes me feel a little weaker. My difficult times are longer, and my better times are shorter. During my good times, I work on my Workers' Compensation case.

CHAPTER 22

Required By Law

~ᴄ

*GOD ESTABLISHED GOVERNMENT FOR THE PURPOSE OF
ORDER FOR THE GOOD OF THE CITIZENRY. A SERIOUS
PROBLEM ARISES WHEN THOSE IN POWER ARE CORRUPT.*

> ...For Magistrates are not to be feared *for* good works, but *for*
> evil....do well: so shalt thou have praise of the same....but if thou
> do evil, fear:...Wherefore ye must be subject, not because of wrath
> only, but also for conscience sake.
> ROMANS 13:3–6

JANUARY 2002

AFTER THE LAST HEARING, I feel very discouraged, because my doctors have
given their best efforts for me in court, but their efforts seem to be in vain,
because of "willful misconduct" which robbed us of justice. I need a long rest
because my many years of research and stressful court battles have been very
hard on my diseased body.

Each morning after breakfast, I study my Bible, and then carefully plan
my activities for the day so that I may minimize stress to my nervous system.
I gently care for my nervous system as if it were a tender wound in need of
loving therapy.

After about twelve restful days, I feel a little better. However, my mind is still very active thinking about my Workers' Compensation case, so I begin to look through my court paperwork, and once again conclude that I actually do have a Workers' Compensation claim, which inspires me to organize paperwork and study labor code again.

As I toil on court paperwork, I discover a section of Labor Code regarding the *State Law of Employees, Injuries and Workers' Compensation*, which greatly encourages me to contact authorities, other than Workers' Compensation authorities. This section of Labor Code states that the employer is responsible for treatment if complications arise due to physician's negligence; and that any person who causes or makes a false or fraudulent statement for the purpose of obtaining or denying Workers' Compensation benefits is guilty of a crime.

The "fraudulent" statements of Dr. Bismarck and Dr. Connive complicated my Workers' Compensation claim, and their "knowingly false" statements make them guilty of a crime. Bashan Oil and Og Construction's two insurance companies are fully aware of the fraudulent activity committed against me. I know that they are, because at my last hearing I carefully explained the fraud in my case to their attorneys who were present in the courtroom. However, those attorneys chose to follow a deceitful course of conduct for their clients' benefit.

The Insurance companies obviously violated the Labor Code, which states that if its agents or employees are deceitful, causing injury to a worker, the insurance company is liable for damages.

My study of labor code gives me great hope and confidence that there is still a remedy for the unjust denial of my Workers' Compensation claim. Though all involved parties are fully aware of the fraud in my case, I intend to confirm, and increase their guilt by mailing copies of the most important reports that clearly reveal the crimes committed against me.

After I make a list of authorities that I will contact, I realize that if I first contact the district attorney, who is the greatest law enforcer in our county, he will likely resolve my Workers' Compensation problem.

With great hope, I go to the Office of the County District Attorney and speak with an authority in the Special Operations Division. After I explain my exposure story, I show him the inaccurate and accurate reports, and ask for his help in resolving this matter. When the deputy district attorney learns about Judge Graft's corrupt involvement in my case, his attitude becomes very negative toward me, and he behaves rudely. Before I leave, I give him copies of my paperwork, and though his attitude discourages me, I fill out an official Office of District Attorney Complaint Form.

A short time later I receive a letter from the District Attorney (Document #166) in which he states that his office looks for a pattern and practice of un-lawful and unfair business activities; but that he is prohibited from represent-ing anyone who seeks the return of money or other personal civil remedies.

The DA mentioned these thoughts during our meeting, so I said to him that I understand these mandates, however, I asked him to help me to correct the fraudulent activity in my case, or at least direct me to someone who can. I am not surprised that he ignores my request, and refuses to help me with my dilemma.

This disease has obviously dulled my judgment and discernment, or I would not have again contacted the following authorities asking them to help me with my case: Mr. Delay, the head of Workers' Compensation Information and Assistance; the Workers' Compensation Medical Board; the Commission of Health and Safety; and another District Attorney. However, they decide that they will not help me after I mention the judge's involvement in my case.

So as it is, like a boxer who is badly beaten, but refuses to give up, I call Dr. Bismarck again and ask him to correct his reports. When I call Dr.

Bismarck's office, I am surprised that he answers the phone. When he learns who I am, I hear nervousness in his voice. I remind him about my exposure story, and while I talk about his reports, I describe his accurate statements, his errors, and other reports that harmonize with his correct statements. I also remind him that his errors caused the denial of my Workers' Compensation claim. I mention that I will mail to him all of these reports so that he can correct his errors. He says, "Okay mail the reports to me and I will take a look at them." I mail him the reports, and am not surprised that he does not respond.

I take these same reports to the Insurance Fraud Unit of the District Attorney's Office of the City and County requesting help. A short time later I receive a letter (Document #170) from the Insurance Fraud Unit attorney which states that I should have taken action on this matter within four years after I discovered the offence, and as a result of my supposed late action I am beyond my statute of limitations, which means that no further action will be taken by the District Attorney's Office.

I am confused about the statement regarding the statute of limitations, because I took action well within the required time limit, and my last court hearing on this matter occurred on January 8, 2003, which is one year and four months ago.

I will not give up, so I go back to Mr. Delay's office. As usual, when I walk into his office he is not at all happy to see me. After I explain the details of my poor health, I ask him if he will please help me with my case. I again mention my exposure story and the mounting problems with my case. When Mr. Delay suggests that I schedule another hearing, I ask why, and mention that another hearing will just be a waste of my time. Before he can open his mouth, I begin to tell him about my last hearing before Judge Sock-Puppet, and though he tries to hide his thoughts, I can see that he is very surprised to hear about how I seized control of the court. When I begin to tell him about the many authorities who I have asked to help me, he suggests that I talk with the Administrative Director of Workers' Compensation. This is the first time that he has given me good advice, which is probably so that I will stop talking with outside authorities.

I call the Administrative Director's Office and mention that the head of Information and Assistance with Workers' Compensation has recommended that I meet with the Administrative Director. I am amazed and very happy when the secretary schedules me for a meeting with the Administrative Director.

My sister knows all about my Workers' Compensation problems, so she is as happy as I am about my appointment with the Administrative Director, and agrees to go with me as my witness.

During our drive to my appointment, I mention to my sister that Mr. Delay probably arranged this meeting for me with the Administrative Director because my documentation is very serious, and possibly, because all involved parties understand that I am unstoppable. Our hopes are very high that this Director will respond favorably to my documentation of fraudulent activity.

We finally arrive, and as I get out of the car, I decide to leave my crutches in the car. A moment later, as we sit in the Director's waiting room, I feel as if I am actually waiting for "justice" to enter the room. The Director finally walks into the room, and after he introduces himself to us, he informs me that he is not able to meet with me. Before my heart stops, he mentions that he has arranged a meeting for me with the head judge of this areas Workers' Compensation.

A moment later that judge walks into the room, and after the Director introduces me to Judge Pretty (he is wearing a pretty earring) the Director excuses himself from the room. When Judge Pretty asks me to follow him to the conference room where we may talk, I ask him if my sister may sit with us. I am surprised when he says that it is best if she waits here, which causes my sister and me to give each other an intense glance. My sister's glance confirms my thoughts; *I do not trust this judge!*

As Judge Pretty and I walk to the conference room, I prepare myself for more Workers' Compensation manipulation.

We enter a very lavish conference room which humbles me, and makes me feel slightly submissive to Judge Pretty. After we are sitting at the very elegant table, I look around at the beautiful room and realize that I must not allow the beauty of this room to affect me improperly, and weaken my discernment, and judgment. When I look into Judge Pretty's eyes, I determine that I must be simple, and circumspect.

As I explain my exposure story, I lay crucial reports before the judge, and after I show him all of the important aspects of the reports, he says, "May I look at the reports?" I smile and say, "Yes" and gladly push them over to him.

While the judge reads, I remain quiet, waiting for him to look up at me and say, *Your documentation is amazing, you have a criminal case.*

However, Judge Pretty reads my reports for about a minute and then looks up at me he says, "Mr. Landon, before our meeting I reviewed your case. I am sorry because there is nothing that anyone can do for you because you have run beyond your statutes of limitations."

Now I know what it feels like when cold water is thrown onto hot glowing metal.

I mention that I disagree with him, and quote labor code as to why I believe that I deserve another hearing so that I may receive justice. However, the judge says, "I am sorry. There's nothing we can do because your statutes have expired."

I then realize that he did not say a word about the errors. Now I understand who he is. So to confirm my discernment about him, I ask, "Judge, what are your thoughts about the altered reports?"

He avoids my question, and when he begins to speak about something else, I interrupt and ask again, "Judge, what are your thoughts about the altered reports?"

He again avoids my question, and talks about something else. Now I know that he is not an honorable judge; he is another Workers' Compensation puppet, manipulated by corrupt people.

As he speaks, I turn and look to my right and then to my left and think, *This lavish room was intended for justice, not for games like this. This puppet is wasting my time.*

With mild command, I look at him and say, "I need to go, this meeting is over."

Although it is always my consideration to let others walk in front of me, this time, as we both stand and head for the door, I make sure to walk in front of him. And when we are almost to the door, I purposely slow my pace, and then abruptly stop. We are now only a few inches apart as I turn my head, lower my voice, look straight into his eyes and say, "If anything happens to me, remember, there are more with me than with you." His increased heart rate dilates his pupils. He has no idea that I am referring to my Father, and the multitude of His angels.

I walk out to my sister, and when she sees my sober countenance I say, "I will explain in the car."

When we step into the elevator, I say with a lowered voice, "I do not think that it is a good idea to talk about my documentation in this building, because there might be listening devices. I especially do not want them to hear what I am about to do."

As we walk to her car I say, "Do you want to have a little fun?" When she looks at me I say, "Let's go to Workers' Compensation and open my case." When she says, "Okay," I grab her arm and swing her around so that we can walk a short distance to Workers' Compensation. As we walk, she grabs my arm and says, "James, you don't have your crutches." I smile and say, "That's okay, I feel well enough to walk without them." During our walk, as I tell my sister about my talk with Judge Pretty, she starts to get upset, until I say, "I am very encouraged because he refused to comment about the erroneous reports." She agrees, and I then describe how we are going to reopen my case.

When we step into Mr. Delay's office I purposely act a little frustrated while I tell him about my meeting with Judge Pretty, and mention that I am done with this stupid state and with Workers' Compensation court. As I look into Mr. Delay's eyes, I say with a hint of needed sympathy, "Mr. Delay, I'm leaving this stupid state. After I leave I will have to live the rest of my life knowing that I should have tried one more time in court." He hands a form to me and says, "Answer all of the questions. Be sure that you explain why you have taken so long to bring your case back to court, and we will schedule another hearing for you." I knew that this ploy would work because of my study of labor code.

I have reestablished my statutes of limitations. My successful ploy is called the art of war.

I now have thirty days to take action with my case. If I can find an authority that will go into court with me, I might prevail. However, now that my case is open, I might prevail if I go back to the Department of Industrial Relations, a division of Workers' Compensation, and ask them again to help me with my case.

With much hope, I go into the Department of Industrial Relations, and again explain my exposure story while I show them my documents, and then leave many documents with them for their review.

A short time later I receive a letter (Document #172) from the Department of Industrial Relations explaining that my documents were reviewed, and that the judges' decision is final and binding and therefore they will not help me.

I am livid! I truly believe that the puppets in this Workers' Compensation building have determined that I receive nothing but injustice. I must transfer my case out of this jurisdiction to another court, with new faces and hopefully honest hearts. I go to the Workers' Compensation offices and speak with one of the Information and Assistance Officers about transferring my case to another jurisdiction. Thankfully, she says yes, and says that she will start the process. As I travel back to my boat, I am very thankful for the transfer of my case.

While aboard my sailboat, I hear a small boat passing through the marina. When I look out my port window, I see that it is the harbormaster, so I step out on the dock and wave for him to come over. When he pulls up to my slip, I grab a hold of his boat and tie it off so that we may talk. I explain the history of my case and the fraudulent activity that is preventing my justice, and ask if he would please allow me to miss a few slip rents so that I may have extra money for court costs. He says yes, as long as I eventually pay all of my unpaid rent.

A few days later, I return to the same Information and Assistance Officer and ask about the transfer of my case. She tells me that my transfer is in process.

For eight days now, I have enjoyed new hope because of the transfer of my case. Christmas is a few months away, and I again hope that the transfer of my case will enable me to receive a settlement before Christmas. I once again look forward to the possibility of spending Christmas with my girls in a nice home.

After about a month, I become concerned because I have not received a notice from Workers' Compensation regarding the transfer of my case.

During the first week of December, I sadly realize that I will not be receiving a settlement by Christmas.

A few days after Christmas I go to Workers' Compensation and file a paper which states that I have not received a notice about the transfer of my case. While here, I discern that something is wrong with my case, and on my way back to the marina I am troubled, wondering what might be wrong.

Back at my sailboat, always hoping, I consider that there just might be an honest judge somewhere in Workers' Compensation. After I look at a list of judges within Workers' Compensation, I choose to write a letter to Judge Silver. In my letter, I explain the history of my case and describe the details of the fraudulent activity therein. I also describe my poor health, and mention that my health problems prevent me from working on my case in a timely manner before my statute of limitations runs out. When I put the letter in the mailbox, I feel good about contacting this new judge.

Days later, I go back to Workers' Compensation and speak with yet a different Information and Assistance Officer about the transfer of my case, and learn that my case was never in the process of transfer. Though I am deeply offended at this news, I cannot express my frustration to this officer because she is presumably innocent in this matter. I left the matter as is, and return to my sailboat.

During the first week of January 2004, I again go back to Workers' Compensation and ask about my request for another hearing. A moment later, they hand me an envelope that I should have received in the mail a long time ago. I open it and see that it is a notice informing me that my request for a hearing is denied, because more than twenty days have passed since my last hearing. When I filed my petition for another hearing, I described my poor health as the reason why I am not able to complete paperwork in a timely manner before the statute of limitations runs out. I feel very discouraged.

However, later in the day when I pick up my mail at the harbormaster's office, I read a very encouraging letter (Document #176) from Judge Silver. Amazing, fifteen years and eight months after my exposure I have renewed hope. The judge states that my case is closed because I have not kept my case open. He also mentions that if my physical problems are the reason for my lack of activity with my case, I may obtain a letter from my doctor explaining that my medical problems did in fact prevent me from proceeding with my case, and possibly reopen my case.

Really? That is all I have to do? I am very certain that my primary doctor will be happy to write this letter for me. I am so thankful for another opportunity in court. I would like to make this next hearing my last hearing.

I need all the help I can get for my last hearing, so I go to the police department and speak with an officer in the fraud division about my Workers' Compensation claim. During our talk, I am encouraged because of this officer's kind concern about the details of my case. After I say all that I need to say, I give my paperwork to him and tell him that I will fax him some additional documents. Before I leave his office, he mentions that he will mail a copy of his report to me in a few days. On my way back to the marina, I feel encouraged about our meeting, because the officer took extensive notes. The officer's concern and care for my case makes me feel as if he is lifting a huge weight off my back.

However, the weight on my back becomes heavy again when I receive a letter from the Office of Revenue Collection. They say that I owe $5,149.48 for past hospital visits. This angers me because all of my hospital visits are because of my exposure. I call the Office of Revenue Collection and become very upset when I learn that I actually owe $10,000. Workers' Compensation owes this money to them, not me!

I briefly tell the collection department about my exposure story and poor health, and mention that I am a man of integrity who pays all of his debts. However, I do not pay bills that should be paid by Workers' Compensation. Thankfully, they understand and agree with me.

However, I am not thankful when I receive a letter from the Police Department Fraud Division (Document #183) explaining that I am beyond my statute of limitations. Therefore, their investigation of my case is closed.

If I had known about all of the intricacies involved with the statue of limitations, I would have contacted the District Attorney after my second hearing fourteen years ago. I think that Workers' Compensation kept me active in court for two reasons. One reason was to cause me to exceed the statue of limitations, and the other reason was for them to learn, through dealing with my uncommon and sustained efforts, how to prevent other justified cases.

Bashan Oil and Og Construction's two insurance companies were aware of the fraudulent activity in my case a long time ago. They remained quiet about the crimes committed against me, because they knew that Mr. Goliath and Judge Graft had given credence to the false reports.

I should call the insurance companies and explain my exposure story to them again, and remind them about what the labor code requires them to do regarding the fraudulent activity in my case.

So, I call both insurance companies, however, neither one of them answers the phone, therefore I leave a message asking them to contact me regarding my Workers' Compensation claim. I am not surprised that they do not return my call.

My Workers' Compensation activities have stressed my damaged nerves, causing a lot of pain throughout my body. About two weeks ago when the back of my head, neck, and spine began to swell, I knew that I should rest. However, because I cannot stop working on my case, additional stress causes my heart to beat irregularly and very rapidly.

This evening before supper, my entire nervous system feels as if something is very wrong, and it seems as if I am experiencing a heart attack. I call the county hospital, and when I explain my symptoms to the nurse, she expresses her belief that I am experiencing a heart attack. She tells me to lie down and wait for the medics. Before I lie down, I call Mom and tell her about my symptoms, and she says that she will meet me at the hospital. The medics arrive and take me to the hospital, and after a few tests, my symptoms are diagnosed to be the result of "mixed motor messages" to my heart. After a few hours at the hospital, Mom takes me to her house, and I rest there for a few days.

When I return to my sailboat, I again mail a large amount of documents to Og Construction's insurance company so that I may increase their awareness of the fraudulent activity in my case. A short time later I receive a letter from Og Construction's claims examiner (Document #190) stating that they will not take any action with my case until the court's denial of my case is set aside.

During my last hearing, after I explained the fraudulent activity to the insurance company's attorneys, I emphasized their required Candor to the Tribunal, which means that they must approach the bench and correct the errors in my case. They know that law prohibits them from knowingly allowing their insurance companies to perjure themselves. If they will not uphold truth and justice, then they must withdraw from my case. However, I do not think that they will withdraw because their involvement in my case reveals that they are disgraceful attorneys.

I go to my doctor and show him the letter from Judge Silver, and ask if he would write a letter to him explaining why my health sometimes prevents me from completing court requirements in a timely manner. I am surprised when he says, "James, I can't write a letter like that." My heart falls to the floor, and after I say good-bye, I drag my heart out to my truck.

Before I start my truck, I bow my head and earnestly pray, "Father, there must be an answer, there must be. Please, what could my doctor write?"

I then hear so clearly in my heart, as clearly as one hears with their ears, "Delayed proximal latency."

I sit up a little taller and say, "That is Dr. Connive's comment in her deposition. Thank you Father! This is an excellent answer."

I hurry back into my doctor's office and say, "Doctor, what about delayed proximal latency?"

He smiles and says, "That will work, I can write a letter like that. Wait and I will write it right now."

A short time later, I am grateful when the letter is in my hand. The letter describes my poor health, specifically stating, "Delayed proximal latency" as the reason why I am not able to complete required court paperwork in a timely manner. On my way to the marina, I mail the letter to Judge Silver.

JULY 2004

EACH OF THE LAW AUTHORITIES that I have asked to help me with my Workers' Compensation case have had an excuse as to why he or she would not help me. Mr. Scout warned me that someone would stay one-step ahead of me and nullify all of my efforts. He also said that the Bashan Oil and Og Construction

Attorney's would approach me and offer a settlement if I said that I would tell my story to the media.

I do have a good story for the media, especially with my documentation of fraudulent activity, so now this media idea gives me a lot of hope.

I call a large news agency who is one hour away, and though the woman who answers the phone seems rushed, I briefly describe my exposure story and the fraudulent activity. She seems very interested in my story and says that she would like to look at my documents. Oh, this is almost too good to true. I tell her that I will call her in a few days when I am ready to meet with her, and she says okay.

I wonder if my Father gave me the truck so that I may now drive to the news agency and talk with the media.

My greatest concern about going to the news agency is the summer heat, because heat intensifies my pain and weakness. Although it gets very hot here at the marina, it is not as hot as the oven heat in where the news agency is located. I would rather stay here aboard my sailboat because it has an air conditioner. Last year during the hottest time of the summer, I kept my boat so cool that I often wore sweat pants and wool socks.

However, I do not think that I have a choice. I must go to the very hot city where the news agency is, and talk with the media about my exposure story. I could leave the marina early in the morning when it is cool and arrive at my destination an hour later, talk with the media, and likely return to the marina before lunch. No, that is not a good idea, because that long of a drive will hurt me. It seems best if I drive to the news agency and talk with the media, and then go to an air-conditioned mall and stay there until evening and then sleep in the truck and return to the marina the next morning. And even that will still be very hard on me. Well, a man must do what a man must do, so I should get the truck ready for an overnight visit even though my destination is only one hour from here.

After I duct tape a blue tarp over the back of the truck, I go to the boat and gather my pillow, blanket, enough food and water for three days, and yes, my Bible. I make a comfortable bed in the back of the truck, and as I put these items in my little mobile motel, I feel like I am about to embark on a fun adventure, and after everything is fixed just right, I step back and take a look and think, *Wow, my little truck is now an RV. My radio, I should get my radio.* I quickly go back to my little ship and get my radio, and hurry back to my RV. After I put my radio next to my pillow, I close the tailgate, step back, and take a look and think, *Perfect! No one will ever know that I am asleep in the back of this truck. Well, I should climb in and make sure that is as comfortable as it looks.* I climb in and lie down on my bed and see that the tarp is only a few inches above my head. That's okay, when I am asleep I won't see the tarp. As I lie here, I realize that I should sleep here tonight and make sure that I can sleep here all through the night. And if I sleep okay, then I will throw the lines early in the morning and head for the news agency.

During my evening bath, I realize that I should put two gallons of water in the truck so that I can bathe tomorrow night.

After dark, it seems odd to leave my boat and go to the truck for a night's sleep. However, as I climb into the back of my truck I feel as if my adventure has begun. I climb into bed and feel very comfortable, and I thoroughly enjoy the sounds of the marina as I slip into a deep sleep.

The next morning I awake at first light, and after a good breakfast, I start the truck and say, "Brake release, throttle up."

Upon my arrival at my destination, I call my media contact and am surprised when she says, "We are very busy. Can you call me tomorrow?" I graciously say, "No problem, I will call you tomorrow."

Great, that is not what I want to hear! Well, I might as well make the best of it, so while it is still cool I go to an enjoyable section of the city and look at the excellent sights. When I begin to feel a hint of summer heat, I head for the air conditioned mall, and I feel a little excitement as I begin to explore this giant cool mall.

However, after about an hour, I begin to feel like I have the flu and wish that I was aboard my sailboat so that I could lie down on my star board couch. As I slowly walk, looking for a place to sit, I wonder if anyone thinks that I am on drugs. Some people probably think that I am, because I am very thin and do not look healthy, so my questionable appearance, and the fact that I am not at work, probably makes me look as if I truly am on drugs.

I feel a little better when I see a coffee shop, so I go in and buy an iced tea and go back out to the walkway and sink into a chair.

I rest for about an hour, and then slowly walk around trying my best to look normal and healthy. Eventually, I see a restaurant, so I venture in and buy a nice meal. As I enjoy my meal, I remember the many cold meals that I ate when I lived in the Grand Hotel.

After dinner, I look for another place to sit out in the mall so that I can rest until it is time for me to drive around and look for a place to park, and sleep. As I rest, I consider that when I drive around I need to also find a place where I can bathe, and think, *Great, where will I find a place to bathe. God will show me where I can bathe. I can do this for one night, and tomorrow night I will be back aboard my sailboat.*

Later on, shortly after the sun sets, I begin to drive around, looking for a place where I can hide and quickly bathe. I eventually find a place, and then drive to a different place where I can park and sleep.

I am so grateful too finally lie down on my pillow. Before I fall asleep, I thank my Father for my bed and ask Him if He will please keep the police away from me tonight.

When I awake at 5:34 a.m., I am thankful to realize that I slept through the night, and I am grateful that the police did not wake me. Well, I for sure cannot go back to sleep now, because I hear people, not far away from my truck. I carefully listen, trying to decide when it is the best time for me to open the tailgate and quickly crawl out. As I listen, I slowly and quietly dress. Well, it is difficult to dress when I am horizontal and my ceiling is only a few inches above me. All of my movements are very slow so that I do not shake my truck or the tarp. After I am dressed I lie very still as I listen to more people arrive. My fear of someone discovering me raises my heart rate, causing me to think about my enjoyable easy mornings aboard my sailboat. No doubt, after I talk with my media contact today, I will be very happy to go back to the marina.

Just after 10:00 a.m. I call my media contact and she again tells me, "We are very busy today. Can you call me tomorrow?" The only thing that I can say is, "Okay."

Through the day, I am careful not to go to the same places that I went to yesterday so that no one will think that I am a homeless person. My concern is that I feel like everyone can see that I am not well. I desperately wish that I were aboard my air conditioned sailboat.

Every day, through the following two weeks my media contact tells me, "We are very busy today. Can you call me tomorrow?" And each time I graciously say, "Okay, I will call you tomorrow."

Through the past two weeks, my lifestyle has exhausted me.

As I begin my third week my media contact asks, "Is your case still in litigation?"

When I tell her that I am trying to bring my case back into court she responds, "We cannot report on cases that are in litigation."

After her statement, I am thankful that my heart starts again.

I say good-bye to this very hot city, and rush back to my cool, beloved sailboat.

A few days before my media contact said, "We cannot report on cases that are in litigation," I began to understand during prayer that it was not yet the right time for me to contact the media. Logic would disagree; however, the counsels in Heaven are trustworthy. I just wish that I had prayed more about this before I left the sailboat.

I am very grateful when I arrive at the marina, and as I walk down the ramp to the dock, I am pleased to hear the enjoyable sounds of this marina. When I see my boat, I look intently at it, as if it were a brick of gold.

During the evening I notice that the tide has come in, making us at high water. So I go top side, and while I recline on my boom leaning against the mast, I enjoy a most beautiful sunset.

Later when I climb into my bunk, the slow movement of my boat, and leisurely rhythm of the dock lines gently ease me into a most restful, deep sleep.

Early the next morning, while I fix breakfast, I reach up and slide the hatch open, and after breakfast I pour another cup of hot coffee, and go top side and sit on the boom. While the sun slowly rises, I slowly sip my coffee. My little ship is good balm for my heart and damaged nerves.

This morning when I awake, I think, *Good deal, today is Friday, the girls will be here this evening.* Later, before dinner, I hear one of the happiest sounds in this marina, and that is when I hear the girls coming down the dock toward my boat. We are always so happy when we are back together.

The next morning we enjoy a good sailboat breakfast, and after Bible time we watch Lawrence Welk and Bob Ross. When we hear the girls' two friends out on the dock we invite them to come aboard and play our favorite card game, My Ship Sails.

Sunday evening after the girls leave, I consider that I have not received a response from Workers' Compensation regarding my request for another hearing. I could call them tomorrow, however, I feel inclined to speak with them face to face.

The next morning after I shave, I head for Workers' Compensation, and as I drive, the summer heat makes me feel very weak and ill, and I wonder how much longer I can strive for justice.

When I arrive at the clerk's window, I am thankful to see the familiar kind clerk who has helped me for about thirteen years. However, when I greet her, I discern for the first time a negative attitude toward me, and I have the impression that she is not going to help me. This is odd, and it seems as if someone has spoken to her about me. Well, I am not going to let this trouble me, as she might just be upset because of a personal matter. I mention that I filed for a hearing more than a year ago, and that I have not received a response. Her reply is short and rude, as if her problem is with me. Now I know for sure that someone has told her not to help me. Now that I clearly understand that she is defiant toward me, I ask her for a piece of blank paper, and after she gives me the paper, I sit down and write the following note:

DOCUMENT #198: NOTE TO WORKERS' COMPENSATION

To: Workers' Compensation,

I have filed for a hearing. I have provided the paperwork you have requested. My hearing request was 14 months ago! I have not received paperwork from you regarding my request!

James Landon

When I return to the window, I say, "Will you please put this paper in my file."

I am surprised that she will not even look at my paper as she boldly looks at me and says that she will not file my paper. I explain to her that fourteen months ago Judge Silver wrote a letter to me stating that he would consider granting another hearing for me if my doctor would write a letter explaining my medical problems that hinder me from filing court paperwork in a timely manner. I mention that my doctor did write that letter. However, after I sent the doctors' letter to Judge Silver he did not responded to my letter or the other four letters that I mailed to him describing the information he requested. I mention that it is very important that she file this paper so that I will have evidence in my file that I am attempting to proceed with my case. However, she defiantly says that she is not going to file my paper, and as she turns to walk away, I boldly say, "It is very important that I have some evidence in my file that I am attempting to proceed with my case."

She returns to the window and rudely says that she is not going to file my paper. As she turns to walk away, I say passionately, "If you don't file my paper, I will call the police. Then my effort will be documented."

She rudely says, "Go ahead!"

I walk out, not believing what had just occurred.

On my way to the lobby, I ask my Father why this problem happened, and what I should think. I clearly understand that there is a unified effort within Workers' Compensation to stop my pursuit of justice, even here at this clerk's window. I have the impression that someone within Workers' Compensation has flagged my name. The honest Workers' Compensation attorney was right when she told me, "After you file your twenty-five page documentation, things are going to heat up," which they certainly have, in all departments.

When I get to the lobby, I stand by the pay phone for a moment, and try to slow my heart rate by taking a few deep breaths before I call the police. After I speak with the police, I sit and wait for an hour and a half for them to arrive. When two officers finally walk into the lobby, I approach them and introduce myself. When they learn that I was the one who called for them, they become upset with me and say, "We have more important things to do." When they start to leave, I feel a little desperate, so I quickly mention the crimes in my case, thinking this will compel them to stay and help me. For a moment, my ploy seems to work. However, after I describe the history of my case and the altered reports, they turn to leave. As they turn from me, I realize that if I artfully persuade them, they will likely stay and help me. So I say to them, with a strong hint of my former boxer/Harley strength, "Officers, when you leave I am going up to Workers' Compensation to file my paper myself."

They quickly turn back to me, and I look into the eyes of the officer who is about six foot three inches tall, and say with a hint of boldness, "When you leave I am going up to file this paper, even if I need to go over the counter and file it myself. This paper will be filed today."

My tactic works. The tall officer looks at his partner and then steps about eight feet away, and uses his cell phone to call Workers' Compensation. I wonder, *How does this officer just happen to have the number for Workers' Compensation in his phone*. I surmise that someone from Workers' Compensation has already contacted him.

A moment later a stocky, well-built man from the Workers' Compensation office comes down to the lobby, and after he tells the officers who he is, he looks at me, expecting me to hand my paper to him. However, before I give my paper to him, I say, "I want a stamped copy."

The tallest officer says, "No copy."

I look at the tallest officer as if I am taller than he is and say, "Officer, I am walking out of here with a stamped copy."

The officer says to the Workers' Compensation man, "Bring back a stamped copy."

Moments later the Workers' Compensation man returns with a stamped copy of my paper. I thank the man and the officers for their help, and all of us gladly part from each other.

During the drive back to my sailboat, I am so happy, because I believe that Workers' Compensation will certainly respond to me now.

Each day I eagerly wait for a response letter from Workers' Compensation. However, after a considerable time, I realize that Workers' Compensation has again chosen to ignore me.

If the media and Workers' Compensation will not speak with me, there must be another way that I can further expose the fraudulent activity in my case and gain justice. I have informed all involved parties about the inaccurate reports in my case, and since labor code requires all involved parties to do what is best and right for an injured worker, I think that I should mail copies of forty-six documents to Og Construction and both insurance companies.

I estimate the cost of copying forty-six documents for each party and realize, *I do not have enough money to do this...no way. But it must be done. I must not give up or slow down, and I must adequately inform all parties about the crimes committed against me, as if they did not already know. Now is the time to establish guilt and call for justice. The time and cost will be worth it, because someone might respond to me in a proper manner.*

By the time I finish making what seems like a billion copies, I quickly pick up all of my papers because the copy store is closing. I am so tired and weak that I do not feel as if I can drive back to the marina, so I walk out to my truck, open the tailgate, climb into my mobile motel, and sink into my bed. I quickly fall asleep, and in the morning when I awake, I head back to the marina so I can write a cover letter. My cover letter states that Judge Silver said that he will grant me another hearing, and I also describe how rude the woman at the window was when I tried to file my paper. I close my letter stating that law requires them to report the fraudulent activity in my case to the district attorney.

After a day of rest, I put my hat on and head to town to purchase large envelopes. After the envelopes are addressed, filled, sealed and mailed, I go back to my boat and rest for a few days. Well, now that I have spent so much money I will have to be very frugal for the remainder of the month.

Through the past year and a half, I have met with almost twenty attorneys in their offices, asking them to help me with my case. Each of them was interested until they learned that a judge was involved. Two of them even yelled at me because I would not give up my court efforts.

Now I think that it is a good idea for me to search for an attorney in the two cities east of the marina, because one of those cities is where the courthouse is, and that is why there is an abundance of attorneys there.

To avoid the expense of commuting, I will sleep in my mobile motel under a train trestle in one of those cities. After I put a few days of food and water in the back of the truck, I head out for another mission in my pursuit of justice.

The first week passes, and I have not obtained an attorney, but I must not give up. My continuing injustice seems like time and tides, which never stop.

By now, I have learned the art of hiding during the late evening so that I can bathe with two gallons of water. A man must do what a man must do.

My activities, and a lack of proper rest, greatly stress my diseased nervous system. However, if I rest as I should, who will fight for justice for my daughters and me?

Toward the end of the second week, my stressed nerves develop a problem with my breathing, especially when I lie down. I hope that my lungs are not also beginning to receive mixed-motor messages. I feel like I should stop my search for an attorney, and return to my boat so that I can properly rest. However, I am very concerned about my breathing problem, so I think that it is best that I stay in this area, close to the hospital, just in case I need immediate medical attention.

Two nights later at about 9:30 p.m., after I lie down, my breathing becomes very labored, and I can only draw about 80 percent of the air that I need. So I quickly go to the emergency room. Through the night, as hospital staff observes me, they eventually believe that the motor nerve to my diaphragm is receiving mixed-motor messages. They do not know what to do for me, so they monitor me for several hours. Then at about 4:30 a.m., they see that my breathing is much better, so they send me on my way. I should return to the marina, but I think that I will remain close to the hospital for another night or two, because my breathing problem scares me.

I return to my spot under the train trestle and quickly fall asleep until a train passes over the trestle at about 6:30 a.m. I would like to look out at the train, but I cannot because commuters are beginning to park their cars all around me.

I turn my radio on, and put it close to my ear, making sure that the volume is low enough so that no one will discover my presence.

The cool morning air feels so good, and the early morning birds sound very happy, so I decide to join them in the woods behind my truck. That is, until I realize that John MacArthur's Christian radio program "Grace to You" is about to start. After his program, I will go on a short walk into the woods so I can spend some time in prayer.

During the radio program, I hear someone walking across the gravel parking lot toward my truck, making my heart rate increase. When the footsteps stop next to my truck, my heart almost beats out of my chest, because it sounds like someone is standing about one foot away from me! I turn my radio off and lie very still, hoping they do not hear my pounding heart.

As this person gets into his car, my truck moves a little, making me think that he is door-dinging my truck!

When the engine of the car next to me starts, I think, *That's amazing. That engine sounds just like mine.*

However, when my truck begins to roll, I realize, *Someone is stealing my truck! How did they open my locked door?* Now I do not care if they hear my pounding heart.

As my truck rolls about twenty feet my old Harley/boxer boldness returns to me. So, I pull the tarp back, and with an authoritative voice I say to the driver, "Hey there. Where are we going?"

He is very surprised when he turns around and sees me in the back of the truck, and no doubt, he can see that I am very serious when I say, "I'm going wherever you are going. We'll talk when we get there!"

A car behind us then pulls up alongside of us, and the driver of that car says to the thief in my truck, "Come on. Let's get out of here!"

As my truck begins to slow, I lower the tailgate at the same time the thief opens the driver's door of my truck. I exit a little before he does, and when we meet face to face, I think God's presence with me frightens him. My truck is still rolling, so I let him go, and jump into my truck and apply the brakes.

After I stop the truck, I am surprised to find his keys in the ignition. He had filed off the edges of some keys to eight different vehicles. That is why he was able to open my locked door and start my engine.

Oh, how grateful I am that I stayed in my truck so that I could listen to John MacArthur. If I had walked into the woods, that punk would have stolen my truck, and all the valuables inside. However, my gratitude turns to disappointment when I discover that he took my small backpack, which contained my wallet. Almost all of my money for this month was in that wallet. The extra activity to replace the things that he took will certainly take a toll on my damaged nervous system. This is not the best way for me to start the morning in this cute little river town. I call the police so that I can report the two car thieves. After they arrive, as I tell them about my ordeal, one of them interrupts me and asks, "Why were you lying in the back of your truck?" Thankfully, they believe me when I tell them why I need to stay close to the hospital. However, I do not think that I should sleep under this trestle again tonight.

Before the sun begins to set, I drive to a remote area about halfway to the marina near the other city, thinking that I will sleep here for the night. After my two-gallon bath, I climb into my mobile motel, put on my pajamas, and quickly fall asleep. At around 2:00 a.m., I awake when I feel my truck slightly move. I immediately realize that someone is messing with my truck, so I quickly pull the tarp back and sit up for a look. When I see that my hood is up, I lean to my left and see a tall man walking away with my battery. I quickly climb out of the truck, and when I discover that the thief broke out my driver's side window, I learn that I am standing barefoot in broken glass. When I turn and look at the thief, I see that he is not aware of my presence, so I quickly and quietly run toward him. When I am a few feet behind him I commandingly say, "Hey there!"

I have never seen anyone turn around so fast, and no doubt, he is very surprised to see me. When our eyes lock on each other, I think that God's presence with me frightens him, because I see great fear in his eyes, until he looks down at my pajamas. However, fear comes back to him, when I say with a slow, sober tone, "Put the battery down and back away."

My authoritative and courageous voice must make him think that I am a former US Navy SEAL, because I now see deep fear in his eyes as he slowly lowers my battery to the ground. His release of the battery is quick, but his rise is cautious and slow. He slowly backs away keeping his eyes on me, until after a few feet he turns and trots to the car that is waiting for him up on the highway. As I watch him go all the way up to the highway until he gets into a car, I cannot help but laugh, wondering what he is telling his friends about the weird courageous man down there who is wearing pajamas.

The police must have watched this ordeal through highway cameras, because two police cars arrive before I climb back into my truck. I am certainly embarrassed because of my pajamas, and when one of them asks for my identification, I feel like an idiot because my wallet was stolen just this morning. I take a deep breath, and tell them where I live, and why I slept under a train trestle. When I mention the two car thieves, I begin to see compassion in their eyes. One of them asks if I know my driver's license number. Thankfully, I actually remember it, and after I state my number the officer steps away, and a moment later he returns and says to the other officers, "He's okay."

As they start to leave, I thank them for their kind understanding and then turn and stare at my truck, wondering how much a window will cost. After a few hours of sleep, I awake and go to the wrecking yard and find a window for my truck, which takes almost all of my remaining money. As I install the window, I realize that I should go back to the safety and comfort of my little ship.

When I return to the marina the harbormaster's office informs me that I have not paid slip rent for twelve months. This stuns me because I thought that I had only missed a few months of rent. Through the past months, my desperate activities have caused the back of my head to remain swollen, which caused me to lose track of time. Now I wonder about other responsibilities I may have neglected. I understand that I am not thinking correctly because I lost discipline with my monthly budget and it is now in a terrible mess.

I owe $2,000 in slip rent, which I do not have. Therefore, I decide to give my $9,000 sailboat to the harbormaster's office. No doubt if my mind was in better condition, I am certain that I would slowly pay all of my back rent. I am very sad to lose my beloved little ship. If I start to complain about the loss of my sailboat, I will put my hand over my mouth so that God does not hear me complain about the lack of discipline with my money. However, I will for sure thank God for allowing me to live aboard my sailboat for eleven good years.

Because of my poor health, I am not able to remove all of my possessions from my boat. That is probably best because my new home, which is my un-safe mobile motel, is very small. Another problem with living in my truck is that it is now early winter.

About a week later, when Mom learns that I now live in the back of my truck, she suggests that I live with Grandma. This idea pleases the family because Grandma and I will be of great help to each other. My first night at Grandma's house brings back many fond memories of when I was a young boy in this home. The best thing about living here is that I am only a few minutes away from my daughters.

MAY 2005 SIXTEEN YEARS AFTER MY EXPOSURE
ONE DAY WHILE I AM out in the garage with my uncle, Grandma opens the door and says, "James, there's an attorney on the phone for you."

I can hardly believe what Grandma has just said, but with enthusiasm I say, "An attorney? My letters! An attorney must be calling me because of my letters!"

Suddenly I feel like a young prince who is about to receive his father's crown. With enthusiasm, I quickly go to the phone. Before I pick up the phone, I calm myself, because I do not want to give this person the impression that I am naïve and vulnerable. After I take a deep breath, I pick up the phone and say, "Hello." The attorney sounds very professional when he says, "Mr. Landon, I am Mr. Musk, an attorney. What settlement amount do you have in mind?"

Tears form in my eyes as I think, *A new attorney! Bashan Oil has hired a new attorney so that we can finalize my case!*

I gain control of my slightly shaking voice before I say, "A settlement amount?"

The attorney says, "We cannot proceed until we know what amount you have in mind."

This is the moment that I have worked so long and so hard for. I gather all of my mental skills, take command of my emotional heart, and say, "Mr. Musk, we should first review my exposure, and my exposure symptoms before we discuss a settlement amount."

Before he has a chance to talk, I describe my exposure, my nerve disease, the doctors' altered reports, and my vast preponderance of evidence. I also mention that we will look at a Range of Compensation Formula before we discuss any settlement amount.

I am very pleased to hear Mr. Musk suggest that we schedule a meeting. His suggestion makes me feel a little numb as I think, *A meeting! All of my hard work and many prayers have prevailed.*

We set the meeting for June 3, 2005, and say goodbye to each other. I sit for a moment, thinking about the many years of failed attempts, and now they have contacted me to resolve this matter.

Grandma stood close to me during the conversation between this attorney and me, so she is very curious to her about our talk. As I explain, tears begin to form in my eyes, especially when I mention that it seems like this long ordeal is almost over. Though the girls and I are not as close as we once were, hopefully a settlement will make it possible for us to live in a home together before they grow up. I call the girls and then Mom and tell them all about my talk with Mr. Musk. I ask Mom if she and my sister will go to the meeting with me, and no doubt, she says yes. My talk with the attorney has caused a lot of excitement in my family.

On June 3, Mom, and my sister and I arrive at Mr. Musk's office. We are awed to see that his office is the entire floor of a prestigious downtown high-rise building. His office is evidence of his great wealth, and power accumulated from a very successful law practice.

When we are seated at his desk and with all of the critical documents in my lap, he begins to talk. However, in less than a minute, I start to question his integrity.

I interrupt him by asking, "Mr. Musk, did you review the Workers' Compensation paperwork regarding my case," as I hand him copies of the documents.

His facial expression gives me a hint that he is surprised that I have interrupted him, but he says, "Yes, I did."

He continues to talk, however, within a short time I interrupt him again by saying, "If you reviewed that paperwork, then you are aware of the fraud, breach of obligation, willful misconduct, and of course, my vast preponderance of evidence."

I see that he is surprised at my knowledge of the law, and I more fully understand his true nature when he says, "We are not going to call it fraud unless a judge states that it is fraud."

He notices the increased soberness in my eyes when I say, "That is exactly what both insurance companies told me. And I can tell you for sure that the judge is not going to declare fraud in my case because it is the judge who is guilty of fraud."

Mr. Musk says again, "We are not going to call it fraud unless a judge states that it is fraud."

As I look into his eyes, I consider that he is wasting my time. I realize that I must take command and direct our talk because this attorney is not harmonious with the law. So I say, "You know about Candor to the Tribunal. It is required of you to approach your client, and the bench, and tell both of them about the errors, and the truth in my case."

He attempts to change the subject, which confirms my conclusion that he lacks integrity, and is just another puppet. I again describe the history of my exposure, my resulting disease, the doctors' altered reports, and my preponderance of evidence. When he does not respond, I am concerned, and completely understand this *puppet's* true nature when he says, "We will offer you five hundred dollars to settle your claim."

I sit up a little taller and say, "That is an insult."

He then says, "Okay, then we will offer you one thousand dollars."

The intolerant expression on my face causes him to say, "Fifteen hundred dollars."

I stand and exclaim, "That is an insult to me. This meeting is over."

Mom, my sister and I briskly walk out, and head for the car. During our drive home, Mom and my sister mention that they are shocked at that attorney's insolent and unprofessional manner of business with my case. They become quiet when I say, "This is exactly what I have been dealing with for many years from numerous people regarding my Workers' Compensation case."

Note to the reader: The following explanation describes why I named this attorney Mr. Musk.

Musk is a strong penetrating odor secreted by certain animals such as the alligator. This perfume scent draws prey to the animal that secrets the odor. Like an alligator, Mr. Musk's perfumed settlement offer drew me to him for cruel reasons that I do not fully understand. I wonder why this attorney contacted me, because a few authorities have told me that my statutes of limitations expired three years ago. Mr. Musk knows something that he is not disclosing! He did however, confirm by his contact with me that my case is still actionable, as I well know. His insult is a strong blow to me, and burns within my heart.

How many blows or insults can a man take before he throws in the towel, especially when he is suffering from enormous mental and physical difficulties? As a constant flowing river erodes a strong rock, so do my unrelenting trials wear me down. I can feel it every day as my heart cries; my situation seems hopeless. I feel so heavy because the many cruel Workers' Compensation puppets, and my many afflictions, have clothed me with exhaustion. I know it, because I wear it every day. No doubt, this is an opportune time for Satan to take advantage of my weak, hopeless state, and easily convince me that there is no hope because of the logic and psychology of my trials. This is truly a convenient, logical time for Satan to shake me until I fall into a state of hopeless despair. However, God's presence indwelling me, and His Word open to me, inspires me, sustaining me with uncommon heavenly might, and God honoring faith, and hope against all hope. This is a great opportune time for me, because trials open my ears, and incline my heart to the mind and will of God. And no doubt, God uses trials to shake me from this world, which means that I must let my trials humble me, and make me truly contrite, which is explained in the following verse:

For thus saith he that is high and excellent, he that inhabiteth the eternity, whose Name is the Holy one, I dwell in the high and holy place: with him also that is of a contrite and humble spirit to revive the spirit of the humble, and to give life to them that are of a contrite heart.

ISAIAH 57:15

Thus, as I walk with God, and sit before Him in prayer I truly enjoy a renewing, sweet time with Him. I am truly a most fortunate man who is learning by trials to walk humbly as an uncommon man of God.

It seems to me that Mr. Musk failed to accomplish his cruel work with me. However, what he did accomplish within me is to provoke me to contact again all of the involved parties. I mail vital documents to all them, and then patiently wait for their responses. After a long time passes, I realize that none of them are going to respond. They have again put their backs to me.

I refuse to give up, so Mom and I mail crucial documents to the following authorities, that we have not previously contacted:

Document 208: Letters to State Attorney General and the State Superior Court Judge
June 27, 2005

Document 210: Letter to Attorney General's Office of Public Inquiry Unit
June 27, 2005

Document 211: Letter to the State Superior Court
June 30, 2005

We are hopeful, and based on the law, we truly believe that these authorities will help us.

CHAPTER 23

Healing Wounds in a Coastal Town

⤳

...My presence shall go *with thee*, and I will give thee rest.
EXODUS 33:14

JULY 2005

THE FIRST EIGHT MONTHS WITH Grandma are very good. However, now at the beginning of summer, it gets very hot here and I am absolutely miserable. Each day when I first begin to feel summer heat, I think about how cool it is under the house, and wish that I could rest there until evening. I mention the idea to Grandma, and she says that would be silly. Thankfully, she thinks that I am joking, but I am not. When the temperature rises above sixty-five degrees, I begin to feel very weak and ill.

The only problem here at Grandma's house is that my drug-addicted uncle also lives here. Before his addiction, I truly enjoyed him. However, now he is a constant problem, and when he threatens to beat me with a large piece of wood, I decide to leave, and go to I do not know where.

When Mom learns about this problem, she invites me to live with her again. I feel better just thinking about living with Mom, because she lives in a coastal town where it is always foggy and cool.

After I arrive at Mom's, she is troubled to see that my boots are almost too heavy for me when I climb the stairs to her bedroom.

Every day she comments about how skinny and weak I am, because she remembers when I was thirty-five pounds heavier with solid muscle. She has no idea how embarrassed I am, because my clothes now hang loose on me, and no longer reveal a hint of my previous strong, healthy body.

Through the first four months at Mom's, my body insists that I lie down for an hour twice each day, and then climb into bed at about seven-thirty. Well, not really into bed because I sleep on the floor at the far end of Mom's large bedroom. However, each day I feel a little better because of the refreshing, salty cool air.

I am pleased to live one-minute from the ocean. But I am sad because I now live one-hour away from my daughters. For now that is okay, because I am learning by God's help to make the best of my situation.

Every day I fill my thermos with hot green tea and head for the beach, where I am safe because it is always too cool for women in bathing suits, and because many of my friends are always there. When they see my truck approach, they rush to meet me. Before I arrive, they gather at the spot where I always park, and when I pull in alongside them, I open the truck door and throw birdseed all over them. These little bird-friends have no idea how happy I am to sit with them.

Today as usual, while I feed my bird-friends, the cool, moist, foggy weather allows me to leave the door of my truck open for only a few minutes. So I close the door, turn on the heater, and while my truck slightly warms, I reach for my thermos and pour a cup of hot green tea. I look to my right at the quiet, pretty meadow, and then to my left at the arrival of continuous ocean waves. Looking at the waves draws my gaze out across the sea, putting me into deep thought about my sailboat.

While I behold my birds-friends, I am intimately aware of the beautiful meadow and the great blue ocean. All three of these delights cause a rare good feeling to flow through my diseased nerves. I then hear in my heart, *These delights are only three of the many delights that the angels above God's throne sing about.* I follow my thought and open my Bible to Isaiah chapter six, and read verses two, three, and four. In this text, special angels above God's throne sing a hymn to each other, saying,

...the whole world is full of his glory.
Isaiah 6:3

With greater delight, I look back to the meadow and ponder the beauty of God's glory, so well displayed in all of the amazing life in this meadow. After a long moment, little chirping birds draw my attention back to them. I slowly open my door and throw more birdseed out to them, and then quickly close the door. While I stare at them, considering God's glory, the arrival of ocean waves draws my attention back to the impressive ocean, and as I look, considering its depth, breadth, and all of the amazing life within this great expanse of water, I am amazed at God's glory. My gaze continues until fog limits my deep strong stare. So I look at what is not foggy, the Bible. After reverently reading my Bible and spending some time in prayer, I go back to the house and tell Mom about my inspiring time at the beach.

Every day my awe of nature is balm for my damaged nerves, and my enjoyment of scripture is balm for my damaged soul, improving the health of my body and inner man.

During my recent study about Labor Code, I learn that the FBI is required to investigate the type of crimes committed against me. So today, I am on my way to the FBI so that I can talk with an agent about my case. When I step into the FBI facility, I am impressed with the astute demeanor of the agent who greets me. While I carefully explain my exposure, and the incorrect and correct reports, the agent listens intently, writing many detailed notes.

When our talk ends, I give him copies of all of my reports, and on my way home, I feel good about this talk with the agent.

The next morning the agent calls the house and tells my sister that the FBI is going to begin an investigation of my case. This good news again causes a lot of excitement in my family.

Through the following days, as I continuously think about the FBI investigating the crimes in my case, I am so very happy.

After about two weeks, I go back to the FBI, and am stunned when the same agent tells me that he cannot find my file. The agent tries to negate the loss of my file by telling me that my statutes are expired. I try to bring him back in harmony with me by telling him that fraud, willful misconduct, and breach of an obligation waives statutes of limitations. He becomes a little stiff before he tells me that the FBI does not deal with my type of problem, and I become a little sober before I tell him that the FBI website states that, "The FBI investigates insurance fraud." Before he responds I say, "We are talking about insurance fraud." When he tries to change the subject, I interrupt him and say, "Your website also states that the FBI investigates public corruption, and Workers' Compensation fraud."

The agent tries again to avoid his obligation by saying that I should take my dilemma to the district attorney. I surprise him when I say that I have talked with the DA, and two other DAs from different counties seven times, and each of them was willing to help me until they learned that a Workers' Compensation judge was involved.

The agent tries again to take the lead by saying that the district attorneys' believe that they do not have the authority to prosecute problems like mine. As I pull a report from my paperwork, the agent prepares himself for another blow. When I look back into his eyes, I say, "This is a report regarding insurance fraud, fraud committed by insurance companies. The investigation of this type of insurance fraud discovered that DA's avoid their duty to investigate dilemmas like mine because they choose to."

The atmosphere becomes very uncomfortable because the agent knows that I have backed him into a corner from which he cannot escape. However, he does escape from me by saying, "Let me go and check on your file."

As he walks away, I think, *Check my file? When I arrived he said that he could not find my file.*

Thirty seconds later the agent returns and says, "I have someone else I need to talk with. Our meeting is over."

As I shake his hand, I look intently into his eyes and say, "Workers' Compensation fraud is very prevalent because there is no accountability, no restraint, and no fear of punishment." He does not respond, so I turn and leave.

A short time after our meeting, I receive a letter from the FBI agent (Document #214). The letter explains that the FBI was created to investigate federal matters, and therefore they are not permitted to conduct any action with my case. I am very surprised to read that no judicial decisions in any court are reviewable by a law enforcement agency. After I read the letter to Mom I say, "This is one reason as to why judges have no concern about committing crimes."

Because of the way in which the FBI handled my case, I understand why there is an erosion of public confidence in the FBI.

I was not asking the FBI to investigate the decision of any court, but to investigate the actual crimes committed against me. Through the past seventeen years and two months, discouragement has weighed me down many times. I refuse to let Agent Silly weigh me down with discouragement.

After I mail yet another letter and a few more necessary documents to a Superior Court Judge, I receive a letter from Superior Court Judge Defer (Document #209). In his letter he mentions that I should take my case to the Workers' Compensation Division of the Department of Industrial Relations.

By now, I am not surprised when an authority shuns me.

Mom takes me to the local hospital for another nerve conduction test (Document #215). This test verifies that my nerve disease is prevalent throughout my entire body.

After Dr. Proof Positive completes my test, he gives me some very bad news when he says, "You have had your disease for so long now that it cannot be reversed." And he also informs me that based on my previous test, the disease is progressing.

If Workers' Compensation and other responsible parties had properly handled my injury, I would have likely recovered my health and returned to work, and I would have enjoyed a good life with my daughters.

The doctors' bad news provokes me to try again to obtain justice. When Mom and I begin to type letters to Senator's [1] and [2], I suggest that we not mention anything about the judge's involvement in my case. She agrees and says, "Everyone has been willing to help you, until you mention the judge's involvement in your case. Do you remember that Mr. Scout told us that if we correct a judge, no one will help us?" I say, "I do, I do remember his comment. However, our legislature drafted laws to prosecute corrupt judges, so we have an obligation to document the crimes within Workers' Compensation, and show these crimes to certain authorities." As Mom nods yes, she says, "I agree." I add, "I am certain that the Senators will offer to help us, and after that we will mention the judge's involvement in my case."

We mail letters to the Senators describing my exposure, and why my Workers' Compensation claim was denied. Within a short time we are very happy with the Senator's response. Senator #1's letter states that the Senator is pleased to file a formal inquiry with the US Department of Labor on my behalf.

Senator #2's letter is also very encouraging; stating that after their staff reviewed my letter they have decided to do all that they can to help me.

Mom and I are elated for their offer to help us. However, as Mom and I prepare to take the documents to the senators' offices, I tell Mom that the senators will likely withdraw their help when they learn that two Workers' Compensation judges are involved in the fraudulent activity of my case.

After we deliver the documents, I am not surprised when we receive a letter from Senator #1's office stating that state officials are in the best position to help me with my Workers' Compensation matter. This Senator's office recommends that I contact a different *state* senator.

We contact the suggested Senator requesting help. However, the senator does not help us.

A short time later we receive a letter from Senator #2's Office stating that the Senator is sorry to hear about my difficulties with Workers' Compensation. The Senator thanks me for my trust in the Senators Office, and yet sends me back all of my paperwork and suggests that I contact the Governor's Office because the Senator has been assured that the Governor's staff will work hard to resolve my matter.

Well, we are very disappointed with Senator #2's change of mind to help me. However, we are pleased with her confidence that the Governor's office will help us. So, Mom and I begin to draft a letter to the Governor's office.

Each evening I listen to a very interesting AM radio program called "Coast to Coast." The guest last night was Dr. Lorraine Day, who talked about how she reversed her own severe, advanced cancer by rebuilding her immune system. Her story was amazing, because even though she rejected western medicine, she healed herself by consuming a proper diet. Her diet consisted of a wide variety of vegetables and unprocessed, organic food. She eliminated all processed foods and white sugar from her diet. Dr. Day's website is rich with information (drday.com).

Because of my dull mind, my monthly budget is still a mess, and as a result, I am not able to order Dr. Day's DVD and workbook. However, I learned enough last night from Dr. Day to get me started on a proper diet.

After my first healthy meal, I feel slightly better, which encourages me to follow Dr. Day's advice. As the days pass, my health slowly improves, which inspires me to start exercising. Each evening I go to the garage and stretch, and then wave my arms from side to side. That is all I can do for now, but that is okay, because I am greatly inspired to improve my health, especially when I recall my former training with John Alacrity. I estimate that I spend about 10 percent more for organic food than I did for nonorganic food.

A short time later, I discover another amazing doctor on the radio. He is Dr. Marshall, a PhD clinical nutritionist who has treated more than fifty thousand patients. His knowledge, experience, and advice greatly encourage me, and give me a lot of hope for the recovery of my health. During his radio program, people call Dr. Marshall and ask various questions about personal health issues, which make his program both educational and interesting. Dr. Marshall's website (QNLabs.com) is also rich with information.

A few months later, I listen to a brain specialist on the Coast to Coast radio station. He describes how important exercise is for the brain, especially for a person who has suffered damage to his brain. He says that if the brain is healthy, the body is better equipped to heal itself from illness or injury. He also mentions that if a person exercises for at least twenty minutes, a certain chemical is produced in the brain that will improve one's quality of sleep.

This brain specialist inspires me to exercise both my body and my brain. No doubt the best way to exercise my brain is to memorize scripture. So each morning after breakfast, I go to the garage and memorize Bible verses for about an hour. I am very happy to memorize scripture again, but I am also saddened to realize that my intellect has become so very weak. When I put a verse into my brain, I try with all of my might to grab the verse and hold onto it. However, it feels as if there is nothing in my brain to grab the verse with, so it quickly slips away, as if I have reached out with my hand to grab a hologram. I am not going to give up; I will try harder. After one month of memorizing scripture, I can only quote a few verses.

Though I am very ill, I feel good about myself, because my daily Bible reading, prayer time, memorization of scripture, proper diet, and exercise are building good character into my life.

Note to reader: Coast to Coast also has a website (CoasttoCoast.com) with information regarding other interesting programs regarding various vital subjects.

CHAPTER 24

Still Seeking

‿

SOMETIMES WHAT WE ASK FOR, AND SEEK AFTER, IS NOT WHAT GOD HAS INTENDED FOR US.

And I say unto you, Ask, and it shall be given you: seek, and ye shall find: knock, and it shall be opened unto you.

LUKE 11:9

EARLY NOVEMBER 2005

As I CONTINUE LISTENING TO the radio, I hear another interesting guest speaker, Julie Simmons. She is a well-known, vigorous advocate for disabled veterans who have been neglected by our government. Since I am not able to find any medical or legal help in this state, I know I must seek advice from her. From past experience in speaking with people on the phone about my case, they did not believe me until I met with them in person and show them my documentation.

She lives about seventeen hundred miles from here, which is a problem. It is too far for me to drive, because when I drive for more than an hour at a time the back of my head and neck become very swollen and painful.

I have also heard a husband and wife talk on the radio that live only a few states away, which I believe would be a great help to me in solving my

Workers' Compensation problem. I call them, and thankfully, they agree to meet with me for some counsel.

Mom is happy to hear that this couple is willing to meet with me, and hands me her credit card to purchase all of my gasoline and pay for hotels. I agree, but only if I can repay her. A few weeks later, I once again pack my mobile motel and in late October head out. A man must do what a man must do, again.

After about an hour of driving on the highway, the back of my head and neck become very swollen and painful, and now because my thinking is so poor, I drive past my exit, and do not realize my error until I am almost at the southern border of the United States. I am so upset with myself! The only thing I can do now is head for my destination and find a place to stop for the night.

Though it is a chilly November evening, I take a two-gallon bucket bath in a hidden place, and then climb into the back of my truck for a night's rest. Thankfully, I now have a camper shell on my truck.

A few days later, when I finally make my way to within a few miles from their house, I call and am disappointed when the husband says that he is too busy to meet with me.

Because of his type of work, I completely understand. He does not know that I have driven so far to meet with him, nor does he know about my poor health. I am certain that if he knew about my sorrows, sufferings, and losses he would try to meet with me because he is a good, sincere, Christian man. After he told me that he cannot meet with me, he asks me to explain more about why I wanted to talk with him, and after I explain my Workers' Compensation problem, he suggested that I meet with Julie Simmons. Now I understand that it is ordained by my Father that I keep driving and meet with Mrs. Simmons. I call Mrs. Simmons and explain my Workers' Compensation problem, and thankfully, though she is very busy, she agrees to meet with me.

As I travel on, my nerve disease is taking a toll on me, and my thinking is so poor that I am not able to find the correct interstate to continue on. I desperately need to find a place to rest for a few days. So I venture up a dirt road that stretches up into the mountains, and at about seventy-five hundred feet, I park and camp for two nights. Though I am in a lot of pain, I am very happy to be here. After a two-day mountain rest, I continue my travels eastward.

After more than a week of traveling, I finally arrive at the little town where Mrs. Simmons lives. When I meet her, she makes me feel like I am where I should be. After I tell her about my exposure, and the incorrect and correct reports she looks at my documents and says, "James, your story is amazing, and your documentation is rare and big. When you are back at your house, attempt justice in the court one more time and then write a book." I reply, "A book! I have actually thought about writing a book." She says, "Your story would be a great benefit to many people, especially my wounded veterans. Do you know how to write a book?" I tell her no, but that Mom has always dreamed about writing a book, so I am sure that if Mom and I work together, we will be able to compose a good book. Mrs. Simmons says, "When your book is finished, I'll help you promote it."

Well, I can hardly wait to go home and write a book with Mom.

No doubt, providence directed me to travel so far to meet with Mrs. Simmons. Though I would like to stay in this little town for a while, especially because snow is in the forecast, I must head for home.

When I arrive at home, Mom and I are so excited to see each other, and talk about the book that we must write, and just as I thought, she is ready to start working on our book.

During my three-week trip, I traveled forty-five hundred miles. My little Toyota truck and I are ready to explore again. However, I am now going to become an author, so I must stay at home because we have a book to write.

Shortly after Mom and I begin to write our book, she becomes weaker and weaker because of her lupus and diabetes. We work as much as we can on our book, because both of us believe that she will soon die.

Since I moved in with Mom nine months ago, her heart has changed and softened toward me. I now enjoy a friendship and love with her that I have always desired. When I moved in with Mom, we thought it was so she could take care of me, but now she needs me to take care of her.

The best way that I care for Mom is by sitting in long prayer for her every morning down in the garage. Although she now looks and sounds like a Christian, I know she is not a Christian, because there is no biblical evidence of true Christianity in her life (2 Corinthians 13:5; 1 John 3:1–15). Each time I read the Bible to Mom she seems more and more earnestly interested in God's word, and I increasingly see good evidence that God is drawing her heart to Him through His word. I am awed to see the word of God do the work of God.

Mom's increasing value of truth is evidence that God is drawing her to Him. One day as we sit at the computer typing, Mom turns to me and says, "James, you are the most honest man I have ever known."

Through the seven laborious months of typing, Mom becomes very week and ill. I am increasingly concerned because I often need to take her to the hospital. However, each time upon her return home, she is ready to start typing again.

Then finally on June 20, 2006, when she types the last sentence we conclude a book that contains 36,632 words. Both of us lean back in our chairs, and for a moment we are silent, because we are so weak and tired. She then turns to me and says, "James, do you remember me telling you about when you were in my womb and I heard a voice within my heart, which I believe was God?" I say, "I do, I do Mom, but I do not remember what you heard."

Though her face looks very fatigued, her eyes brighten when she says, "When you where in my womb, I heard a voice in my heart that said, 'Your baby will not live a normal life.' When God said that to me, it scared me, and later when you bought your Harley I thought that you were going to die because of a motor cycle accident." I softly say, "Wow, that is amazing!" Mom says, "Because of your exposure you haven't lived a normal life." I laugh and say, "No, I haven't."

Now, we understand why my Father did not warn me about the toxic fumes at Bashan Oil. God allowed me to climb the ladder and breathe the toxic chemicals because he ordained my trials before I was born. One of the many benefits of my trials is that we have written a book about why God allows afflictions, and how to benefit from trials.

After working on the book, Mom has a much better understanding about my trials, and since she is well convinced that we have documented "insider fraud" she suggests that we write yet another letter to our state Attorney General. We quickly draft a letter, and wait for a response.

After a few weeks we receive a letter from the State Attorney General, Department of Justice (Document #223). The letter describes the many duties of a State Attorney General, and toward the end of the letter I learn that our Attorney General is not permitted to intervene in matters like mine.

On May 12, 2006, I speak face to face with an authority at the Commission on Judicial Performance about the judge's involvement in my case. After I tell my exposure story, and show my documents that prove fraudulent activity in my case, I am once again disappointed when they put their back to me.

Though I am very disappointed about the lack of help with my Workers' Compensation case, I am very happy because God has given mercy and grace to my mother. Today as Mom walks toward me, I can see that she is very passionate about something, and as she begins to speak, she seems different. I understand why when she says, "James I'm different! I am a Christian! I prayed and now I am a Christian! From this day forward, I see good biblical evidence that she is in fact a child of God.

Mom often talked with me about how much fun it would be to travel on a book tour together. However, today, only a month and a half after she became a Christian, as I stand next to her hospital bed, I whisper into her ear, "Mom I love you" before she dies. I am very sad, but amazed, because she now glistens as she walks through God's pearl gate into Heaven.

After Mom's death, two family members take the inheritance that she had left for me and close down the house, leaving me with an urgent need to find a place to live.

My brother kindly invites me to live with him and his two teenage boys, which is about twenty minutes from my Mara's house where two of my daughters live.

One day as I sit in my bedroom looking at the manuscript, I realize that it needs a lot of improvement before it is ready for publishing. Though I learned to type in high school, my diseased intellect, great fatigue and palsied coordination in my fingers, will make this a very difficult, slow task.

As I ponder improving the manuscript, I conclude, *I can't do it. No way, I cannot do it.* However, I know that I must improve this manuscript.

As I go to the floor, I lay the manuscript there before God, and humbly say, "Father, thank you for your mercy and grace to me, and thank you for allowing all of my sorrows, sufferings and losses." I reach up and grab my Bible from my desk, and as I behold it reverently, I recall so many good memories of when I met with God in this Bible. My heart enlarges with deep gratitude, causing me to look to Heaven. As I gaze up to where God dwells, I feel so beholden to Him, because He also dwells within me. As my heart resounds with deep inexpressible words of awe, I am thankful that my Father hears every heart-felt thought. I then say, "Father, I must inspire many others with your Word. Please enable me to write a most excellent book that will greatly warn, and strongly inspire many from your Word." After a little more time in prayer, I rise with great confidence, knowing that I can do it. I can improve this manuscript.

Though my typing is slow, it is earnest, because I know that I am doing a great work for many who will read this book, and for God. Each day my typing is difficult, but progressive.

Through the past year, I thoroughly enjoy living with my brother and his sons. However, my diseased body desperately needs quiet rest. I mention my need to the Father, and a short time later I was silently awed when my brother and his sons move out and move into his fiancée's house, leaving me alone in my brother's newly remodeled home. My brother shows great kindness to me by refusing to collect rent from me.

A few years ago when I had mentioned to Lauren that she would meet her husband in another state, her response was an emphatic "no!" After much prayer, God specifically put upon my heart the mountain area of which we are to move. However, for now that does not seem possible, because when I mention to Lauren that we should move to that mountain area, she says, "No way daddy, I'm staying in this state." That's okay, because I have asked the Father to talk to Lauren about moving to the mountains, so it is only a matter of time before Lauren agrees with me and we move.

Each day my exercise and organic diet help me to feel a little better. However, I do not feel good about a comment someone recently said to me. "When you talk or smile your lower face does not move like it did before your exposure." Their comment struck me hard, because this can only mean that my nerve disease is now also deteriorating the motor-sensory control of my lower face.

My neck and esophagus have also become very weak. Today while I was eating, when I swallowed, the food stopped in my throat, causing great pain and panic because I could barely breathe. When I realized that I could not remove the food, I attempted to wash it down with a drink of water. That made the problem worse, because now the water was also stuck in my throat. I then knew that I was in serious trouble. I quickly ran to the bathroom and threw myself against the toilet thrusting the food out of my throat.

So now, each day I vigorously exercise my entire face and neck, hoping to restore good motor control.

Lauren arrived at my house about thirty minutes ago, and as we talk, she mentions a brief thought about the mountain area, which indicates to me that my Father has begun to scribe good thoughts within her heart.

During each of Lauren's following four visits with me, she increasingly mentions thoughts about the mountain area. And no doubt, each time she mentioned her ordained interest about the mountains, I listened with absolute amazement.

This evening, as I sit before God in prayer, I am just amazed at how gracious and good my Father is to me, because earlier today during my visit with Lauren, she said, "Daddy, I'm moving to that mountain area, and you are going with me!" Well, I could only say, "I am? When are we leaving?" With heart-felt excitement, she said, "In four months!" I say, "In four months! That means that we will arrive in the mountains during the first part of June (2009.)"

Two years after I began to live alone at my brother's house, and four months after Lauren told me that we are moving to the mountains, Lauren and I throw the lines, and head out.

After we arrive in the mountains, we are very happy to make a home together, and I must say that I am very grateful. We are very curious to visit the natural foods grocery store, because Lauren transferred her employment from such a store in the state we left, to this one. So before we finish unpacking we hurry to the store. When we step through the door, we are very impressed with both the store and the employees. All of the employees kindly greet us because they were anxious to meet the new girl who had transferred from another state. After our brief talk with some of them, and a walk around the entire store we sit at a table and enjoy a good wholesome meal, and then go home.

I am a most fortunate man because Lauren and I often enjoy spiritual edification with each other.

The next day, when I walk through the door of the store, all of the girls who work at the registers run to me and say, "James, Jeremiah wants to meet you!" I smile, and say, "Jeremiah, who is Jeremiah?" With much excitement, two of the register girls say, "See that tall man over there?" I look and say, "Yes." Two of them respond, "That's Jeremiah!" I say, "Alright." As I turn and walk in that direction, I look intently at the tall young man and realize that he is different. All of my senses rally, and discern that he is a simple, good man.

While I stand at the counter, Jeremiah steps over to me and says, "Hi, may I help you?" When I mention that all of the girls over at the registers told me that he wanted to meet me, he turns just as red as can be, making both of us laugh. As we talk, I realize that he is truly a simple, sincere, gentle, good man, and a man of virtues. A few minutes later, I mention that I should let him go back to work, so we say goodbye. As I walk through the store, I put favored things in my cart, as Jeremiah has put his Christian benevolence into my heart.

Since we live only a few minutes from this grocery store, I visit the store almost every day. Each time that I step through the door, I pass by the registers so that I can greet my dear Lauren, then head for the food section where Jeremiah works.

After a year of many enjoyable talks with Jeremiah, and much prayer about him I know what I must do. So I ask Lauren if she would like to go to an air show with me, and thankfully, she says, "Yes." I then say, "Let's take Jeremiah with us."

We enjoy our day at the air show, and now Jeremiah and Lauren enjoy every day together. That was my hope, and my prayer.

This evening, I walk about two minutes from our home to a bluff, and while I watch the day close, I meet a kind, kindred spirit whose name is Pete. Now when I visit the bluff, he usually comes out of his house and greets me, always blessing me with true simple Christian friendship. As one feels so nourished and satisfied after a special meal, Pete nourishes my life with true friendship, sincere love, and God's Word.

Early each Sunday morning, while Lauren is in her room, I put home-made sourdough biscuits in the oven, and then with a thermos full of hot green tea, I go to the bluff and wait for Pete. After he comes out, we head for my house. While we walk, we can hardly wait to open the front door and smell percolating coffee and hot sourdough biscuits. After we step into the kitchen I pull the biscuits from the oven and butter a few, pour some coffee, and then we sit at the table with these delights, and open our Bibles. While we edify each other with God's word, Lauren comes out of her bedroom, ready to go to church. The three of us climb into Pete's truck and head for church.

My health continues to improve because of my organic diet, earnest exercise and prayer. Though I still have symptoms of my disease, I feel blessed because I now at least look as if I am healthy.

Sometime later, when I step into the grocery store, I see Jeremiah walking through the store, so I run after him like a puppy runs after his favorite ball. After a brief walk with him, we stop at the registers, and continue our good talk. As we talk, I see through the glass doors that a tall pretty woman is walking toward the door. When she walks through the door, she steps right into my heart, and Jeremiah says, "There's Mom." And I say, "That's your Mom?"

After Jeremiah's widowed mother, Sophia greets Jeremiah, he introduces me to her. As I behold her pretty face, the lovely tone of her voice, and the playful way that she expresses her thoughts, my heart is well pleased, causing all of my senses to understand that she is a simple, genuine, tender, good woman. The three of us talk for a moment, and then as Sophia and I walk through the store, I fall in love with her. After our talk, I hurry home and shut myself in my bedroom, so that I can talk with my Father about Sophia.

After many days of prayer about Sophia, my desire for her is bounding. One evening while I sit on the bluff, I hardly notice the quaint old town down below me, nor do I enjoy my usual gaze up at the beautiful mountains, wishing that I could explore those famed old mountains. This evening my heart inclines me to only look up toward the little mountain town where Sophia lives. While I stare, my heart wants to go up there and see her again. I have no idea when I will see her again, because she lives so far away. Reality then cries out in my heart, *what will she think about me when she learns that I do not work because I am recovering from a nerve disease? What will she think about me when she learns that I do not have a vehicle?* I silence my logical thoughts when I look to Heaven and say, "Father, she seems to be a very good, very patient, understanding woman. It seems to me that she will see me for who I am, and I believe that if You have opened a door for friendship, and love between us then it is only a matter of time before you bring us together. Will you please help me to become a proper man for her, and will you please move me up to the little town where she lives?" I sit for a moment, communing with my heart where God dwells, and as I bow my head, I put both of my hands over my face and earnestly say, "All things are possible with you. I am not asking you to bless us only for our good, but so that our lives will please you, and greatly honor you."

It was a year and a half ago when I took Jeremiah and Lauren to the air show, and now today up on the side of a mountain, Jeremiah asks my daughter if she would be his wife for life, making both Lauren and I feel very fortunate.

Sophia mentions to Jeremiah and Lauren that the three of us should come up to her house so that we can start preparing for their wedding. Well, that sure pleases me, because I have been ready for a long time to go up to Sophia's house. No doubt, the four of us will enjoy a great time together.

When we arrive at Sophia's house, I feel like a shy schoolboy in her presence, until her playfulness engages me. After a very good dinner, we sit at the table and start making things for the kids' wedding. Though the house feels nice and warm, I can feel a hint of the cool autumn evening outside. After about forty-five minutes of fun at the table, Sophia and I go out to the garage and enjoy a warm fire as we sit before her woodstove.

Through the following five months we venture up to Sophia's house many times, always accomplishing much for the kids' wedding. Each of those times, while Sophia and I sat before her woodstove, we enjoyed heart-felt friendship, fun and laughter.

This morning, after I finish reading and studying my Bible, I sit on the floor for meditation and prayer. During my prayer, I reach to my desk and pick up a Mennonite catalog, and open it to the page where there is a picture of my favored Mennonite suit. After I look at the suit, I lay the catalog in my lap, and say, "Father, I don't have the money to buy a suit for the kids wedding." And as noble thoughts about this suit fill my heart, I am pleased to consider that my thoughts are words to God. I pick up the catalog and show the suit to God, and say, "Father, all things are possible with you. Will you please give me the money for this suit?" A few minutes later, while I am still in prayer, Lauren knocks on my door. After I say, "Enter," she opens the door, and as she extends her hand and says, "Here's the money for your suit." With absolute astonishment I say, "Money for my suit!" While her hand is still extended, I rise from the floor and reach for the gift from God. After I count $300.00, I laugh as I say, "That's exactly how much the suit cost." I then show the picture to Lauren, and mention that only a few minutes ago I had showed the picture to God, and asked if He would please give me the money for this suit.

The day of the kids' wedding, when all of us and our guest are in our proper places at church, the lovely wedding march song begins. Everyone in the sanctuary quickly becomes tenderly silent; while out in the foyer, a most beautiful bride slips her arm into my arm, uniting our hearts. We then begin a slow, reverent walk toward her man. When we turn and enter the sanctuary doors, I surprise Lauren when I gently stop our walk. As I turn to her, she follows my lead, just as she did when she was a little girl. The wedding guests slip from my attention when we look into each other's eyes. After a brief heart-felt moment of silence, I say, "Daughter, do you remember when we were aboard my sailboat and God told me that you would meet your husband in another state?" "Yes daddy," she says. As I lift my arm and point my hand toward her man, I say, "Behold, your husband in another state." I then, with much heart, begin our walk toward her amazing man. A moment later when I hand my first daughter to her man, I am amazed to consider that this marriage is truly made in heaven.

A few weeks later I borrow Lauren's car and drive straight up to Sophia's house. After a good mountain dinner, we light another warm fire, and while we sit close to the wood stove, I tell her more about my exposure story and the book that I am writing. I am thankful, but not surprised, when she offers to help me improve the manuscript. After we start working together on the manuscript, I am pleased with her excellent literary skills, and so very thankful because of her great improvements.

Through the cold winter, we sit before many warm fires, talking and laughing as if there is no end of our time together.

Through winter, as we wash many dishes together, our simple friendship grows, and during spring when flowers bloom, our friendship grows as we work together on household chores. When autumn flowers fade, our friendship thrives. Through it all, we often edify each other with God's word.

We often refer to each other by the nicknames of James and Sophia. Our nicknames for each other began one day when we were in town, and after we finished our errands, Sophia said, "Home James." We laughed saying that James was a good name for me, and Sophia suggested her name for her.

During a cold snowy morning in February 2010, as Pete and I stand on the bluff, I tell him about the time in 1991 when the Spirit of truth told me that in twenty years we will lose our Constitution, which will be next year in 2011. His response is very brief, and seems to question my comment.

Sometime later during the spring, as Pete and I stand on the bluff, I say to Pete, "God has given me insight about your wife that I should mention to you." Pete is surprised because I hardly know his wife.

He discerns that my insight is not good, which causes sentiment for his wife to form in his eyes. As we look intently at each other, I say, "A year from now your wife will inherit a lot of money, and then she will leave you." He remains silent because he and his wife enjoy a good marriage. However, I mention to him that God will now start preparing him for his wife's departure.

Before church, early on a very cold Sunday morning in January of 2011, as I stand out on the bluff waiting for Pete, he comes out of his house, and though he is not yet ready to go to my apartment, he hands a piece of paper to me and says, "You were right."

As he turns to go back to his house, I read the paper which states that the US Supreme Court issued a landmark decision that serves to allow judges to void the Constitution in their Courtrooms. The Court did not even explain this decision that was issued on January 18, 2011.

As I look out over the sleepy town below, I am sad for the people, but not surprised at this news. Through the years, I wondered how I would learn, or who would tell me about the loss of our Constitution in 2011, exactly twenty years after God warned me.

It has now been a year since I warned Pete about his wife leaving him, and now he is deeply hurt because his wife recently inherited a lot of money and left him. Memories about his wife are still in his house, so he knows that he must move to different house, and begin a new life.

During the early part of March, while I am shopping at the natural foods grocery store, Pete calls my cell phone and asks, "Do you want to ride up the mountain with me so that I can look for a place to rent?"

I respond that I can't because I am too busy and need to get back to my desk and work on the manuscript. God then gives me the insight that this trip to the mountains is providentially meant for me, so I say, "Let me think about it, and I will call you in twenty minutes." After Pete's call, I ask the Father what I should think about Pete's invitation, and I quickly understand that I should go with him. Less than an hour later, we are in his truck driving up the mountain.

When we drive past the first off-ramp where Pete intended to exit, I mention that the second off-ramp is a little further ahead. And when we drive past the second off-ramp I mention that the last off-ramp is just a little further ahead. When we drive past the last off-ramp I laugh as I say, "Because I do not have my own vehicle, God is taking me somewhere, for some reason." To my delight, I realize that the little town where Sophia lives is just a little further ahead. Before we pull into her town, I call Sophia and mention that we are about in enter the town where she lives, and thankfully she invites us to come to her house.

While at Sophia's house, I mention that we had intended to go to the town just below here so that Pete could find a place to rent. However, now that we are here in this cute little town, I ask if there is a place here in town for me to rent. Sophia says that earlier today she saw in the paper an advertisement about a little cabin for rent not far away. Sophia takes me to look at the cabin, and when I see it, I am greatly pleased at its old rustic mountain appearance. However, if it were a cardboard box I would still be happy to live in it, because it is a nine minute walk away from Sophia's house.

During our drive back down the mountain, I call the property manager and ask about the cabin. I am very disappointed when he tells me that the cabin was rented earlier today. I try to hide my disappointment as I graciously thank the manager and say goodbye. Pete heard my talk, and feels my disappointment. As I bow my head, I take my hat off so that I may properly talk to my Father, and pray, "Father, please, I want to move into that cabin." Though my prayer is short, I am certain that God heard in my heart my other thoughts about that cabin. After I raise my head and put my hat back on, my Side Kick cell phone rings. I am amazed to hear the property manager say, "It's yours if you want it." After our short talk, I can feel Pete's strong stare at me, so I turn and look at him, and see that he is just stunned, and says, "Was that the property manager! Did he just call and say that the cabin is yours!" As I begin to laugh I say, "That *was* the manager, he said the cabin is mine if I want it!" It almost seems like Pete is going to stop the truck, jump out, and dance on the highway.

My cozy little mountain cabin; everything within my cabin was given to me.
Thank you Father.

The following weekend I go back to the town where Sophia lives, and where I will soon live, and sign a contract to rent the little cabin.

A little more than a year after Jeremiah and Lauren became one in marriage, their daughter Abby enters this life, and into our hearts.

One evening while Sophia and I are refurbishing my cabin we hear a kind voice say from the open front door, "Knock, knock!"

In walks a man who is old enough to be my dad. His warm smile fills my cabin with much happiness. His name is Richard, a simple, earnest, good man. After a brief visit he goes home, but blesses me again the next day when I hear at my front door, "Knock, knock!"

Thankfully, Richard lives right next door, making it easy for him to come to my cabin almost every evening. As one visit follows another, our friendship and love for each other grows. When I begin to tell Richard about my exposure story, he offers to help me with the manuscript. I am pleased when he tells me that he learned excellent literary skills, and proper English, from his Pulitzer Prize winning father, and that he acquired other literary skills when he worked as a French teacher. He will no doubt be of great help in rewriting the manuscript.

Through many days and evenings, both of us enjoy good talks and much laughter, as we improve the manuscript together. After two years of work we are very happy when we draw close to the end of our work, and often talk about how the book will bless me, and many readers. However, it is with great sadness when Richard dies, leaving us to go on without him.

The evening after Richard's death, when it is time for me to say good night to Sophia and go to the cabin, Sophia tells me that she does not want me to go to cabin because she knows that through the night I will lie awake grieving about my dear friend's death. So I gather some fire wood and build a fire in the fire pit behind her house that Richard made for us, while she gets a few blankets. We then put the porch swing close to the fire pit, and after we make ourselves very comfortable on the swing, we talk, and laugh until sunrise. After her dad died about a year ago, I did the same thing for her.

Days later, as I ride with Pete in his truck he turns into the parking lot of his bank. And while he is in the bank, I step out of the truck and go to the river that flows next to the bank. When we meet back at his truck he hands me a lot of money, and says, "You'll need another suit for your book tour." I decline his offer. However, he prevailed, and soon after Sophia and I purchase a very nice suit.

A few months later, as we are close to the finish of our work on the manuscript, I begin to wonder how God will send me out on a book tour, because I do not own a vehicle. Yesterday, I began to realize God's provision for me after I mentioned to Sophia that her neighbor Tom wanted to post his truck and travel trailer for sale on the internet. After I told her that I offered to take pictures of the truck and trailer, and post them on the internet for Tom, she said, "Well, let's go take some pictures."

After we arrive at the very cute 19 foot Scamp fifth wheel trailer, I open the door so Sophia can step inside. Before I enter, I hear her say, "Wow, this is in beautiful condition!" She is very pleased to see the custom oak cabinets, and cozy appearance. We then learn that Tom bought the trailer new in 2006, and had never used the bathroom.

Well, both of us wonder if the truck is as nice as the trailer, so we hurry out of the trailer and go to the side of the house for a look at the truck. When we arrive, we are just as amazed to see a very nice 2003 Chevy extended cab truck that looks new. Sophia says, "James, how many miles are on this truck?" I quickly open the driver door, and surprise her again when I say, "37,000."

While we talk with Tom about the amazing truck and trailer, Tom mentions that he will not sell them separately. I am quite surprised to hear Sophia offer to buy both for the price Tom is asking.

The next evening as we sit on the back deck, she says, "You can use the truck and trailer to start your book tour!" I am very humbled by God's provision for me.

Lord willing, after the book is published, Pete and I will tour together; he in his truck, and me in this one. Pete will be a great comfort and inspiration to many who are afflicted with sorrows, sufferings and losses, because through fifteen long years, God has taught him many valuable lessons about living with fibromyalgia.

I began the research and writing of this book twenty-three years ago. The great literary skills of Richard and Sophia richly improved this manuscript. Through two and a half years of work with them, we added a little over one hundred pages to this book, and after our dear Grandmommy completed her excellent edit, we concluded a manuscript with 105,774 words. That means we added about 69,356 words to the manuscript Mom and I concluded. My exposure happened 10,227 days ago, and now after so much work, we are finally ready to publish our book. It is amazing that my exposure occurred on Friday, May 6, 1988, and that we are uploading the manuscript to our publishers website for publish on Friday, May 6, 2016. We are grateful to God for enabling us to finish this great work for you the reader, and God.

Lauren worked very hard through many months researching and forming our 501(c)(3), LLC, our website (COFMinistries.com) and our ministry, and I did my best to keep up with all of her homework assignments for me. Who would have thought that my daughter, and her husband, would be so vital in the formation of our book and ministry? After I wrote the back cover statement for this book, Jeremiah and Lauren created the picture of the Cestus glove in this book.

Lord willing, when we start Call of Faith Ministries, many of you will slip into God's yoke with us in serving God and in earnest prayer, pulling with us all the way into Heaven.

My dear Maribelle is blessed with a good, responsible husband, and may I say that they have the cutest little boy, my grandson. All three of them are firmly fixed within my heart. I earnestly wish that we lived closer to each other so that we could visit with each other more often.

Madeline is very busy in college, and no doubt, someday when a good man sets his eyes on her and learns who she is, he will bless her with true life-long love. We are also separated by a great distance, and I wish we could visit more often.

Two years ago before dad died, he attempted to deeply hurt my feelings. However, I am grateful for God's comfort to me.

In this book, I have not mentioned all of the cruel things people did to my daughters and me, nor have I mentioned all of God's amazing answers to my prayers. The answered prayers that I did mention are not meant to lift myself, but to emphasize that if you are a true Christian, and properly draw near to God, He will draw near to you.

Submit yourselves to God: resist the devil, and he will flee from you. Draw near to God, and he will draw near to you. Cleanse your hands, ye sinners, and purge your hearts, ye double minded.
JAMES 4:7–8

CHAPTER 25

And The Lord Blessed

⤚⟋

Then the Lord turned the captivity of Job, when he prayed for his friends: also the Lord gave Job twice as much as he had before... So the Lord blessed the last days of Job more than the first:...

JOB 42: 10–12

THROUGH FORTY-ONE CHAPTERS IN THE Bible, Job was afflicted with great sorrows, sufferings, and losses. It was not until chapter 42 that God turned Job's afflictions into great blessings.

During my times of sorrow, suffering and loss, my prayers and hopes were that God would turn my afflictions into blessings. After I understood that He was going to bless me, I often wondered if the progression of my life was symbolically in Chapter 28 or possibly in Chapter 41, or closer to the blessings in Chapter 42 of Job. Whatever the case, I always knew that by God's word, and by His Spirit, I must walk worthy of my calling while I wait for God to turn my trials into His blessings. I knew that when God turned my trials into His blessings, as my sorrows, sufferings, and losses faded; God's blessings would occupy my life.

Surely he will not much remember the days of his life, because God answereth to the joy of his heart.

ECCLESIASTES 5:19

He will take no great thought for the pains that he hath endured in time past.

GENEVA BIBLE COMMENTARY

Now that God's blessings occupy my life, my past trials are but a faint memory. And because God has restored my life, giving me a second chance, my heart-felt desire is to die to self and live for Him. The earnest expressions of my obedience to God, my love for God, and my fear of God must always increase, renewed daily in God's Word and by His spirit.

When I became a Christian, God's Word and His presence in my life caused an earnest desire within my heart to live obediently, righteously, and to walk in true holiness (Romans 6:16–19). It is very important to understand what holiness is because of the high standard set forth in the following verse:

Follow peace with all men, and holiness, without the which no man shall see the Lord.

HEBREWS 12:14

A brief understanding about holiness is that Christians separate from sin, separate from all that is contrary to God's character, and conform to His word. Holiness is the opposite of common, that which belongs to the generality. To live and walk in holiness means that the Christian makes an earnest effort to not expose ones-self to that which is unclean and unfit for the holy city, which is Heaven (Rev 21:27).

Which do you live for, and which is more important to you, earthly gold, or the heavenly city of gold?

Gold Statement #7: **And I saw a new heaven, and a new earth:... And I John saw the holy city... and the city was pure gold, like unto clear glass.**

REVELATION 21:1, 2, 18

The interior part of the new Jerusalem. We have seen its strong wall, and stately gates, and glorious guards; now we are to be led through the gates into the city itself; and the first thing which we observe there is the street of the city, *which is of pure gold, like transparent glass.* The saints in heaven tread upon gold.

MATTHEW HENRY

CHAPTER 26

There is a Day of Renewal When All Things Will Be Made Right

↶ꝰ

Take, my brethren, the Prophets for an example of suffering adversity, and of long patience, which have spoken in the name of the Lord. Behold, we count them blessed which endure. Ye have heard of the patience of Job, and have known what end the Lord *made*. For the Lord is very pitiful and merciful.

JAMES 5: 10–11

"I AM GOING TO BE okay!"

CHAPTER 27

Collusion – Racketeer Influenced Corrupt Organizations (RICO)

—⤚

WHEN TWO OR MORE PEOPLE join, mutually agreeing to implement fraudulent or deceitful plans for the purpose of benefit or profit, they are guilty of collusion.

The enterprise has deliberately formed a continuous and related pattern of racketeering activity. This crime becomes very artful when the guilty party offers to resolve collusion for the purpose of protecting their deceitful plans.

These high profile crimes are known as RICO violations.

Contact with authorities who are responsible for the punishment of RICO violations must be made in order to expose and discourage these continuous patterns of fraud.

The citizenry must be equipped with insight and the ability to judge these enterprises for themselves.

This is called push back!

CHAPTER 28

My Life is Like the Apollo 18 Flight to the Moon

⟋⟍

AN 1828 DICTIONARY DEFINES "IMPOSSIBILITY" as that which cannot be; the state of being not possible to exist. There are two kinds of impossibilities; *physical* and *moral*. A *physical impossibility* is contrary to the law of nature. A *morally* impossible matter gives the appearance of being impossible when in itself it is possible, but attended with difficulties or circumstances.

All things are possible with God. However, He often requires of us great patience as we wait upon Him.

Man almost cancelled all of my dreams, and my life. However, because of God's great mercy and grace to me He lifted me out of my sorrows, sufferings, and losses for many reasons. One is so that many may know about the power of His abundant mercy and grace.

God's restoration of me is like the Apollo 18 flight to the moon.

In 1972, Apollo 17 was the last flight to the moon. Apollo 18, 19, and 20 were paid for, assembled, and ready to go. Astronauts were trained and prepared for flights to the moon aboard Apollo 18, 19, and 20. However, these scheduled flights were cancelled and redirected to earth's orbit for the building of Sky Lab.

When God put it into my heart that I must make an earnest effort to recover my life, many believed that recovery of my life was impossible; it was as if NASA had announced that Mom, and I and God had seized the Saturn Five Rocket/Apollo 18 because we needed it for our own mission to the moon.

Bashan Oil and Og Construction considered our early efforts in court as incredulous, as if they had heard that we had pushed the mighty Saturn Five only one inch toward Launch Pad 34.

However, the recognition that we eventually gained in court was as if NASA had announced that we were half way to the launch site.

On the day that I seized control of the court, it was as if NASA had announced that Apollo 18 was at the launch site and we were in the capsule, preparing for launch.

When the two judges from Workers' Compensation, Bashan Oil and Og Construction realized that we had become a serious challenge, it was as if NASA had announced that Apollo 18 had completed their status check and confirmed that the oxidizer tanks were fully pressurized.

When I lost crewmember Mom, my Father provided me with a most capable and genuine friend, Sophia.

As flight controllers, Richard and Pete, worked with Sophia and me on our book, it was as if Apollo 18 was on automatic sequence, with no deviations from our plan, and we were go for launch.

As we drew near to the completion of our manuscript, it was as if flight controllers had said that the launch tower swing arms are fully retracting.

We finished our work together with one goal for our readers and God. And that was as if we were finally at T-minus nine seconds and the ignition sequence had begun.

When we were ready to publish our book, our thrill was as if we had sent the launch commit command to the five powerful Saturn Five engines.

Our great hope is that our book will bless you with true hope, and the ability to harmonize with God's mind and will for your life. And that is as if all five Saturn engines are burning at 103 percent, and we have cleared the tower.

Our Father's abiding mercy and grace has sustained us, and we believe it will continue to comfort, support, and aid us. And that is as if my hand is not on the abort handle because that is not an option.

I am finally a most fortunate, healthy man enjoying life with Lauren, Jeremiah, Abby, Pete, and Sophia. And that is as if Lauren has confirmed that our telemetry is good, our pitch and roll program is complete, and we are on a good heading. Yes, we are on a very good heading, because by God's Word and by His spirit we make an earnest effort to harmonize with Him. Thank you, our kind Father!

When a previous Apollo command module was about to slip around to the backside of the moon, static developed in radio communications. Before radio contact was completely lost, one of the astronauts said to Ground Control, "See you on the flipside," meaning that they would reestablish communications when they came around to the other side of the moon.

As you come to the end of our book, we are about to lose communications with each other. However, Lord willing, we will reestablish communications with you again when you visit our website, COFMinistries.com (Call of Faith Ministries) and through public speaking, and Lord willing, if we produce a movie based on this book. So we say, "See you on the flipside."

"WOO-HOO!"
SOPHIA

Father, thank you for enabling me to write this book, please
be merciful and gracious to those who read our book.

NOTE: November 9th, 2016 - As I advanced through each long year of writing this book, the spirit of my heart intensified with an earnest desire to enlarge your heart with God's wisdom, so that you will choose correct knowledge, providing for you a proper understanding; forming joy in the office of your soul, and the joy in that office influencing happiness in the office of your heart, and the happiness in that office producing peace in the office of your mind.

However, as we drew near to the end of our work, one day when I was alone at my desk working on this book, I said to God, "Father, my nerve disease! I am not able to properly finish writing this book because I feel so very ill. Please give me strength of heart and clarity of mind so that I may properly finish this book." Shortly afterward, I was absolutely amazed and very grateful to God after He took all of my nerve disease symptoms away from me. Ohhh, with all of my happy heart I worked with Sophia on this book, until we confidently understood that my story, God's Word, and the spirit of this book was just right for you dear reader.

We were like two giddy kids as we pulled our chairs close to the computer, and after Sophia brought the print house web-site up on the computer screen, she uploaded the manuscript to their site. We then looked at the "Publish My Book" button, and said, "Let's press the button together!" So as we slowly and reverently placed our index fingers on the button, Sophia counted to three, causing all of my sorrows, sufferings and losses to rejoice as we press the button.

A few days later when I feel a hint of my nerve disease, my heart begins to moan. And as intimate memories of previous suffering rudely enters into my heart, my Father also tenderly enters into my heart. His presence brings immediate order and comfort. He then inclines me to read certain Bible verses again that I have read so many times in the past. Through these verses He establishes understanding that my afflictions are appointed by God, for His perfect purpose (Job 23:10-15; Psalm 37:23; Proverbs 16:1, 9, 16:33, 20:24; Ecclesiastes 3:1-14).

As my symptoms increase with severity, God increases His grace and comfort, preventing discouragement. He then begins to build purpose into my life as He leads me to other verses that I have also read many times before. Through these verses I realize that I am so very fortunate because trials are a means whereby saints purge themselves of ungodliness, and become stronger in godly attributes (Psalm 119:71-77; 2 Corinthians 12:1-10; James 1:1-4; Romans 5:3-4; 1 Peter 1:6-7, and 2 Corinthians 1:3-4). During the last hour of my life, when at the end of that hour the pen in heaven will stop recording my life in God's book, I want to look ahead with confidence, not shame (1 John 2:28; Philippians 1:20). I must be able to look ahead, knowing that I did more for God than what was required of me, so that I may be worthy to hear, "Thank you, well done." (Luke 17:7-10; Luke 19:11-27).

A few weeks later, we are told by a neurologist that my nerve disease is "a bad one" and that "the end will be very difficult." Another computer test reveals that my disease has advanced since my last test in 2005.

The greater my trials, the more grace to me, powerfully enabling me in so many ways to be used by God for His immeasurable glory.

One example of how God has used me occurred on a Friday morning while Pete and I sipped on coffee at one of our favorite restaurants. As we sat at our usual place at the end of the counter I told my exposure story to two men who were seated at the counter three stools away from us. During my story I had no idea that at a nearby table a husband and wife were intently listening until they rose, leaving half of their breakfast on the table so that they could stand next to me. About twelve minutes later when I finished my story the husband looked into my eyes with all of his heart and said with passion, "I don't get it. You don't seem bitter. With all that happened to you how is it that you are not bitter?" I was then able to tell them about the comfort from my Father, and His Word.

If my afflictions enable me to understand and comfort some of you, I am grateful to God.

CHAPTER 29

Understanding Forgiveness

—⸹

A GIFT FROM GOD, AND OUR EXPRESSIONS OF HIS FORGIVENESS

THE SPIRIT OF TRUTH GUIDES us into all truth (John 16:13).

However, with man there is often a spirit of error (1 John 4:6).

Correct doctrine is from God (1 Timothy 6:3–5; 2 John: 9–11).

There is reason to be ashamed if we incorrectly interpret the Word of God (2 Timothy 2:15).

We must take the greatest care to accurately speak God's Word as it is given to us (1 Peter 4:11).

The New Strong's Concordance Expository Dictionary defines "heresies" as "a choosing, choice; then that which is chosen, and hence, an opinion, especially a self-willed opinion…"

For first of all, when ye come together in the Church, I hear that there are dissensions among you: and I believe it *to be true* in

some part. For there must be heresies even among you, that they which are approved among you, might be known.
I Corinthians 11:18–19

God's word exposes self-willed opinions. Therefore, 1 Corinthians 11:18-19 must be considered every time we hear someone teach the Word of God.

A Great Injustice and a Willingness to Forgive

Jesus allowed cruel, ignorant men to nail Him to the cross, and while He suffered on that cross, He allowed other cruel, ignorant people to mock Him. They were truly ignorant of whom He was, and because Jesus understood their ignorance about Him, He had mercy for them. If, while Jesus hung on the cross, His murderers and persecutors had realized who He was, I am certain that they would have feared that He would say, "Father, let thy angels destroy them!" However, Jesus revealed His true, heart-felt abounding love for them when He said:

...Father, forgive them: for they know not what they do...
Luke 23:34

The New Strong's Concordance Expository Dictionary defines "forgive" as; "(1) to send away: (1a) to bid going away or depart, (1a1) a crowd (Mt 13:36); (1b) to send forth, yield up, to expire (Mt 27:50; Mk 15:37);" and "(1d) to let go, give up a debt, forgive, to remit (Jn 20:23)."

Jesus is still patient with us sinners regarding our indifference about His death on the cross. He is gracious to sinners, full of compassion toward those who need Him, slow to be angry with all who offend Him, and of great mercy to each of us who is persuaded by His word to change his own mind (repent) about his disobedience to Him (Psalm 145:8).

For God so (intensely) loves the world (John 3:16) and is willing to forgive sinners if they repent. If a person changes his mind about his disobedience to our Creator, God will see his change of thought, and when God also sees within an earnest heart a sincere, correct belief in Jesus, God knows that the penitent sinner is now worthy (imputed righteousness of Jesus) to be forgiven.

Though Jesus asked God to forgive His murderers and persecutors, we know that God did not forgive them unless they repented, as Jesus said in the following verse:

> **...except ye amend your lives, ye shall all likewise perish.**
> LUKE 13:3

In the next verse, Peter preached the same warning:

> **Amend your lives therefore, and turn, that your sins maybe put away,...**
> ACTS 3:19

Our sins are blotted out (forgiven) if we have a proper change of mind about our sins and demonstrate our change of mind, as Paul says in the following verse:

> **For if thou shalt confess with thy mouth the Lord Jesus, and shalt believe in thine heart, that God raised him up from the dead, thou shalt be saved:**
> ROMANS 10:9

Here is a comment from John MacArthur's Study Bible about the previous verse of Romans 10:9:

> confess...the Lord Jesus. Not a simple acknowledgment that He is God and the Lord of the universe, since even demons acknowledge that to be true (James 2:19). This is the deep personal conviction, without reservation, that Jesus is that person's own master, or sovereign. This phrase includes repenting from sin, trusting in Jesus for salvation, and submitting to Him as Lord...

If we truly repent, we are "saved" from personal guilt and the wrath of God (1 Thessalonians 1:10). However, those who are not persuaded to repent, *the wrath of God abideth on him* (John 3:36).

When God forgives, He sends the offense *away* the same as when Jesus sent the crowd *away* in Matthew 13:36; or we can also say, God lets the offense *expire*, making the offender free from his offense. When God pardons an offense, He removes the offense far from us as the following verse shows us:

> **For as high as the heaven is above the earth, so great is his mercy toward them that fear him. As far as the East is from the West: so far hath he removed our sins from us.**
> PSALM 103:11–12

Our gracious God expects *us* to be gracious and willing to forgive others as He forgives us.

> **Be ye courteous one to another, and tender hearted, freely forgiving one another, even as God for Christ sake, freely forgave you.**
> EPHESIANS 4:32

> **Forbearing one another, and forgiving one another, if any man have a quarrel to another: even as Christ forgave, even so do ye.**
> COLOSSIANS 3:13

We have read that God will not forgive a sinner until he repents. The question is what should we do if someone offends us, and that offender will not repent of his offense? The answer is in the following verse.

> **Take heed to yourselves: If thy brother trespass against thee, rebuke him: and if he repent, forgive him.**
> LUKE 17:3

Matthew Henry's explanation of Luke 17:3:

> The forgiving of offences is a great duty, and that which we should every one of us make conscience of:...when your brother trespasses against you, does you any injury, puts any slight or affront upon you, if he be accessory to any damage done you in your property or reputation, take heed to yourselves at such a time, lest you be put into a passion; lest, when your spirits are provoked, you speak unadvisedly, and rashly vow to revenge (Pro 24:29): I will do so to him as he hath done to me. Take heed what you say at such a time, lest you say amiss.
>
> If you are permitted to rebuke him, you are advised to do so. Smother not the resentment, but give it vent. Tell him his faults; show him wherein he has not done well nor fairly by you, and, it may be, you will perceive (and you must be very willing to perceive it) that you mistook him, that it was not a trespass against you, or not designed, but an oversight, and then you will beg his pardon for misunderstanding him; 2. You are commanded, upon his repentance, to forgive him, and to be perfectly reconciled to him: If he repent, forgive him; forget the injury, never think of it again, much less upbraid him with it. Though he do not repent, you must not therefore bear malice to him, nor meditate revenge; but, if he do not at least say that he repents, you are not bound to be so free and familiar with him as you have been. If he be guilty of gross sin, to the offence of the Christian community he is a member of, let him be gravely and mildly reproved for his sin, and, upon his repentance, received into friendship and communion again. This the apostle calls forgiveness, 2 Co 2:7...

If the offender will not repent to the offended, we must respond to him as God responds to us. And that is, that the offender is not worthy to be forgiven, his offense must be kept in his possession, he must not be allowed to escape from his guilt, as the following verse states:

Whosesoever's sins ye remit, they are remitted unto them: *and* whosesoever's sins ye retain, they are retained.

JOHN 20:23

If we are justified by God's word in not forgiving an unrepentant offender, we know by God's word that God agrees with us. Therefore, if an offender will not free himself from the guilt of his offense, we should, if possible, tell the offender that his offense is still bound to him, and that our decision to not forgive him means that his offense is also bound to him in heaven. We should also encourage the offender by saying that if he will repent he will be loosed from his offense on earth and in heaven, as the following verse says:

...whatsoever thou shalt bind upon earth, shall be bound in heaven: and whatsoever thou shalt loose on earth, shall be loosed in heaven.

MATTHEW 16:19

The following rule encourages repentance and promotes peace:

Moreover, if thy brother trespass against thee, go and tell him his fault between thee and him alone: if he hear thee, thou hast won thy brother. But if he hear thee not, take yet with thee one or two, that by the mouth of two or three witnesses, every word may be confirmed. And if he refuse to hear them, tell it unto the Church: and if he refuse to hear the Church also, let him be unto thee as an heathen man, and a Publican. Verily I say unto you, Whatsoever ye bind on earth, shall be bound in heaven: and whatsoever ye loose on earth, shall be loosed in heaven.

MATTHEW 18:15–18

If the offender will not repent, he is not fit for communion with God. Before he approaches God, he must first go to the one he has offended and reconcile his wrong.

If then thou bring thy gift to the altar, and there rememberest that thy brother hath ought against thee, Leave there thine offering before the altar, and go thy way: first be reconciled to thy brother, and then come and offer thy gift.
MATTHEW 5: 23–24

If the offender repents, it is important for him to understand his obligation to the offended, and the nature of restitution. The laws regarding an offense, guilt, or justice for the offended, and restitution for the offended, are stated in Exodus 22:1–27, Leviticus 4:1–35, and Leviticus 6:1–7. These laws were intended to strictly govern Old Testament saints. However, New Testament saints must consider the character of God in these laws, and make an earnest effort to harmonize with God's character in all that they do. We further understand God's character in these laws by reading the following two verses:

Jesus said to him, Thou shalt love the Lord thy God with all thine heart, with all thy soul, and with all thy mind. This is the first and the great commandment. And the second is like unto this, Thou shalt love thy neighbor as thyself. On these two commandments hangeth the whole Law and the Prophets.
MATTHEW 22:37–40

Therefore whatsoever ye would that men should do to you: even so do ye to them: for this is the Law and the Prophets.
MATTHEW 7:12

It is very simple; the offender and the offended should treat each other, as each would want to be treated, keeping in mind that God is watching, and will someday call both to account.

If the offender repents, the offended will surely accept his repentance when he considers how God has forgiven him. God's children have reason to ask their Father for forgiveness every day, because of their wrong attitudes, wrong actions, or neglect of proper actions. If we refuse to forgive a repentant offender, God will not forgive our sins. The following verse does not relate to our salvation, but to our daily walk:

> **For if ye do forgive men their trespasses, your heavenly Father will also forgive you. But if ye do not forgive men their trespasses, no more will your father forgive you your trespasses.**
> MATTHEW 6: 14–15

The offended is further encouraged to be very merciful toward the repentant offender, because God says that the same measure of mercy that we show to others, will be that same measure of mercy that God will show to us (Luke 6:36–38).

The following verses should encourage the offended and the offender to reconcile any wrongs between them:

> **Blessed *are* the merciful: for they shall obtain mercy.**
> MATTHEW 5:7

> **But I say unto you, Love your enemies: bless them that curse you: do good to them that hate you, and pray for them which hurt you, and persecute you, That ye may be the children of your father that is in heaven: for he maketh his sun to arise on the evil and the good, and sendeth rain on the just and unjust. For if ye love them, which love you, what reward shall ye have? Do not the Publicans even the same? And if ye be friendly to your brethren only, what singular thing do ye? do not even the Publicans likewise? Ye shall therefore be perfect, as your Father which is in heaven, is perfect.**
> MATTHEW 5:44–48

"Retaliation does not create a repentant heart in the offender."
SOPHIA

"Wrongs always create an obligation."
SOPHIA

"Tears are like glasses for the heart and soul; allowing one to see more clearly God's Word and presence in your life.
SOPHIA

The following verse should frighten every Christian, and provide the deepest motivation to take the greatest care, and diligence, to do that which is best and right.

For we must all appear before the judgment seat of Christ, that every man may receive the things which are *done* in his body, according to that he hath done, whether *it be* good or evil. Knowing therefore that terror of the Lord, we persuade men,...
2 CORINTHIANS 5:10–11

Our disobedience and obedience to God is recorded in His books. Our choices of attitudes and actions dictate the recording in those books. During the judgment of Christians, the quality of every man's work will be tested (2 Corinthians 3:12–15).

The following verses are examples of when God would not forgive, and therefore, by these verses we know a right mind for us.

Example 1:

If thou do well, shalt thou not be accepted? and if thou doest not well, sin lieth at the door:...
GENESIS 4:7

This is Matthew Henry's explanation:

> God sets before Cain life and a blessing: *"If thou doest well, shalt thou not be accepted?* No doubt thou shalt, nay, thou knowest thou shalt;" either, [1.] "If thou hadst done well, as well as thy brother did, thou shouldst have been accepted, as he was." *God is no respecter of persons,* hates nothing that he had made, denies his favor to none but those who have forfeited it, and is an enemy to none but those who by sin have made him their enemy: so that if we come short of acceptance with him we must thank ourselves, the fault is wholly our own; if we had done our duty, we should not have missed his mercy...if now thou do well, if thou repent of thy sin, reform thy heart and life, and bring thy sacrifice in a better manner, if thou not only do that which is good but do it well, thou shalt yet be accepted, thy sin shall be pardoned, thy comfort and honor restored, and all shall be well.

Example 2:

> **...The Lord, The Lord, strong, merciful, and gracious, slow to anger, and abundant in goodness and truth. Reserving mercy for thousands, forgiving iniquity, and transgression and sin, and not making the *wicked* innocent, visiting the iniquity of the fathers upon the children, and upon the children's children, unto the third and fourth *generation*.**
>
> EXODUS 34:6–7

Here is Matthew Henry's explanation:

> *He will by no means clear the guilty.* Some read it so as to express a mitigation of his wrath, even when he does punish: *When he empties, he will not make quite desolate;* that is, "He does not proceed to the greatest extremity, till there be no remedy." As we read it, we must expound it that he will by no means connive at the guilty, as if he took no notice of their sin. Or, he will not clear the impenitently guilty, that go on still in

their trespasses: he will not clear the guilty without some satisfaction to his justice, and necessary vindication of the honor of his government.

Example 3:

And Joshua said unto the people, Ye cannot serve the Lord: for he is an holy God: he is a jealous God: he will not pardon your iniquity nor your sins. If ye forsake the Lord and serve strange gods, then he will return and bring evil upon you, and consume you, after that he hath done you good.
                        JOSHUA 24:19–20

This is Matthew Henry's explanation:

He thus expresses his godly jealously over them, and his fear concerning them, that, notwithstanding the profession they now made of zeal for God and his service, they would afterward (drawback), and if they did they would find him just and jealous to avenge it…you cannot serve the Lord, except you put away all other gods for he is holy and jealous, and will by no means admit a rival, and therefore you must be very watchful and careful, for it is at your peril if you desert his service.

Example 4:

And for the innocent blood that he shed, (for he filled Jerusalem with innocent blood) therefore the Lord would not pardon it.
                        2 KINGS 24:4

Here is Matthew Henry's explanation:

All that Manasseh did was called to mind, but especially the innocent blood that he shed, much of which, we may suppose, was the blood of God's witnesses and worshippers, which the Lord would not pardon.

Is there then any unpardonable sin but the blasphemy against the Holy Ghost? This is meant of the remitting of the temporal punishment. Though Manasseh repented, and we have reason to think even the persecutions and murders he was guilty of were pardoned, so that he was delivered from the wrath to come; yet, as they were national sins, they lay still charged upon the land, crying for national judgments.

Example 5:

The Lord *is* slow to anger, but *he is* great in power, and will not surely clear *the wicked*:...
NAHUM 1:3

This is Matthew Henry's explanation:

He will not at all acquit the wicked that sin, and stand to it, and do not repent. Those *wickedly depart from their God* that depart, and never return (Ps 18:21) and these he will not acquit. Humble supplicants will find him gracious, but scornful beggars will not find him easy.

Example 6:

Repent therefore of this thy wickedness, and pray God, that if it be possible, the thought of thine heart may be forgiven thee. For I see that thou art in the gall of bitterness, and in the bond of iniquity.
ACTS 8:22–23

Here is Matthew Henry's explanation:

What it is that he advises him to: He must do his first works. First, He must repent,—must see his error and retract it,—must change his mind and way,—must be humbled and ashamed for what he has done. His repentance must be particular: "Repent of this, own thyself guilty in this, and be sorry for it." He must lay a load upon himself for it, must not extenuate it, by calling it a mistake, or misguided zeal, but must aggravate it by calling it wickedness, his wickedness, the fruit of his own corruption. Those that have said and done amiss must, as far as they can, unsay it and undo it again by repentance. Secondly, He must pray to God, must pray that God would give him repentance, and pardon upon repentance.

The following verses teach us about the mind and will of God, and therefore the mind, and will for our lives:

A soft answer putteth away wrath: but grievous words stir up anger.

PROVERBS 15:1

An angry man stirreth up strife: but he that is slow to wrath, appeaseth strife.

PROVERBS 15:18

He that is slow unto anger, is better than the mighty man: and he that ruleth his own mind, *is better* than he that winneth a city.

PROVERBS 16:32

He that covereth a transgression, seeketh love: but he that repeateth a matter, separateth the prince.

PROVERBS 17:9

A brother offended *is harder to win* than a strong city, and *their* contentions *are* like the bar of a palace.

PROVERBS 18:19

The discretion of man deferreth his anger: and his glory *is* to pass by an offence.

PROVERBS 19:11

Be thou not glad when thine enemy falleth, and let not thine heart rejoice when he stumbleth, Lest the Lord see it, and it displease him, and he turn his wrath from him.

PROVERBS 24:17–18

A man that refraineth not his appetite, *is like* a city which is broken down *and* without walls.

PROVERBS 25:28

Blessed *are* the peacemakers: for they shall be called the children of God.

MATTHEW 5: 9

Recompense to no man evil for evil: procure things honest in the sight of all men. If it be possible, as much as in you is, have peace with all men. Dearly beloved, avenge not yourselves, but give place unto wrath: for it is written, Vengeance is mine: I will repay, saith the Lord. Therefore if thine enemy hunger, feed him: if he thirst, give him drink: for in so doing thou shalt heap coals of fire on his head. Be not overcome of evil, but overcome evil with goodness.

ROMANS 12:17–21

Finally, be ye all of one mind: one suffer with another: love as brethren: *be* pitiful, *be* courteous. Not rendering evil for evil, neither rebuke for rebuke: but contrariwise bless, knowing that ye are thereunto called, that ye should be heirs of blessing. For if any man long after life, and to see good days, let him refrain his tongue from evil, and his lips that they speak no guile. Let him eschew evil and do good: let him seek peace and follow after it. For the eyes of the Lord are over the righteous, and his ears *are open* unto their prayers: and the face of the Lord *is* against them that do evil.

I PETER 3:8–12

Many religious leaders have mixed psychology with the word of God. When secular reasoning is mixed with the word of God, the cross of Christ is "made of none effect" (1 Corinthians 1:17). This is why many Christians are powerless, and this is also why many are confused about forgiveness, and do not obtain true help from God. It is very important to keep God's word pure, because it is the word of God that does the work of God. We must carefully endeavor to harmonize with scripture so that God may apply His graces to our hearts.

Now consider the following self-willed, Biblically incorrect, opinions taught by many religious leaders:

1. You must unconditionally forgive, or God will not forgive you.
2. Forgiveness must occur even if you do not agree.
3. Forgiveness does not mean you forget.
4. We are not to hold anything against those who have done us wrong.
5. You must forgive, even if the offense is so bad that you cannot fellowship.
6. I am going to love them no matter what they do. My responsibility is to avoid retaliation.
7. Forgiveness is grossly misunderstood. Forgiveness has little to do with the other person.

My many offenders have not repented to me, so I have not forgiven them. Those who are familiar with me are amazed that I am not bitter toward my offenders. I am though, afraid for them because my Father saw what they did to me. If they do not fear His divine retribution, I do fear it for them. This is why I pray for them, asking my Father to be merciful and gracious to them.

There are many reasons as to why I am at peace with my offenders. When I became a Christian, God put His Spirit within me. His Spirit is both a helper and a comforter (John 14:16–17, 14:26, 15:26, 16:7 Romans 8:15; Galatians 4:6). The creator of my soul intimately dwells within me, and through His

Word He tenderly assists, and comforts the office of my heart; the office of my intellect, and the office of my soul. Through His Word each office understands His mind and will, and when the Word of God brings harmony with all three offices I am at peace with God, regardless of what His purpose is through me. And when someone offends an office my Father uses His Word to comfort that office.

There is much more to discover about forgiveness in the Bible. Two excellent sources that will inspire you with rich spiritual insight are "The MacArthur Study Bible" and "Matthew Henry's Commentary on the Whole Holy Bible; Complete and Unabridged" edition.

CHAPTER 30

Doctrinal Statements

~~⟋⟋~~

THE HOLY SCRIPTURES

WE BELIEVE THE BIBLE IS the written revelation of the mind and will of God to man, which when God inspired Holy men with His words, the Holy Spirit controlled them as they wrote the Holy Bible (2 Timothy 3:16; 1 Corinthians 2:7–14; 2 Peter 1:20, 21; John 5:46, 47 and 17:11).

We believe the first-century original documents that comprised scripture are absolutely infallible (Jeremiah 1:4, 9; Luke 1:1–4; 1 Thessalonians 2:13; 2 Timothy 3:16; 2 Peter 1:16–21; 1 John 1:1–4; Revelation 1:1, 2).

We believe the original scriptural documents inspire different applications; however, there is only one interpretation (John 16:12–15; 1 Corinthians 2:7–15).

We believe the Word of God is living and powerfully active in seizing our ruined consciences. It is able to instruct the most secret parts of our deceived hearts, and tame our rebellious souls. The Word of God is a true comfort and perfect balm for our damaged hearts and souls. The Word of God is a lamp for our eyes, filling our minds with the splendid glories of God, and helps us guide our feet in this dark, misguiding world (Hebrews 4:12; Psalm 119:105; Proverbs 6:23).

GOD

We believe there is only one living, true God (Deuteronomy 6:4; 1 Corinthians 8:4) and that this Supreme Being is infinite, self-sufficient, and all knowing, and exists as in three persons—Father, Son, and Holy

Spirit (John 4:24; Colossians 1:15; Hebrews 11:27; Genesis 1:26; Luke 3:22; Matthew 28:19; 2 Corinthians 13:14).

We believe the magnificent beauty of God is clearly understood when we behold the marvelous variety of colors adorning our earth. The magnitude of God is clearly manifest when we behold the great ornaments in our daytime and nighttime sky. The almighty strength of God is clearly manifest when we behold the amazing exactness of the earth, the sky, the solar system, and beyond. (Genesis 1: 1–5 and 14–19; Psalm 19:1; Romans 1:20; Isaiah 40:12, 21, 22, 26, 28).

GOD THE FATHER

We believe the supreme love of God is clearly manifest when we understand that God as our loving Father is willing to forgive us through Jesus, though we are rebellious and fallen (John 3: 16, 17; Romans 5:8; Ephesians 2:4, 5; 1 John 3:1 and 4:9, 16).

GOD THE SON

We believe God the Father, who is Spirit, appeared to us in human form as Jesus Christ (Philippians 2:5–8; Colossians 2:9). And Jesus, being the second person of God is equal, and eternal with God the Father (John 5:17–23; 10:30; 14:9–11; Hebrews 1:2, 3).

We believe Jesus was conceived in Mary's womb by God, and therefore sin was not transferred to Jesus during conception and birth (Isaiah 7:14; Matthew 1:18–25; Luke 1:26–35). And because Jesus lived a sinless life, He was able to submit Himself to crucifixion on the cross as a pure sacrifice to God as payment to redeem sinful man from God's penalty and punishment of sin, conditioned on each person's repentance (John 1:29; Hebrews 7:25, 26; 1 Peter 1:18, 19; Romans 5:8,9).

GOD THE HOLY SPIRIT

We believe the Holy Spirit is the third person of God, equal and eternal with God (Acts 5:3, 4; Hebrews 9:14; 3:7–11; 10:29; 1 Corinthians 12:4–11).

We believe the Holy Spirit is active in accomplishing the will of God. A few examples are the creation of the earth (Genesis 1:2, 26); the conception of Jesus (Matthew 1:18); as the divine author of scripture (2 Peter 1:20, 21); and of salvation (John 3:5–7; Titus 3:5). The Holy Spirit also works within our conscience convincing us about "sin, righteousness, and of judgment." And He also guides us into all truth (John 16:7–13; Titus 1:1).

We believe the Holy Spirit dwells within the true Christian (Romans 8:9–11; Ephesians 1:13) and uses the Word of God to transform the child of God, making him more like Jesus (2 Corinthians 3:18; Ephesians 2:22; John 16: 13, 14; 2 Timothy 2:15).

Man

We believe our great Creator created man, and later woman, each in a moment, in His "image and likeness" from the dust of the Garden of Eden, intending them to enjoy fellowship with God in the Garden of Eden (Genesis 2:7; 20–25; 3:8a). Adam and Eve's comforts, provisions, and bliss were gracious gifts from God. Both Adam and Eve understood that they might eat from every tree except from the tree in the middle of their garden. The forbidden tree represented a test of obedience to God. The glorious man and woman knew that it was God's right to rule over them, and that their bliss would continue as long as they were obedient to God. They also understood the threat of severe punishment if they disobeyed God (Genesis 2:16, 17; 3:2, 3). However, when Satan spoke with Eve, he deceived her as he drew her into shameless defiance of divine law, and when she bit the forbidden fruit, her perpetual happiness dissolved as spiritual death evolved. Eve then offered the fruit to Adam, who was not deceived when he partook of it. Impending doom alarmed his heart as spiritual death alienated him from God (Genesis 3:6; 1 Timothy 2:6, 7). At the very moment of their sin, divine purity faded from them as corruption filled them. The sad consequence is that nothing unclean will enter heaven (Revelation 21:27), and our sad consequence is that Adam and Eve's corruption was passed to all mankind (Romans 5:12; 18; Job 14:4; 15:14–16; 25:4; Psalm 51:5).

We believe that fallen man loves his fallen nature (John 3:19) because his fallen mind is vain and darkened. And because his fallen heart is hardened, he is senseless, continually giving himself unto sensuality, and all manner of uncleanness. And therefore, fallen man is alienated from life with God (Ephesians 4:17–19). While God observes our rebellious party against His will, He sees that there are none righteous (Romans 3:10–18) and declares all to be "abominable," "filthy," "children of disobedience," "children of wrath," and "enemies" to God (Job 15:14–16; Ephesians 2: 2, 3; Philippians 3:18; Colossians 1:21). Nothing unclean will enter heaven, so at the "Great White Throne Judgment," our angry Creator will say too many, "Depart from me, ye cursed, into everlasting fire, prepared for the devil and his angels" (Revelation 20: 11-15, 21:27; Matthew 7:13, 14; 21–23; Luke 13:23–28; 1 Peter 4:18; Matthew 25: 41).

SALVATION

We believe God will save a sinner from hell if the sinner agrees to the following conditions:

> **For if thou shalt confess with thy mouth the Lord Jesus, and shalt believe in thine heart, that God raised him up from the dead, thou shalt be saved: For with the heart man believeth unto righteousness, and with the mouth man confesseth to salvation.**
>
> ROMANS 10: 9–10

If a sinner is persuaded that Jesus has the right to rule over him, and if God hears from that sinner an earnest, heartfelt profession that his resolve is self-denial, complete obedience to Jesus, and true belief that God raised Jesus from the dead, God will pardon that sinner, and adopt him as His son or daughter (Romans 8:15; Galatians 4:6). However, the sinner must examine himself and make sure that his heartfelt prayer also includes a sincere change of mind about ungodliness (repentance) because God will not accept a heartfelt prayer for salvation unless God also hears that the sinner is repentant (2 Corinthians 13:5).

> **...but except ye amend your lives, ye shall all likewise perish.**
>
> LUKE 13:3

Many incorrectly say that repentance means to make a turn in life. However, the fruit of repentance is that one turns from ungodliness and turns to the ways and paths of God, according to His Word (Acts 26:20; Matthew 3:8; Mark 4:20).

We believe many committed followers of Jesus will not enter heaven because they did not make every effort to repent; they only prayed a heartfelt prayer to be saved (Luke 13: 23–28; Matthew 7:21–23; 1 Peter 4:18).

JUSTIFICATION

We believe Jesus willingly gave Himself to crucifixion on the cross as a perfect and complete payment for the penalty of our uncleanness and sins. God accepted Jesus' payment and now offers a free pardon to all sinners. Through the scriptures, this favorable judgment is made known to the world. The divine legal judgment is:

Now then there *is* no condemnation to them that are in Christ Jesus,...

ROMANS 8:1

There is no fear of condemnation to those who are in Christ Jesus, because God has taken the sins of true Christians and put them under Jesus' payment for sins, and He has applied Jesus' righteousness to His adopted children. The justified may now enter heaven (Romans 5:19; 1 Corinthians 1:30; 2 Corinthians 5:21; Philippians 3:9; Colossians 2:13, 14; Matthew 25:34, 46).

SANCTIFICATION

We believe the moment a sinner surrenders himself to God for salvation, he or she becomes a "purchased possession" of God (Ephesians 1:14) because the price paid to God for the redemption of a sinner was the shed blood of Jesus (Exodus 12:1–13; Acts 20:28; Romans 3:24; Galatians 4:4, 5; Ephesians 1:7; Hebrews 9:11–17). God's purchased possession becomes His temple, because He sends His Holy Spirit to reside in His child (1 Corinthians 3:16;

6:19). Within a true Christian is the place where God dwells. Therefore, the child of God must by God's word learn what must not enter God's temple, so that God is not provoked (2 Chronicles 29:1–18; John 2:13–17; James 4:4). Anything that God forbids to enter through His gates in heaven, must not be allowed to enter through the Christian's eye-gates, ear-gates, nose-gate, mouth-gate, or any of the touch-gates which allows entry to the heart where God dwells (Revelation 21:27; 1 Thessalonians 5:22, 23; Romans 12:9; Ephesians 5:3–6; Proverbs 4:23). Progressive separation from ungodliness increases sanctification (1 Thessalonians 4:3, 4; 2 Timothy 2:19–22). Obedience to God leads to righteousness, and righteousness leads to holiness, which is separation from that which is "common" or that which belongs "to the generality." To live and walk in holiness means that the Christian makes an earnest effort to not come in contact with that which is "unfit for the holy city" Heaven (Romans 6:16–19; Revelation 21:27).

> **Follow peace with all men, and holiness, without the which no man shall see the Lord.**
> HEBREWS 12:14

FAITH

We believe true faith in God is a gift from God (Ephesians 2:8). By reading God's word, faith is strengthened, becoming a strong persuasion that gives the soul possession of that which God has revealed as holy, good, and true (Acts 20:32; 1 Thessalonians 2:13; 2 Timothy 3:16, 17; 1 Peter 2:2). A proper walk of faith honors God. However, without faith it is impossible to please God (2 Corinthians 3:2, 3; Hebrews 11:6).

SIN

We believe that sin is an inherited contrariety to God and His Word; evident as an inward corrupt power, manifesting as the unintentional or willful thought, or step from God and His Word. Sin is insidiously prosperous through logic, reason, and the religious traditions of man.

Regarding TV, and radio preachers; YouTube errors of (*and type their name*), and see what is posted about them. Because some preach "wholesome doctrine," Titus 2:1,7,8, and 10, and some preach "doctrines of devils," 1 Timothy 4:1; 2 Corinthians 11:13-15.

www.ingramcontent.com/pod-product-compliance
Lightning Source LLC
Chambersburg PA
CBHW021351090426
42742CB00009B/817